THE POLITICAL ECONOMY
OF NATIONAL SECURITY

THE POLITICAL ECONOMY
OF NATIONAL SECURITY

A STUDY OF THE ECONOMIC ASPECTS
OF THE CONTEMPORARY POWER STRUGGLE

by

JAMES R. SCHLESINGER

FREDERICK A. PRAEGER, *Publishers*
NEW YORK

BOOKS THAT MATTER

First published in the United States of America in 1960
by Frederick A. Praeger, Inc., Publishers
64 University Place, New York 3, N.Y.
© 1960 by Frederick A. Praeger, Inc.

Library of Congress catalog card number 60-7984
Manufactured in the United States of America

PREFACE

Writing a book on a contemporary issue poses a dilemma for the author. He may confine the discussion to generalizations and avoid the inclusion of concrete illustrations, or he may include illustrative material which, by the time of publication, will no longer be current. It would be impossible to stay abreast of the most recent developments in the Soviet bloc and in the non-Communist world, and to keep up with the latest changes of American policy. Perhaps the best compromise is to emphasize the general propositions and to use contemporary developments merely for illustrative purposes, while hoping that the further unfolding of events will validate the approach and the concepts employed in the work. This is the method chosen here.

My interest in the connection between national security and economic analysis was crystallized during the period of my participation in the National Security Studies at the Naval War College, and this may be an appropriate place to indicate my appreciation for the help, encouragement, and stimulation that I received from the staff and students of the War College. Other individuals have contributed both their time and their special knowledge in discussing the issues raised in the book or in commenting on the text. I am especially indebted to Almarin Phillips, who painstakingly examined both the content and organization of the book in its early stages. Among others whose help was much appreciated are Robert Loring Allen,

v

James M. Buchanan, G. Warren Nutter, Eugene R. Schlesinger, and Gordon Tullock. Each has read the book either in whole or in part and has made valuable suggestions. Finally, I should like to acknowledge the most generous assistance given by the Institute for Research in the Social Sciences of the University of Virginia and by the Old Dominion Foundation.

                                                                    J. R. S.

Charlottesville, Virginia
November, 1959

CONTENTS

THE POLITICAL ECONOMY
OF NATIONAL SECURITY

INTRODUCTION

In the far-flung engagements of the cold war, the West has been losing ground. Partly for domestic reasons, the United States has assumed an attitude of intransigence. We have indulged in rash statements, yet when the chips are down, we have been readier to retreat than to pay the costs of defending our position. Eager as we have been to denounce appeasement, we have—like the lady of easy virtue in Bryon's poem—while "vowing we would never consent, consented." Part of the erosion of American, and of Western, power has been inevitable in the light of the changes that have come about in the nature of the international conflict—the unfreezing of the fixed lines of power that marked the period of the Korean War, the rise of the Afro-Asian bloc, and the gradual deterioration of the "great deterrent" that has been evident since the collapse of our fitful Indo-China policy in 1954. In countering a politico-economic offensive based upon subversion and penetration, as opposed to direct military aggression, it appears that we are overextended in our commitments. The vulnerability of our position in certain areas means that some losses have been and still are in the cards. The unhappy feature of our present policy is that we have been unwilling to consider just where our long-run interests lie. Obeying a vague injunction to oppose Communist penetration wherever it may appear, we have been weakening our position in regions that we must and can hold, in order to bolster Western influence temporarily in regions where we are living on borrowed time. Engaged, as we are, in a deadly game of poker, we have not known when to cut our losses, have drawn consistently to "inside straights," and have refused to raise the stakes when our hand is strong.

A nation's foreign policy is, to be sure, a reflection of its internal compulsions. Unfortunately, the American traits that shape our foreign policy do not provide grounds for confidence either in the realism of our objectives or in our patience and firmness in their implementation. We are the satisfied power—with a touching, but irrational, confidence in both the rightness and the stability of the *status quo*—living in a restless, unsettled world in which certain nations seem to desire nothing more than strife and the upsetting of what we consider to be law and order. Since we tend to project our own stable patterns of behavior onto the world stage, it is not surprising that the American people view international frictions as brief and unruly periods of strife culminating in the restitution of order through international settlements or international organizations. We have not reconciled ourselves emotionally to the need for the continual exercise of power to protect our interests. On the contrary, we have quixotically urged the disputants in international crises to "renounce the use of force," irrespective of their differences. Force, however, remains inextricably a part of international relations, though the grim facts may be partially obscured if we view the world through spectacles tinted by our own moralizing.

Dedicated, as it is, to a peaceful order, the American public has not been prepared to sanction the piecemeal use of force in small but embarrassing disputes—in counteracting diplomatic pressures, threats, subversion, or proxy wars. Our political machinery, ideally designed to respond to the public's mood, will, in satisfying the public's yearning for peace, be ready to acquiesce in small nibbling actions rather than to delineate the realities of our position and to call for the necessary sacrifices. In order to deceive ourselves, we tend to be led into designing policies that cope with nonexistent situations, since we are unwilling to accept the policies necessary to deal with our actual problems.

Despite our hopes and our actions, however, we ought to be under no illusions with respect to Soviet purposes. The Russian does not share our view of the world. The Communist ideology cannot envisage an orderly and stable world so long as a vigorous—and hostile—capitalist civilization survives. While Communism remains in its active stage, no true believer can conceive of benevolent relations between two antagonistic social systems, nor of a *competitive relationship* between the two systems which we would consider to be *orderly*. For the foreseeable future, and until Communism loses its *élan*, we may as well take Khrushchev at his own words—"We will abandon Communism when the shrimp learns to whistle"—with all they imply. On the other hand, we ought not waste any time speculating on this futile riddle: "Is world domination *or* Soviet national interest the motivating force behind Soviet policy?" No doubt the Russians would view with favor a world in which all nations shared their views and respected their advice, but they also recognize the limits of their power. They are not all afire to dominate the world. The immediate goal is security for the Soviet state. Yet, Soviet national interests are viewed from the perspective of Communism, and international Communism is a weapon to be used to serve Soviet interests. The menace to the West is, of course, Soviet expansionism or imperialism, but in practice it is difficult to separate Soviet expansionism from either its ideological roots or its weapons. From our position, it matters little just what supplies the motivation for the outthrust of Soviet power. Whether it be world domination or national interest, the path along which the two forces express themselves is the same. We can only discern the indisputable fact of the threat to our security.

At present, the Soviet leadership is unwilling to reach an over-all settlement—first, because it runs against the grain of its ideology, but secondly, because from the Soviet viewpoint, things have been going so well that it would be foolish to accept an interim settlement, except on terms unacceptable to the West. Whenever the possibility of a settlement is bruited about, however, we have launched into a dispute on the pointless "either-or" proposition—whether peaceful coexistence is possible or whether war is inevitable. From time to time, the Soviet leaders will emphasize the one theme or the other, and provoke another round of debate in the West. It would be foolish, it seems to me, to devote too much energy to speculation about this issue, since in Soviet parlance both terms mean approximately the same thing. Coexistence must be tried, since its alternative is nuclear suicide or mutual homicide. But the adjective "peaceful," in Soviet semantics, means simply the absence of general war, with a continuation of strife in marginal areas— probe and counterprobe, subversion, and even limited warfare. It certainly does not imply the acceptance of permanent frontiers of power or the restraining of the competition by fixed rules of the game. In this way, peaceful coexistence may come to mean the same thing as the inevitability of war. We must not, therefore, permit ourselves to be lulled into inactivity; instead, we must maintain a constant sense of urgency about our international posture.

The Communists are, to be sure, different from the Nazis. War is a means to an end, rather than an end in itself. Lenin made the significant comment that "war is a part, politics is the whole." This implies that real peace is unobtainable, so long as the world is divided; yet, since warfare is viewed as a tool, we may hope that it will be used rationally. The Russians will not be inclined to waste their power in thrusting against superior strength—whenever their foes have superior strength and have the willingness to use it. Thus, we may face the curious condition that Trotsky has described as "neither peace nor war." Any weakening of Western strength, cohesion, or resolve under these circumstances will elicit further Soviet advances.

Soviet propaganda may be relied upon to take advantage of Western attitudes on the questions of stability and order— hinting that only reasonableness on the part of Western statesmen (and, perhaps, a few minor concessions) blocks the pathway to peace. The "siren's song" of peace (on Soviet terms) has had its effect on many in the neutralist countries. Even in the West, its influence has been far deeper and gone much higher than the pitiful support given by well-meaning inno- cents to such devices as the Stockholm petition would indicate. Periodically, the demand to "negotiate with the Soviets" arises, not atypically when some critical decision must be made to shore up Western defenses. Statesmen who should know better continue to snap at the lure. Was it not Clausewitz who stated that the "conqueror is always a lover of peace; he would like to make his entry into our state unopposed"?

Recognition of the unlikelihood of a settlement ought not be construed to imply the futility of diplomatic negotiations. The diplomatic channels should always remain open. There are always concrete issues that can be settled on a mutually ad- vantageous basis, but such action can be achieved at the am- bassadorial level, and through the normal channels. What should be resisted is the ever-present demand for the so-called "summit conferences," which foster the illusion that a general settlement may be reached. Summits are not especially fertile places. In the course of events, the only purpose served by meetings of heads of governments is to initial agreements that have already been hammered out at a lower level. If we participate in such conferences, we should not deceive ourselves into believing that anything will be accomplished. As a result of Mikoyan's visit, it appears that the year 1959 may be marked by the pleas for high-level negotiations with the Russians that have blos- somed biennially since the death of Stalin. The pressure of our allies, combined with the pressure on Berlin, may make such a conference unavoidable, although the Administration has resisted such overtures in recent years. However, it should be noted that on previous occasions the Administration was not so discerning. During the summer of 1957, for example, it was widely reported that the President desired to reach an accord with the Soviets as the capstone of his career. At least for purposes of public consumption, the President permitted him- self to toy with the notion that if only he and his old com- rade-in-arms Marshal Zhukov could get together in a position of authority, our differences with the Soviet Union might be patched up. (The prevalence of this illusion partially explains

American consternation over the Marshal's subsequent fall from grace.) The Geneva Conference of 1955 unhappily illustrates the dangers of hoping to reach a settlement in this manner. The rapid erosion of Western power, particularly in the Middle East, more truly reflects the "spirit of Geneva" than did the saccharine atmosphere which pervaded the conference itself. At the very moment of the conference, the Russians were polishing their techniques for their later and successful incursions into the Middle East. It should be emphasized that, from the Soviet point of view, there was no inconsistency. This was no violation of trust; on the contrary, it was in perfect harmony with peaceful coexistence.

Apparently, we have been unable to adjust our defenses to the more subtle maneuverings of Soviet policy since the death of Stalin. The breakup of the bipolar world of the Stalinist era has left in its wake a situation of much greater fluidity in the network of relationships stretching between a larger number of power centers. A variety of forms of psychological and economic warfare have replaced the Stalinist battering ram, though the latter is still associated with the threat of a limited use of force. During the period of nuclear supremacy, we were prepared to cope with limited war, infiltration, and subversion, although our strategic ideas and our military policy remained wedded to the concepts of the era of total warfare which had already passed. Now that the Soviets have reached a rough parity with us—or, in some respects, have even surpassed us—in terms of nuclear capabilities, we are engaged in the unilateral reduction of our conventional forces, despite the fact that we maintained conventional forces during the period of our supremacy. It is an illogical policy. The danger of limited war has increased, just because the massive retaliatory power of both sides makes recourse to strategic bombing increasingly unlikely.

We have now reached the point at which the power of nuclear weapons has become so awesome that their effectiveness as deterrents has been undermined. We must recognize this fact, with its implication that we are not presently in a position to counter the advanced techniques of the new Soviet offensive. In both Southeast and Southwest Asia, the Western position is crumbling. The upsetting of pro-Western governments proceeds through propaganda, *coup d'état,* or normal electoral processes. We are not able to prevent this retreat. Both the defectiveness of our military posture and the emotional unpreparedness of the American people make unlikely a resort to force to maintain Western power. This was made clear not only in Indo-China, but at Suez and by subsequent events in the Middle East. If, however, the President and the American public, as well as our allies, are willing to acquiesce in small "nibbling" actions rather than permitting the quest for peace to be disturbed, there is little question what our policy will be in the face of the advance of Soviet power—to use the horrid word, *appeasement.*

What is required is a radical reorientation of our traditional framework of beliefs. The basic nature of the American attitude on international affairs is, however, not likely to change rapidly, and it will be some time before we are in a position to make the best use of our potential power. In the interim, we must be prepared to write off our losses. Some Western withdrawal is undoubtedly in the cards, but if we weigh our longer-run advantages and do not allow ourselves to become obsessed with the shorter-run disadvantages, there is no reason for despair. The great danger lies in the possibility that the withdrawal of the West from overexposed positions may generate the pessimistic conviction that the onrush of Soviet power is unstoppable.

In order to strengthen our long-run position, we must understand present Western weaknesses—and we must be prepared to make the necessary adjustments in our strategic plans. The chief weakness of the latter has been the obscurity of our ultimate goals and purposes. Caught up in the crisis of the moment, we fail to distinguish between national interests and national objectives. National interests, which are few in number, are broad and are valid for long periods of time; whereas national objectives are specifics that emerge, fortuitously and temporarily, from immediate conditions. Specific objectives must be reviewed and modified as circumstances change; but in a democracy, the painfulness of the process of review and the ill feelings engendered by our great debates on national policy make us reluctant to undertake the process of reappraisal at the most propitious moment. Instead, we tend to cling to specific objectives—after the conditions that gave rise to their embodiment in policy have changed, when the objectives have become obsolete and unrealistic—rather than reopen the bitter controversies.

The current situation illustrates this problem of the lag of policy reappraisal behind the obsolescence of objectives. At the present time, despite occasional genuflections in the direction of the goddess of liberation, we are still dedicated to the strategic doctrine of containment. Yet, the circumstances that gave rise to the strategy of containment—to wit, the preponderance of American power in the bipolarized postwar world—have now altered, as has been recognized (perhaps even overrecognized) by the formulator of the containment doctrine, George Kennan. We cling to the objective of containment, despite the fact that we are psychologically and militarily unprepared to devote the necessary resources to containing Soviet power within its present frontiers. Western power and influence in Asia, already much reduced, is likely to be further diminished in the years to come. We are not in a position to preserve the "vast arc of free Asia" stretching from Japan to Turkey. Communist power is advancing southward; it now threatens even Africa. We only deceive ourselves if we believe that aid for development purposes, with "no strings attached" and in competition with the Soviet Union, can possibly arrest the anti-Western wave that is sweeping the former colonial areas—a revolution directed not merely at Western power but at Western civilization, and at Westerners *per se*. It is not merely *anticolonialism*; we would be foolish if we confused the issue and believed we could disassociate ourselves from France and Britain. We are today the leader and the great symbol of the West—and an object of distaste for that very reason. We can neither guide nor propitiate this ferment of which the Russians are the immediate beneficiaries.

However, we should not view the onsweep of Soviet power as monolithic, for the spread of Communist power in Asia in itself gives rise to centrifugal forces within the rival power bloc. The

deep fissures in Asia, based upon ancient and recent antagonisms, make it inevitable that disunity will prevail on that
continent—and neither power bloc will have things its own
way. Although parts of what is referred to as "free Asia" may
appear like rather overripe fruit, they would remain a source
of weakness and discord even if they should fall under Communist control. We should not concern ourselves unduly with
names of principalities, or inconsequential real estate, or the
size of populations falling within the Communist maw. It is
misleading to speak of the underdeveloped areas *in general*—as
if they were homogeneous, all likely to go in the same direction,
or all of equal importance to us. The chief unifying element
is hostility to the West, but as this factor recedes in importance—
as inevitably it must, as the West withdraws—the underlying
antipathies will come more to the surface.

In the place of undue concern with the areas that we cannot affect, we should look to the areas that are vital to us, that
are bound to us by mutual interests—and strengthen both our
alliances and long-run defenses. Latin America is of fundamental importance to the West. Happily, it has been far from
the front lines, though the significance of recent Soviet trading
offers and of anti-American demonstrations ought not to be
overlooked. Plainly, Latin America should not be neglected,
simply because it is an element of strength.

To my mind, our principal national objective is now—and is
likely to remain—the preservation of a strong, free, and viable
Western Europe. This implies the preservation of Western
influence in Africa—by association, if possible; by force, if necessary—and the forging of a Euro-African geopolitical unit. (It
is not generally realized to what extent Africa has already replaced Asia as a European source of supply, and what its future
promises to be.) A second vital objective is the preservation of
offshore Asia and Oceania, though Europe looms a little larger
in the over-all perspective. Preserving offshore Asia implies a
willingness to open Western Hemisphere markets to the Japanese.

If these, indeed, be our vital national objectives, we ought
not to confuse them with the merely desirable goals in the

years ahead, because of continued Communist pressure in South Asia. In parts of Asia, the West is living on borrowed time—valuable time, to be sure, because it permits Americans to make the necessary psychological adjustments to a world of continual strife and to the use of force, before our most essential interests are brought under heavy pressure. As the West retreats, and as the problems facing the non-Communist world grow more grave, our attitudes will change. For the time being, we will not be mortally injured by retreat, but in the long run it will be necessary to make a stand and be prepared to use force. We must become adjusted to the heavy costs of limited warfare as a condition of life. This is not to say that we may dismiss or ignore the need to maintain adequate nuclear power as a deterrent to all-out war. It is particularly necessary in view of the recent Soviet technological breakthrough, which carries with it the threat of possible and instantaneous destruction of our strategic bases through the use of missiles. This threat may be countered, however, if we proceed as rapidly as we can with the development of mobile and relatively invulnerable missile bases—especially the submarine-based Polaris missile system, which can so effectively be hidden in the depths of the sea. But such a development will do little more than restore the nuclear stalemate, and reintroduce the necessity of being prepared for limited war.

The bulk of the material in this volume was developed as a series of lectures which constituted a part of the course in National Security Studies at the Naval War College during the summer and fall of 1957. For those interested in the problem of security—particularly those who stress the advantages of balanced military forces—it was not an altogether happy period. Vast cutbacks were being made in military spending and in military forces in order to keep total Department of Defense expenditures for the fiscal year within an artificial limit of $38 billion. In an expanding economy, this decision meant that a declining proportion of gross national product (GNP) would be spent on national security. Because of the continuing rise of prices and salaries, it also meant that the real amount of defense that we were purchasing was actually decreasing—in the face of mounting international pressures. In view of the great flexibility that the nation possesses in the use of its economic resources, the cliché-ridden propositions advanced to justify the artificial budget limit and the spending cuts would have been ludicrous had they not been macabre. These decisions followed by some months similar steps proposed in the British White Paper of April, 1957—calling for a reduction of conventional armed strength, a curtailment in the size of the British Army of the Rhine, and reliance on nuclear deterrence.* It was also a period of increasing enfeeblement and disunity of the Western alliance.

In preparing a series of lectures for Naval officers, one must make clear the limits of the role of the professional economist. There is a natural affinity between the professional officer and the professional economist. No professional, in his role *as* professional, should formulate policy. No policy decisions ought to be made on the basis of purely military or purely economic advice. Professional advice can only cast a light on policy; it cannot determine it. The professional is a purveyor of expertise gained from specialized training, but supplemented by a broader knowledge of the functioning of the society. His role is to analyze and to clarify certain facets of a problem, so that the policy-makers are better able to reach decisions. The professional indicates the limits placed by the realities—military, political, economic, and the like—on the policy-maker's freedom of action. At the same time, he should indicate the range of freedom of the policy-maker and the possibilities open to him.

---

* Compare the British action with the earlier words of the present Prime Minister, Mr. Macmillan, at a meeting of the Foreign Press Association in September, 1955: ". . . There can be no victor in nuclear war . . . since the sanction is so terrible we must realize that men, however resolute, will shrink from using it—even against unprovoked aggression—unless they are convinced that to be conquered is worse than to be annihilated. . . . It follows that ruthless and daring men, counting on this hesitation and exploiting it, may risk minor and even substantial acts of aggression, because they believe that the sanction may be made impotent by its overwhelming strength. Thus, what are called conventional forces will be made necessary, not merely for what might be called police operations, but to take away this temptation. . . ."

Despite these meaningful words, British conventional armed strength has been reduced. In the annual White Paper on defense issued in February, 1958, it was stated that Britain would resort to nuclear retaliation in the event of any Soviet attack in Europe. Thus the West increases rather than lessens its reliance upon strategic striking power. In the United States, despite brave words about the need for sacrifices in the period after the Russians launched Sputnik, the budgets for fiscal 1959 and fiscal 1960 have called for further cutbacks in conventional armed strnegth—in manpower, divisions, ships, and planes.

In short, the professional role is to *present* alternatives, not to *choose* among them. In this volume, I have attempted to indicate inconsistencies in policies—and this is a proper professional role. At times, and especially in Chapter IX, I have discussed policy. I have, however, tried to recognize that fact—policy conclusions should be distinguished from professional observations, and any conclusions with respect to policy clearly transcend the professional role.

Professionalism in military science and in economics has an additional affinity. It is in the nature of a military estimate, first to assess the limits imposed by capabilities. Strategy itself, designed to obtain maximum achievements from limited resources, is fundamentally economic in its nature. "Economics" has been defined as the science of choice; it is, therefore, not surprising that the economic element in a strategic problem provides the yardstick by which the other components of the problem may be judged. Moreover, the further the strategic problem is projected into the future, the more important the economic element becomes—since the greater the time period considered, the greater the convertibility of resources becomes.

The softening of the lines in the cold war since 1955 has increased the importance of the economic element in the formulation of strategy. Political economy provides a *method of approach* to national issues—a point of view that stresses the possibility and the costs of several alternatives. With the crumbling of the rigid cold-war positions of the period 1948–1955, and the development of more fluid lines of conflict, has come the need to re-assess our strategy in the face of this more dynamic challenge. In any such re-assessment, economics—with its belief that *natura non facit saltum* and its principles of compensation and alternative cost—has much to offer.

During the period of intransigence, economic concepts were not palatable. It is pointless to talk of alternative policies and their costs, if no suggested alternative is regarded as acceptable. At the time, we viewed the struggle between East and West as a possible Armageddon: in a critical moment, the victory might go decisively to either the forces of evil or those of righteousness. Now, with the softening of the lines of conflict, we can see that the struggle will be an enduring one—and if, in the ebb and flow of events, we desire a little bit more of this, we must pay with a little bit less of that. As Arnold Toynbee has frequently emphasized, the type of struggle in which we are now engaged has confronted other civilizations in the past; it could continue for centuries, with fortune favoring first one side and then the other. Thus the study of alternative policies, in which the economic element predominates, has been furthered by the likelihood of limited engagements, as opposed to a nuclear Armageddon. To say that the mild thaw in international relations since Geneva has provided additional scope for the consideration of the economic element is, however, not to say that political economy re-appears only when the intensity of the struggle lessens. Quite the contrary: we may fight as determinedly as we know how; and political economy, by clarification of the alternatives, may allow us to extract maximum advantages in a long-run struggle, with the minimum use of resources.

Economic concepts have been introduced piecemeal into the discussions of possible American policies. It has been argued that the amount that the state can spend under a system of free enterprise is quite restricted, and that we are in danger of courting economic bankruptcy if we attempt too much. It has been argued that we are protected by the superiority of our economic potential. It has been argued that we will be conquered by the rapid rate of industrial growth in the Soviet Union, or by what is described as the "massive Soviet economic offensive against the underdeveloped areas." It has been argued that sponsoring more rapid rates of economic progress in the underdeveloped areas through foreign assistance will protect the West from isolation in a hostile world.

All of these arguments attack individual aspects of the relationship between political economy and national security. Many of them are contradictory: it is plain, for example, that we cannot speed up the American rate of industrial growth to match the Soviets, and at the same time diminish the gap between *per capita* incomes in the West and in the underdeveloped areas. Much of the difficulty may be ascribed to the fragmentary nature of discussions of the national security problem. We have budgetary experts, mobilization experts, Soviet experts, China experts, development experts, trade experts, and the like; yet, to my knowledge, there is no work that attempts to present a comprehensive picture of the various economic factors bearing on national security. It is hoped that this book will help fill that void. In it, all of the major security issues confronting the West in the area of economic policy have been brought together. If it helps to reveal the inconsistencies in piecemeal discussion of these issues, the book's purpose will have been accomplished.

Finally, I must admit that we should all recognize the "awful irresponsibility of the academician." Logic may lead to conclusions that should, in practice, be tempered by caution. In trying circumstances, the policy-maker will always find it difficult to act on the basis of advice so easily tendered in the "academy." It should also be admitted that one's style may be less tentative than one's beliefs: in such matters as these, there is the inclination to assert conclusions with greater certitude than is felt—and the reader must make allowance for this fact.

1

THE PERSPECTIVE OF ECONOMICS

Economic analysis is not—as it is frequently, but erroneously, believed to be—concerned solely with the satisfaction of *material* wants. On the contrary, the fundamental issue with which it deals is that of choice, a phenomenon that transcends the material realm. Almost every human problem will have its economic aspect. Desires are unlimited, yet no individual or institution has command of either the resources or the time (which is a type of resource) to achieve all the ends that may be regarded as desirable. Therefore, it becomes necessary to exercise choice among the many possible alternatives, to establish a scale of priorities—in short, to economize. Arising as a result of scarcity, economics examines the disposal made of available resources to achieve goals which, although boundless in themselves, must ultimately be limited because of that scarcity of means.

National security is the problem of our age. By its very nature, economic analysis is intimately related to the broader issues of strategy. The very heart of a strategic estimate is to assess the limits imposed on one's actions by one's capabilities. Admiral Robert B. Carney, former Chief of Naval Operations, succinctly defined strategy as "a plan of action best to employ resources toward the achievement of aims"—a phrase that is remarkably similar to the classic statement of Lionel Robbins that "economics is the science which studies human behavior as a relationship between ends and scarce means that have alternative uses."[1] The assumption in Admiral Carney's rubric that ends are *given* provides the only distinction between the two definitions. The economist would hold that ends themselves are alternatives, since limited resources must impose restrictions on the ends that can be attained. Selection of ends is necessarily a part of the problem of allocating resources.

In all human affairs, the selection of goals and the disposition of means are fundamental, and this is reflected in the primacy in economics of the problem of allocation. The basic propositions of economics, which we shall briefly treat, all touch upon the issue of allocation. From time to time, economists have been inclined to suggest that other problems had become more pressing—economic stabilization or the distribution of income in the thirties, or economic growth at the present time. But broadly viewed, these issues may be regarded as reflections of, and subsidiary to, the main problem of allocation. Economic stabilization must be considered in terms of other goals that must be sacrificed in order to provide full employment or price stability. The price of stabilization must be measured in terms of the possibilities of reduced efficiency, a slower rate of growth, and so on. The goal of achieving a more equitable distribution of income must similarly be analyzed in the light of possible costs: What degree of intervention is justifiable in the levels of compensation determined by the free market, and what will be its impact on incentives and on output? The rate of growth must be judged largely in terms of allocation, for in advanced economies the rate of growth is, to no inconsiderable degree, simply a reflection of the proportion of resources that can be devoted to capital formation. It must, therefore, be considered in terms of the willingness of the society to provide resources for investment activity by abstaining from the present consumption of the total available product. Finally, military preparedness must be weighed on a similar basis, for military expenditures are in competition with consumption and investment activity for the available resources.

1. Some Fundamental Economic Principles

Considerations such as these bring to light a major aspect of economic analysis. Since economics is concerned with the disposal of scarce resources, it will be perceived that the price (or cost) of any given end must be measured in terms of the other goals that must be sacrificed in order to accomplish this particular aim. This basic proposition that the achievement of any goal must be weighed in terms of sacrifice—of the substitution of one end for others—is sometimes referred to as the "principle of alternative cost." It is this principle that helps to explain why, on so many occasions, economists tend to view human events as compensatory[2] in nature, whereas others may view them as one-way movements. Every human action has its cost side. The basic issue involved in reaching policy judgments is whether or not the advantages are viewed as outweighing the disadvantages, but in no case is it wise to ignore the liability side of the balance sheet.

In dealing with the question of the disposal of resources, we need to clarify one additional insight which helps to explain how resources may be rationally allocated. This is the principle of marginalism, which goes to the very heart of economic analysis and makes its pervasive influence felt in many branches of analysis. We might also refer to it as the "law of diminishing benefits." [3] Fundamentally, the law states that the contribution to well-being of any type of economic goods or economic resources must be measured incrementally or *at the margin,* and that at the margin the contribution of a particular good or resource to satisfaction or physical output will eventually tend to decline. The usefulness of this concept lies in the fact that it provides a notion of how we attain a condition of balance or equilibrium in the allocation of resources—how a household reaches an optimal position in making its expenditures on consumer goods and services, or how a business firm reaches an optimal position in its combination of different factors of production. By analogy, it provides a vague but useful yardstick for the state in its allocation of resources for different programs, as planned in its budget.

The law has two major corollaries—one for the distribution of expenditures, the other for the combination of resources. In the first instance, if we consider any particular goal among a range of goals, we discover that as we increase the levels of expenditure devoted to the achievement of that one purpose—be it housing, transportation, or beer on the household level; slum clearance, reclamation, or air groups on the national level—after a certain point has been reached, the additional satisfaction or usefulness obtained *per unit of allocated expenditures* diminishes. In terms of economic jargon, the *marginal utility* of the goods or service in question falls. To state it another way, the additional satisfaction obtained from greater expenditure on a product depends not only on the *intrinsic value* of the class of commodity (quite high for food or water) but also on the number of units of that commodity available, and that generally the added satisfaction decreases at the margin as the number increases. To take a household example, in some ways the satisfaction obtained from a second television set will be greater than that obtained from the first, for it may permit parents to see the programs that they would like to see. But after the purchase of a second set, the amount of additional satisfaction obtained from additional expenditures on television sets declines. Finally, when each member of the family has been equipped with a set, the satisfaction to be obtained from additional sets may become zero or even negative. Each family in making its expenditures would, in principle, obtain maximum satisfaction by arranging its expenditures so that the additional satisfaction obtained from the final dollars spent on all commodities is as nearly equal as possible.

The second corollary of the law is concerned with the combination of resources in productive activity. We may come to similar conclusions with respect to the need for balance among the *several factors of production* that are *jointly* devoted to the attainment of *each* goal. All business concerns must use some capital and some real estate, in addition to labor; but each firm must seek the optimal combination of these factors, or it will be at a competitive disadvantage. The excessive use of labor or the insufficient use of capital on small acreages devoted to the production of cotton, to take a contemporary example, will not yield maximum returns and does not represent the economical use of resources. The more of a specific factor of production that is used, while the other factors are held constant, the less will be added to final output per unit input of that factor of production. For maximum returns, the factors of production in all enterprises should be used in such proportions that the increment (or marginal product) that an additional unit of each factor adds to production is exactly in ratio to its price. The relative prices of the several factors of production—labor, land, capital, natural resources, and managerial ability—reflect the relative scarcities within the particular economy in question. In the United States, we may be relatively short on labor and perhaps some of the natural resources, and so we must be more careful to economize on the use of these factors than, say, the Russians.

In any economy, in order to obtain maximum material well-being and physical production, balance should be achieved in the allocation of resources—both in terms of the composition of output and in terms of the relationship among the several factors of production in every branch of industry. The marginal principle demonstrates that this ideal allocation of resources occurs when both households and firms have made equal the marginal return for the last dollar's expenditure on either goods or factors of production, as the case may be. At base, "marginalism" simply expresses the rudimentary mathematical notions of maximum returns and minimum costs.

2. THE ECONOMIST AND HIS ROLES

So much for a few of the fundamental principles of economic analysis. From what has already been said concerning alternative costs, it might be anticipated that the chief role of the economist under ordinary conditions is that of the nay-sayer. Since resources are limited, the price of any one goal must be reckoned in terms of the necessary sacrifices of other goals. All of us are familiar with such household adages as: "You can't get something for nothing" or "You can't eat your cake and have it, too." In economic and in strategic matters, these are almost universally true, and these simple precepts, oddly enough, represent the economist's chief stock-in-trade. Occasionally, in strategic matters, an opportunity may present itself in which a nation can extract advantages without any compensating disadvantages; in economic matters, however, such occurrences are as rare as manna from heaven. The existence of scarcity must be recognized, and usually the economist is forced to emphasize the price that must be paid for a proposed course of action in terms of the alternative possibilities that must be sacrificed. Public policies, for example, ought not require for their implementation resources that are in excess of the nation's capacity. The immediate cost of failure to recognize the limitation of resources is the failure to achieve overly ambitious goals; a likely symptom is inflation.

Generally, economists are forced to reiterate some simple observations, not because they are particularly *penetrating*, but because they are *true*. Among such elementary bromides are the following: the limits on resources place a limit on our goals; we cannot consume more than we produce; a nation cannot afford a higher standard of living than its population has the energy and the will to maintain; and so on. Such banalities need to be repeated frequently because hope springs eternal in the human breast, man's desires outrun his capacity—and, above all, in a complex society such as our own, men may hope that the costs of increased benefits for themselves might be foisted onto some other group. In large measure, it is his role of nay-sayer that has made the public view of the economist a slightly jaundiced one. It helps explain why economics has been and is still called "the dismal science." For a century and a half, it has been puncturing the high-flying balloons of both reformers and dictators with its plaintive and insistent query: Where are the resources to come from?

Yet, happily, economics has a yea-saying role as well. On occasion, the economist must remind the public of the broad freedom of action that it possesses in the allocation of resources. If the attainment of a particular goal is considered imperative, the resources can be found, simply by reducing the amounts allotted for other goals. It is at this point that economic analysis transmutes itself into political economy—that is, when certain goals (or social values) are so widely accepted as given that there can be a narrowing of the range choice, and the economist is required to identify the means by which particular ends may be achieved. At times, the economist may rise to the defense of unpopular programs, reminding the public that such programs are not untenable, as is so often asserted, on economic grounds.[4] Larger military expenditures or increased foreign aid, for example, may not be popular, but they must be weighed in terms of the national interest; they will not cause "national bankruptcy." In such circumstances, the economist must do battle with preconceptions, even misconceptions, concerning the economic capacity of the country. In principle, resources may be allocated with great freedom, although as a practical matter the question will arise whether a proposed allocation will prove tolerable to the public. It is here that economics touches politics and social psychology. To be sure, there are limits to public expenditures, but economists must stress the fact that these limits are basically political in nature. They are not "economic facts of life." We could have more defense expenditures; we could have a more rapid rate of growth—provided the public is willing to bear the cost, which is a reduced proportion of the nation's resources devoted to consumption and to present welfare. There is a wide range of alternative policies open to the American people, and for this reason the economist need not always appear in his nay-saying role.

2

THE GROSS NATIONAL PRODUCT
AND ITS ALLOCATION

One fruitful method of demonstrating the significance of the concept of alternative cost is to examine the allocative process in terms of total national output. National production reflects in a rough-and-ready manner the availability of resources. The various social goals, measured in aggregative terms by components of national output, are in competition with each other for the use of economic resources. The nation as a whole allocates national output among various end uses, and since these end uses are competitive with one another for resources, the cost of each must be measured in terms of the sacrifice of other end-use components of the national output.

In order to study the national allocative process in detail, however, we must dispose of two preliminary problems—one theoretical, the other statistical. The theoretical problem may be dealt with simply by an admonition. In Western democracies, we ought not think of the nation as a whole disposing of resources, except in a statistical sense. A nation is composed of individuals and private organizations which separately reach their own decisions as to the best way of using the resources at their command. The collectivity, in itself, does not decide how resources are to be used, except for that portion of total resources that falls under its control through its tax and expenditure policies. Outside its own sphere of operations, the state is limited to attempting to *influence* the use of resources by private parties through its monetary and debt-management policies and through the *structure* of its fiscal operations. Therefore, when we examine the over-all use of resources, we must remember that we are dealing with a statistical aggregate resulting from countless decisions by private individuals and organizations, which we should be hesitant to criticize. The only proper route by which collective decision enters the allocative process in a free society is in determining whether or not the state should control a higher proportion of total resources, and whether or not it should take steps to influence the decisions that are reached privately.

The statistical problem, on the other hand, must be considered at greater length. It requires us to diverge briefly from the main thread of our argument, in order to examine the technical problems that confront the economist when he attempts to devise measures of total national output. Before we can assess the significance of resource allocation in practice, it is advisable to understand the purposes for which aggregative measures are derived, and their limitations in application to the problem of national security. The measure that we will use is the "gross national product," which provides not only an estimate of national output but also a crude approximation of the volume of resources available to the society. But the GNP has its drawbacks, chief among them being the fact that it measures current output of goods and services without any allowance for the depreciation of plant and equipment in the turning out of those goods and services. This means that the GNP overstates real national output by the amount of depreciation. Net national product (GNP, minus an allowance for the consumption of capital) is a derived measure, not guilty of such overstatement of output. The NNP is, however, not necessarily more accurate, since any allowance for depreciation is bound to be dubious. We shall use the GNP, not merely because it is somewhat more reliable, but because in the short run a nation has the opportunity of briefly expanding the resources immediately available by permitting its capital plant to run down. This was one of the ways that Great Britain, for example, obtained the resources to prosecute World War II. In the longer run, we must recognize, however, that the GNP is inflated, and that the degree of inflation depends on the relative importance of depreciation in total national production. It should also be emphasized at the outset that, statistically speaking, the attempt to obtain any measure of aggregate output represents an exercise in the performance of the illogical as logically as possible. It will be impossible to examine in any detail all the pitfalls that loom before the national-income statistician, but it is vitally important to understand the chief difficulties and the limitations of aggregative measures.

1. THE ESTIMATION OF GROSS NATIONAL PRODUCT

The "gross national product" may be defined as the *total market value of all final goods and services produced by an economy during a stated period of time*, generally one year. Two innocent-appearing aspects of the definition should be noticed—the phrases "market value" and "final goods and services." They supply the key to an understanding of the strengths and the limitations of GNP.

Every statistical estimate is designed for a specific purpose. The GNP is designed to ascertain the *market value* of total output, and its relevance for other purposes is debatable. Market values are merely that; they need not reflect aesthetic excellence, or the degree of satisfaction or happiness of the population that obtains them; they simply represent the prices at which the goods sell. We must accept as given the prices, costs, and *relative efficiencies* of the industries of a nation. For this reason, the final figure cannot be applied mechanically to questions of national security, for example. It will indicate not the efficiency of expenditures on national security—but only the market value.[1] The lower the relative efficiency of the armaments industry in a nation, the higher will be its expenditures on national security, without representing any addition to military-force levels.

Secondly, we must be alert to the statistical implications of measuring *final goods and services*. We must be sure to exclude the intermediate goods and services that are used up in the production of final goods. We must not include, for example, the steel, rubber, and other materials used up in the production of automobiles, as well as the value of automobiles produced. Failure to exclude intermediate goods would be a form of double counting of production, and would result in a massive overstatement of national output. Another way of putting the problem is to say that we wish to include only the value added in each stage of industry, and to eliminate the costs of production represented by supplier industries.

Obtaining an estimate of GNP is by no means a simple task, even if we keep in mind the limited purpose of the aggregate—to show the market value of final goods produced. It will be recognized that the size of the final figure will be influenced by the treatment accorded certain doubtful categories of expenditures, and also by certain broader characteristics of the economy in question. We shall treat each of these difficulties in turn:

The problem of intermediate expenditures. How, in practice, can we distinguish between final goods and the intermediate goods that are transformed in the process of production? In many cases, to be sure, the decision is simple: the consumption by industry of raw materials or electric power is an intermediate expenditure; whereas summer vacations for the public are final services. Many expenditures, however, pose difficult problems, and inevitably an element of arbitrariness must creep into the decisions. Business entertainment expenditures are viewed as a cost of production—an intermediate expense—yet businessmen may mistakenly view them in terms of consumption and might possibly extract some enjoyment from such expenditures. Some unfriendly souls have even hinted that such expenditures are not legitimate costs of business, and that national output is understated by regarding them as intermediate expenses.

On the other hand, many so-called "consumption expenditures" are business-oriented and may be considered necessary for maintaining one's standing in the business community. In certain activities, maintaining a suitable establishment is necessary for the career-inclined individual. Moreover, some consumption expenditures are absolutely essential to the productive process. Take the question of commutation expense. In our suburbanized society, the transportation costs of hauling people to and from their places of employment are heavy burdens, both individually and socially. In the absence of commutation, the economy would suffer a partial breakdown, in view of our present residential patterns. Yet commutation expenses are considered to be consumption rather than intermediate expenditures. It is difficult to draw the line properly between intermediate and final goods and services; inevitably, the final decision will represent a compromise that is unsatisfactory for some purposes.

The problem of government expenditures. The tricky problem of how to deal with the government's contribution to output arises, in large measure, as a side aspect of the problem of intermediate expenditures. Some people profess to believe that government expenditures are essentially nonproductive and add nothing to total output. Others feel that any form of economic activity carried on by the state makes a distinctive contribution to social welfare, and that government expenditures somehow are more productive than those handled in the private sector of the economy. There is considerable leeway, in between these two extremes, for differences of opinion as to how the government's contribution should be weighed.

A considerable proportion of government expenditures is designed simply to provide industry with intermediate services that will facilitate the production of goods and services. In theory, any such expenditures constitute a part of the cost of production and should be excluded from the GNP. Examples are police protection for industrial property, the industrial use of highways, the activities of regulatory and advisory departments, and so on. Yet, on the other hand, certain government expenditures clearly add to the output of final product—schools, highways for the use of consumers, public parks, and various government enterprises. It would be difficult, if not impossible, to draw any firm statistical line between the intermediate-goods and the final-goods activities of the government. In practice, no such attempt is made; it has been arbitrarily decided to include *all*

government expenditures on goods and services in the GNP. Such
a decision immediately implies an overstatement of final output,
because of the inclusion of the intermediate services of the
government. Moreover, the amount of inflation of the GNP on
this account tends to increase *progressively*, since historically
the scope of the government's activities and expenditures has
expanded over time.

To illustrate the tendency for the final output figure to increase as the government's activities expand, one might cite the
increasing effectiveness of police protection, which has permitted business firms to discharge night watchmen and factory police. What had been an intermediate expenditure for
private constabulary services now becomes a final expenditure
and swells the GNP. The double counting arises because both
the salaries of policemen and the taxes (paid by business concerns for intermediate services supplied by the government)
are included in the final estimate.

The extent of the market. The fact that the GNP measures
only those values that flow through the market creates a third
problem. Aside from imputing values for a few factors such as
owner-occupied housing or food produced and consumed on
the farm, the GNP makes no attempt to measure the vast amount
of output represented by the efforts in the household economy.
Traditionally, most production takes place for the household
rather than for the market. In a subsistence economy, the population may live comfortably, despite extremely low *per capita*
incomes, because of the difficulty of accounting for production
that does not flow through the market. Since household efforts
do not pass through the market, a rise in GNP may simply reflect the encroachment of the market on the household, rather
than representing an increase in real output. If all American
households were to take in each other's wash at a price of $5
a week, total real output would not change at all, but GNP
would rise by approximately $15 billion a year. On the other
hand, when a man marries his housekeeper, and ceases to pay
her a salary, GNP shrinks.

In the United States, in particular, the size of the GNP reflects in no inconsiderable degree the relative width of the

market. The rising GNP exaggerates the rise in real output. This is especially true for the service component; services that were performed in a rough-and-ready manner fifty years ago may now be represented by high-priced talent. Therefore, the rising GNP figure reflects the increased marketability of services and a spreading division of labor. In such manner, the GNP figure may well overstate the secular rise in national output.

Other difficulties. Two other problems might be mentioned briefly: those posed by a "hardship economy" and by the legal framework. It requires more effort—in terms of food, clothing, shelter, and energy—to survive in Labrador than in Egypt. Greater output may not be reflected in higher standards of living. Yet, in the computation of the GNP, the problem of the hardship economy is necessarily ignored. Nevertheless, greater effort may be required merely to leave the populace as well off as it would be in more congenial climes.

Finally, we must remember that the national-income statistics measure only those values that *legally* flow through the market. Illegal activities are omitted, irrespective of their marketability or their contribution to national satisfaction. Thus, the earnings of moonshiners, bookmakers, or hired killers are not included in the final statistics. (There is some doubt that government officials could make an accurate estimate, even if it were desired.) In some societies, however, a significant proportion of consumption enjoyment may be obtained illegally. If there is a change in the law, GNP is suddenly affected. For example, the commencement and the demise of prohibition posed tricky problems for the national-income statistician, as well as for other citizens.

Even without a mention of the difficulties introduced by price fluctuations, enough has been said to indicate that one must be prepared to take the raw statistics with a very large grain of salt. The statistics on GNP are constructed with a limited purpose in mind, and therefore, their applicability to other purposes cannot be assumed. They do not necessarily measure psychological well-being or military capacity, and before using these statistics, one ought to fully understand their limitations. The statistics are especially suspect for comparisons between countries or between periods of time. Since they are based on market valuations, any differences in price systems or in the structure of the economies or in the extent of the market will reduce their usefulness for purposes of comparison. Yet, crude as the figures are—and all aggregates must, by their nature, be imprecise—they are perhaps the best guide that we have with which to compare the *total resources* available to the economies of the several nations. They are, however, as we shall see, much less useful for comparing the separate sectors of different economies.

2. ALLOCATION IN THE SOVIET UNION

The purpose, methods of construction, and limitations of the GNP figure all suggest that the analyst must display a touch of healthy skepticism before he applies the crude statistics to questions of national security—or even to economic capacity itself. Let us now turn to the actual process by which nations allocate their resources, and the way in which the allocative process places constraints upon the formulation of national policy and, by posing issues in terms of alternatives, creates puzzling dilemmas for the political leaders.

The Soviet leaders are confronted with a question of choice in determining the proper degree of emphasis to be placed upon the several components of their broad national strategy, just as the American people and their leaders are. Viewed broadly, the issues facing the two countries are surprisingly similar, but a number of sharp distinctions occur as a result of the disparity in the decision-making processes. Two of these differences help to explain why we will first discuss the allocation problem with reference to the Soviet case. First, resource allocation in the Soviet Union may be attacked *directly*, since it does not have to be examined in the context of a complicated market mechanism; in the market economy, the political leaders can only approach the problem obliquely. Secondly, the pressure of public opinion cannot be a direct force influencing the decisions. Since no open way exists to mobilize or organize public attitudes independently of state decision, the regime is freer

to allocate resources in the light of its own interpretation of
the needs of the state.

Broadly speaking, the Soviet leaders are faced with four
allocational questions:

1. How much is it necessary to devote to the consumers in
   order to maintain political stability and quench dissent?
2. How much must be devoted to the physical maintenance
   of the security of the state—that is, the allotment for the
   armed forces?
3. How much can be devoted to the future through investment in the industrial capacity of the country?
4. How much can be spared to supply aid to friends, lures
   to neutrals, and trouble for enemies on the international
   scene?

Since these questions are interdependent, the decisions must
be reached simultaneously, and these decisions will both reflect
and determine the main lines of Soviet policy. If the demands on
resources exceed the available resources, the leadership may be
faced with a dilemma. It will be forced to reduce commitments,
and the decision as to where to retrench will alter the direction
of Soviet policy.

The first question—how much should be devoted to consumption—goes to the heart of Soviet strength. Since the end of World
War II, we in the West have repeatedly underrated Soviet
capacity and the menace that it posed to our civilization, because we persisted in interpreting Soviet goals in terms of our
own priorities. We have assumed that the primary use of productive capacity is to augment the well-being of the populace.
But the great increases in Soviet power—both industrial and
military—may be ascribed to the iron discipline with which the
aspirations of the Soviet citizen have been suppressed. When
one considers the state of the Soviet economy at the end of
the war—with its industry decimated and its citizens destitute—
it would have been difficult to predict the speed with which it
revived and narrowed the gap between it and the West in output, in military technology, and in education. Though we have
occasionally been obsessed with the nature of Communism and

the threat it poses, we have been blind to the fact that *the mission of its leadership is to preserve and to extend the power of the Soviet Union,* and that in the process, consumption could and would be ruthlessly sacrificed. In the early postwar years, Stalin decreed that the levels of consumption would be held as closely as possible to those prevailing during the war, and all residual capacity devoted to refurbishing and extending Soviet industrial and military power.

In Figure I, I have indicated the percentage allocation of GNP by final use for the United States and the Soviet Union during the year 1955. I have used the conventional figures, and shall leave until later a discussion of why the conventional figures probably are biased *in favor of consumption.* In will be remembered that by the year 1955 the postwar pressure on Soviet living standards had been considerably alleviated. The national product of the Soviet Union is now estimated to be roughly one-third of our own. Nevertheless, despite the much lower levels of living (estimated at no more than one-fifth of the U.S. level), the proportion of the total that is devoted to household consumption has been held below 50 per cent without provoking widespread unrest. This provides a partial explanation of the wide margin of resources that has been available to the Soviet leadership for strategic purposes. Needless to say, the Soviet citizenry has not been entirely happy under this pressure, and its silent support has been available to any Soviet leader who promised relief. In the Stalin era, the undisguised emphasis was upon defense and heavy industry. Malenkov, prior to his deposition, was promising relief in the form of consumers' goods. Khrushchev's rise to power, in a series of well-managed *coups,* has been interpreted, oddly enough, as a victory for the alleviation of the Stalinist pressure, largely due to the departure of Stalin's faithful subalterns, Molotov and Kaganovich.

In his quest for higher living standards, Khrushchev has devoted much of his attention to agriculture. The virgin-lands program, announced in 1954, involved the plowing of 32.5 million acres of semi-arid land mainly in Kazakhstan, formerly devoted to a pastoral economy. Cultivation of such land involves risks, since the reduction in soil moisture, if accompanied by

FIGURE I

PERCENTAGE ALLOCATION OF GROSS NATIONAL PRODUCT
BY FINAL USE—UNITED STATES AND U.S.S.R., 1955

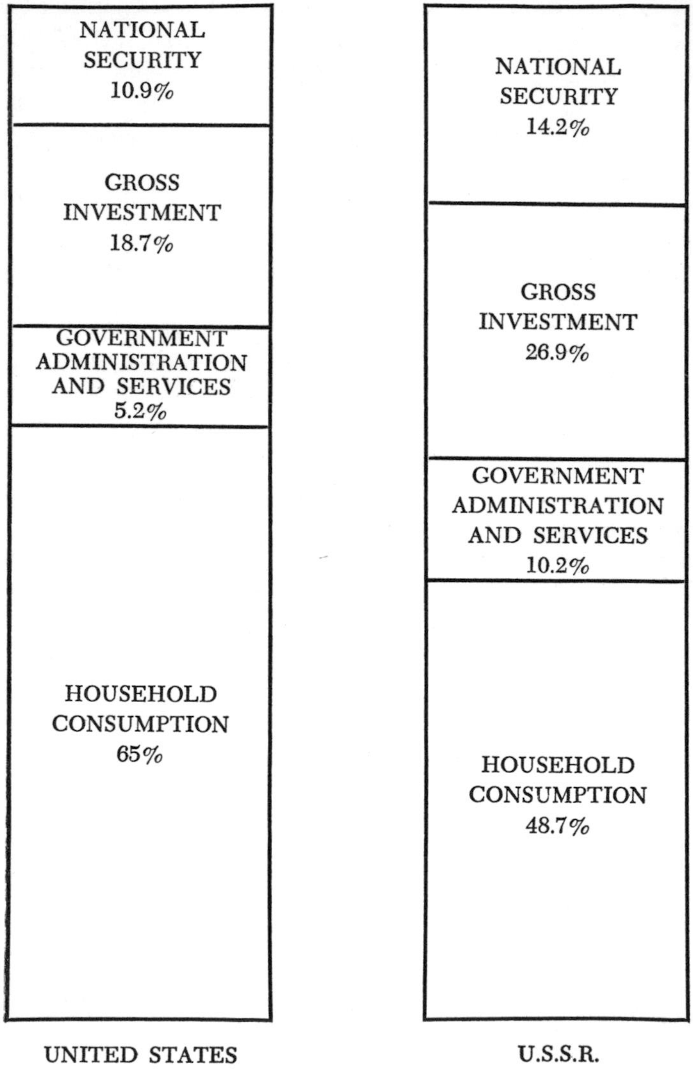

UNITED STATES	U.S.S.R.
NATIONAL SECURITY 10.9%	NATIONAL SECURITY 14.2%
GROSS INVESTMENT 18.7%	GROSS INVESTMENT 26.9%
GOVERNMENT ADMINISTRATION AND SERVICES 5.2%	GOVERNMENT ADMINISTRATION AND SERVICES 10.2%
HOUSEHOLD CONSUMPTION 65%	HOUSEHOLD CONSUMPTION 48.7%

Source: *Soviet Economic Growth; A Comparison with the United States*,
a study prepared for the Subcommittee on Foreign Economic Policy of the
Joint Economic Committee by the Legislative Reference Service of the
Library of Congress (Washington: Government Printing Office, 1957), p. 127.

drought, may set the soil to blowing. In both 1956 and 1958, good results were obtained; in 1957, however, production fell sharply as a result of drought—and rumors of dust-bowl conditions emerged from the Soviet Union. During the summer of 1957, Khrushchev also pledged, somewhat rashly, that Soviet production of meat and dairy products would catch up with that of the United States within three years—which, particularly in the case of meat production, will require some doing. In 1957, Soviet milk production was reported to be at 95 per cent of the U.S. level, and in 1958, it was reported to have exceeded American output. Here, however, as not infrequently happens, the Russians seem to have benefited from the peculiar nature of their statistics, since milk production is calculated on the basis of biological yield and includes both spillage and milk consumed on the farm by livestock, whereas the comparable American figure includes only milk for human consumption. Meat production, on the other hand, continues to hover at about one-third of the American level, and little has been said about it recently. Since it is about seven times as costly, in terms of calories, to feed men indirectly through livestock production as it is to feed them directly through grain production, Khrushchev's promise implies an enormous increase in the supply of feed, and consequently a substantial diversion of Soviet resources into the production of grain.

Despite the striking inferiority of the Soviet agricultural base, there is no doubt that the Soviet Union could eventually surpass American levels of agricultural production, if the Soviet leaders so desire and are willing to invest the resources. American farmers, it is presumed, produce for a market, and the market for agricultural products is limited by the size of the population. American consumers do not seem to desire more agricultural production, preferring to spend their incomes on other goods and services. The Soviet Union—with its control over resources and with no need to produce for a market—could outstrip the United States in agricultural production if that is the goal. The support of Mikoyan, reputedly a light-industry man, in the *contretemps* with the Stalinists may indicate Khrushchev's sincerity in attempting to improve the lot of the Soviet citizen. Despite the continued emphasis on heavy industry, the

Seven-Year Plan does promise more to the consumer than is customary. On the other hand, the military will undoubtedly continue to urge a hard policy, and should be able to prevent actual coddling of the consumer. Just what future policy will be with respect to consumption is difficult to say; even the experts in the field can do little more than hazard a guess.

The second issue confronting the leadership—providing for the physical defense of the realm—is not one on which the Russians have shown any tendency to shirk. Considered in terms of their total resources, their performance has been remarkable indeed. Despite the strains and the rapid pace of weapons technology, they have maintained military forces that compare not unfavorably with our own. For reasons that will be developed later, it seems likely that the figure of 14.2 per cent of GNP, as given in Figure I, drastically underestimates the proportion of real resources used for national security purposes. There can be little doubt that armaments production has constituted an immense burden on the Soviet economy, and in view of the over-all resource position, *there can be little doubt that substantial disarmament would be a greater boon to the Soviet economy than to our own.*

The third question—what proportion of total resources may be allocated to investment activity—is partially independent and partially dependent. The over-all degree to which consumers may be deprived of the benefits of present production may lie within the discretion of the state, but the pattern of investment activity as between heavy and light industry must reflect the decisions that are reached with respect to the other questions. If, for example, the state is determined to concentrate investment in capital-goods and in defense-sensitive industries—to invest in depth, as it were—the desire of the citizenry for consumer goods must be even more firmly repressed. On the other hand, if a steady rise in the standard of living is desired, a high proportion of investment must be carried on in light industry. Investment in depth, in the capital-goods industries, provides additional leverage for growth in the long run, but less immediate return for the citizenry. The rate of growth of industrial production is dependent in large measure upon the over-all proportion of production that can be plowed back into capital formation; but it is also a question of the degree to which emphasis can be placed upon the production of capital goods within the over-all investment program.

Once again, the Soviet performance in this respect has been outstanding. In 1955, according to the conventional statistics, 26.9 per cent of Soviet GNP was devoted to investment activity, as contrasted to 18.9 per cent in the United States. But these figures understate the real difference—not only because of the systematic lowering of prices on capital goods, to which I will return later, but because the direction of investment activity differs so greatly in the two nations. A high proportion of investment in the United States goes into residential construction; in the Soviet Union, it is held to a minimum. But even the portion devoted to producers' goods is used in different ways. In the United States, a very large part is used to provide amenities for producers—deep carpets and paneled offices for corporate executives, commodious washrooms with fluorescent lighting for the workforce, and comfortable snack bars for white-collar employees' coffee breaks. Granted that investment in neon lighting, new store fronts, or leather-covered wastepaper baskets may enhance both trade and morale, and may be considered a legitimate form of business capital, it is not nearly so productive as producers' equipment. In the Soviet Union, investment is directed to a higher degree to producers' goods and to a much smaller degree to the amenities. As we shall see later, it is the single-mindedness of Soviet economic activity that accounts for its impressive rate of growth of industrial production. Despite a smaller margin of resources, the proportion of Soviet national product available for "strategic production"—defense and capital formation—has been better than 40 per cent as opposed to less than 30 per cent in the United States. In recent years, the Soviet rate of net investment has been about double our own; its rate of industrial growth similarly impressive, compared with our own. It is probably unnecessary to dwell upon the fundamental long-run importance of such divergences.

The final question—what proportion of total resources should be devoted on the international scene to aid, pseudo-trade, or the mischievous provision of armaments—has been a negligible one until the last few years. Even now, there is far more fanfare than concrete assistance. A minute proportion of Soviet output, less than 1 per cent of the total, is devoted to aid to allies and neutrals or to pseudo-trade with neutrals. The niggardliness of the Soviet Union in its dealings with its associates has hardly reflected the spirit of socialist brotherhood. The limits on foreign assistance up to, and even since, 1953 may simply reflect a deep-seated assumption of Soviet economic policy that gives preference to the needs of "socialism in one country," rather than following the ideological direction implicit in the slogan "Workers of the world, unite." Moreover, Soviet trading credits, sometimes confused with aid, which have been extended to some of the neutrals have been quite limited; the credits have not been drawn upon completely, and when drawn upon, the shipments have been unsatisfactory. Aside from the arms shipments since the launching of the new program in 1953, the neutrals have received less than a half-billion in assistance—either in the form of direct aid or the provision of credits. It is doubtful whether any but a few of the neutrals have benefited from their economic association with the Soviet Union, and these latter (with the exception, to date, of India) only to an insignificant degree.

The upshot of our brief discussion of Soviet allocation problems is the necessity of seeing the limitations imposed upon opportunities by insufficient means. The quest for national power cannot be viewed as a monolithic advance on all fronts; instead, there must be a choice among alternatives. If a nation is straining to build up its heavy industry, it may, for example, have difficulty in promoting agricultural expansion. The doctrine of alternative cost suggests that success in one line implies risks in others, yet there seems to be a fundamental propensity of the human mind to extrapolate trends or even imaginary tendencies, without consideration of the compensating growth of obstacles. If the Kremlin's long-run design for the engulfment of the free world depends, as is sometimes suggested, upon the maintenance of a rate of growth that will simultaneously narrow the material gap between the Communist world and the West and also exert an attractive force to lure the underdeveloped lands within its orbit, then it will be forced to defer other goals. It cannot at the same time reduce working hours, liberalize the regime, rapidly expand the production of consumer goods (including agricultural products), improve the dreadful housing conditions, replace obsolescent industrial facilities, maintain an enormous military program, *and* devote considerable resources to aiding other countries. Since it cannot accomplish all things at once, improvement of domestic conditions plus expansion of aid abroad both imply a reduction in the rate of growth.

The events of the past few years have underscored the problem posed for the Soviet Union by limited resources. The East European upheaval of the fall of 1956 resulted in the rapid expansion of Soviet commitments; the satellite nations ceased to be a source of substantial profit and may even have become a source of drainage. Within a period of a few months, net obligations rose sharply: cancelled Polish debts equaled 2.1 billion rubles, new credits of 1.1 billion rubles to Poland and 1 billion rubles to Hungary were extended, and the cost of Yugoslav *rapprochement*, temporary as it appears to have been, was some $285 million.[2] At the same time, the annual charge to East Germany for the upkeep of the Soviet garrison was halved—a loss of 1.5 billion rubles a year. In January, 1957, Otto Grotewohl, the East German Premier, announced that East Germany could not look indefinitely to the Soviet Union for assistance and must increase her own production, for the aid to East Europe was straining the Soviet economy. In the following month, the Soviet government announced a cutback of defense outlays, admitted a decline in the rate of growth, and indirectly announced the scrapping of the Sixth Five-Year Plan. Goals for steel, coal, pig iron, and electric power were revised downward, although at the same time investment in housing was slated to rise by 20 per cent. Even the fanfare that accompanied the announcement of the new Seven-Year Plan late in 1958 could not disguise the fact that Soviet targets were being stretched out and that a substantial retardation of the growth rate had occurred. These events, coupled with a decline in the rate of investment, have promoted a more skeptical appraisal of the *willingness* of the Soviet Union to extend large-scale aid to neutrals.

3.   ALLOCATION UNDER FREE ENTERPRISE: A COMPARISON

The problem of resource allocation in the United States, operating as it does under a system of free enterprise, is considerably more complicated, and the differences between it and a centrally controlled economy need to be underscored. It is far easier to understand the direct allocation of resources in accordance with a "plan" as practiced in the Soviet Union, since one may avoid dealing with the complexities of the price system and the mechanics of the government's taxation and expenditure policies. Under free enterprise, prices, quantities, and quality of output are determined largely by the mechanism of the market and by the host of factors that fall under the catch-all headings of supply and demand. Consumers may freely purchase the commodities or services they desire. If they desire more of a particular commodity (increasing the demand), either prices will rise or stocks will be depleted; in either event, there is a signal and an incentive for the producers to expand the output of this particular item. Producers base their output decisions on prospective revenues and costs. Just as consumers select their purchases on the basis of price, producers will base their combinations of factors of production on the respective prices of those factors, thereby creating a market for the factors of production. By and large, the incomes of individuals in a free-enterprise economy are based upon the price that their possessions or labor may bring in the market. It is hoped that the individual's income is closely correlated with the contribution that the resources under his control make to the productive process. No individual is forced to put all his property or labor in the market for productive factors; he is merely given the incentive to do so. The larger a man's income, the greater will be his spending power—which brings us back to the force that initiates the productive cycle, consumer demand.

The market economy in the United States has proved itself to be a tremendously efficient mechanism for the satisfaction of the material desires of the citizenry. It provides consumer satisfaction based upon individual preferences, rather than upon government fiat. It has proved its adaptability to the short-run exigencies of total war. Its mettle, however, is yet to be tested in coping with the strains of an international conflict of indefinite duration, such as the one we now face with the Communist world. Probably the most ticklish question facing the American system is whether or not its economy, which was developed to satisfy the inclinations and tastes of individuals in accordance with the libertarian tenets of the nineteenth century, can achieve the pattern of resource allocation that is essential to provide for collective goals and for national security.

The root cause of the difficulty of adapting to the permanent stresses of national security lies in the fact that collective expenditures on the part of the government represent a superimposition upon—and, in some sense, a distortion of—the market mechanism. In the main, in order for the state to carry on collective expenditures, the citizenry must provide the resources by paying taxes. In a democracy, the citizenry must impose taxes upon itself. It must accept the burden of doing something that is individually unpleasant, and which runs against the grain of a consumption-oriented, market-oriented economy, in which individualistic goals have traditionally been paramount.

A second issue arises from the fact that, in this age, investment and the expansion of heavy industry may have strategic significance. In a market economy, however, capacity will only be expanded when it is felt that the goods produced can be sold profitably. Thus, in a society in which production is mainly carried on to satisfy consumers' desires, investment activity that might be desirable on broad strategic grounds (in steel capacity, for example) will occur only if it happens to coincide with consumer preferences. Thus strategic investment, which might be necessary as risk insurance, may be at the mercy of the consumers' whims instead of being determined by state policy.

In these two ways, then, a market economy oriented toward

the consumer creates a problem for the achievement of the pattern of resource allocation most conducive to national security. Democracies do seem to find it necessary to devote a much higher percentage of total resources to consumption than do totalitarian states. This, perhaps, simply reflects the nature of a society in which the purpose of the state is to provide a framework that protects and fosters the achievement of the aims of private groups and individuals. In the case of the United States, we may note from Figure I that some 65 per cent of GNP is devoted to household consumption, as opposed to less than 50 per cent in the Soviet Union. Our relative outlays for national security and investment are correspondingly lower— 10.9 per cent and 18.7 per cent, respectively.

Our total output is, however, so much greater than that of the Soviet Union that we can afford to devote a smaller percentage to strategic expenditures and still remain ahead of our chief rival. In Figure II, I have indicated the relative magnitudes of the GNP's of the United States, the Soviet Union, and Communist China for the year 1957, making a somewhat more generous estimate for the Communist powers than is usual. American output is about three times that of the Soviet Union, about ten times that of Communist China. It would appear that although we spend a smaller relative amount on national security, we are spending twice as much, dollar for dollar, on national security as is the Soviet Union—some $44 billion, as opposed to some $23 billion for the Soviets. This suggests the pleasant conclusion that we really have nothing to worry about. Unfortunately, all estimates of Soviet military capabilities indicate that their over-all position compares quite favorably with our own. If money expenditures meant the same thing in the two economies, this would not be true; we must, therefore, be suspicious of the relevance of the GNP figures to this problem.

If we recall the definition of "gross national product"—the value of the annual flow of goods and services *at market prices*— we have a clue to the cause of our difficulties. If prices have the same meaning and if the structure of production is roughly similar in the two economies, then the GNP figures will provide a fairly reliable index of the importance of the different sectors

FIGURE II

RELATIVE MAGNITUDES OF THE GROSS NATIONAL PRODUCTS
OF THE UNITED STATES, U.S.S.R., AND COMMUNIST CHINA, 1957
(in billions of American dollars)

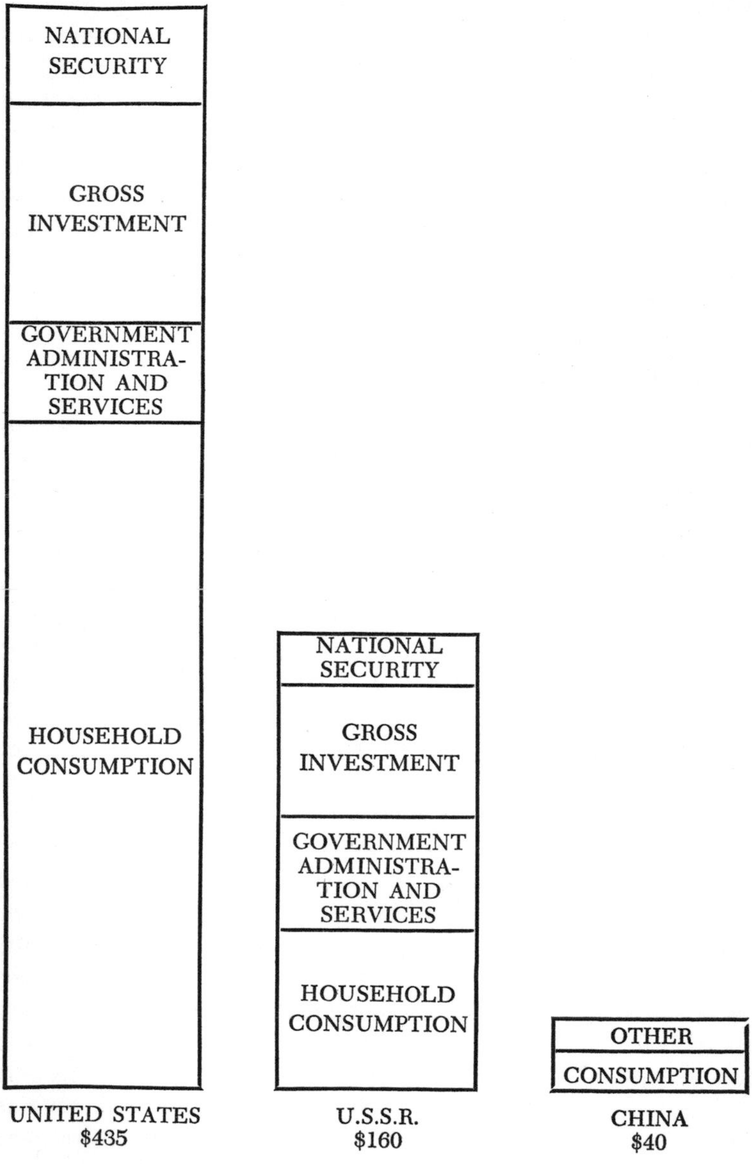

NATIONAL SECURITY		
GROSS INVESTMENT		
GOVERNMENT ADMINISTRA- TION AND SERVICES		
HOUSEHOLD CONSUMPTION	NATIONAL SECURITY	
	GROSS INVESTMENT	
	GOVERNMENT ADMINISTRA- TION AND SERVICES	
	HOUSEHOLD CONSUMPTION	OTHER
		CONSUMPTION
UNITED STATES $435	U.S.S.R. $160	CHINA $40

of the economies. But the structure of Soviet prices, wage rates, and the relative productivities in the several industries differs entirely from that prevailing in the United States. In the first place, prices in the Soviet Union do not reflect the costs of production as do American prices. Instead, the entire price structure is manipulated by centralized control to achieve state goals. Soviet industries need not pay the costs of the use of land or of capital, which biases the prices downward in the more heavily capitalized industries. Moreover, the price structure is used to subsidize indirectly certain industries at the expense of others; consumer-goods industries must earn profits that are not required of the capital-goods industries. The prices of capital goods have been artificially lowered, relative to consumer-goods prices, so that those industries that are heavily capitalized may charge prices lower than would otherwise prevail.

The role of prices in the Soviet system raises some question concerning the usefulness of information conveyed by estimation of gross national product (based upon prevailing prices). But even more surely, it indicates that the GNP figures provide no useful guide as to the relative efficiencies of similar sums spent in the military sectors of the two economies. In the consumer-goods sector, 20 rubles may not buy what a dollar can in the United States; yet, in the defense sector, perhaps 2 rubles will achieve the same results as the American dollar. It would be erroneous to assume that the dollar or its ruble equivalent has the same effectiveness, industry by industry, but this is the implicit assumption when shares of GNP are used as an index. The Soviet economic system is so organized that the productivity of labor is raised and the prices are lowered in the defense-sensitive industries. The capital-goods industries supply cheap producer goods to the defense industries. If American wages are four times as high in defense industries, but productivity in these industries is only twice as high, the Soviet goods may cost only half as much. Soviet expenditure of the equivalent of $20 billion may go as far or further than American expenditures of $40 billion. *In terms of American prices*, it may well be that the Russians are devoting 30 per cent of their output to national security. Certainly, it is clear that the proportion of real resources devoted by the Soviet Union to national security is much higher than is suggested by the conventional GNP figures.

This brings us back to the problem of allocation in the American economy and the difficulties of meshing the necessity for heavy collective expenditures required by international tensions with the ethos of an individualistic, market-oriented economy. In order to achieve our national objectives, it may be necessary to maintain military-force levels higher than we have today; yet, in democracies, the public begrudges the diversion of a higher proportion of output to the military. It may be strengthened in its reluctance by public statements that we cannot "afford" to spend more on defense, lest we court "national bankruptcy." The problem of achieving the pattern of resource allocation most suitable for national security is, however, not insoluble if the public has the firm determination to meet it. Though undoubtedly there do exist economic limits to a nation's taxable capacity and its ability to provide for collective expenditure, we have not yet approached these *economic* limits. The immediate limit has been a political one—the unwillingness of the public to tax itself sufficiently to bear the necessary burden. There is no economic reason why this should be so. We can, if we possess the firmness, provide the combination of incentives, penalties, accolades, and subsidies to attain the pattern and rate of investment and the degree of collective spending most conducive to national security. We can encourage the growth of a firmer mobilization base, but in the process we must possess the political cohesion to overcome the opposition of various interest groups whose short-run aims are adversely affected by economic activities along certain lines. It must be reiterated that the barriers to resource allocation most advantageous from the strategic point of view are political rather than economic in nature. Economics points to the wide latitude of choice that we possess if we are willing to accept all the ramifications of the proffered alternatives.

4. Some Final Observations

The fundamental problem in economics remains the allocation of scarce resources, and the delineation of the methods by which this allocation is achieved. In dealing with national economies, we have noted how the scarcity of means imposes the necessity of choosing among goals and limiting commitments. In the case of the Soviet Union, we have observed that it is not in a position to pursue concurrently all the courses of action that would create difficulties for the West, and which in our imaginations we can conceive as theoretical dangers. A similar assessment is in order for Communist China—she, too, cannot accomplish all things. As indicated in Figure II, her resources relative to our own are small. If she foments subversion in South Asia and struggles over Formosa, maintains an enormous military machine (relative to her resources), and engages in a conflict with her own peasantry, her opportunities for rapid industrial growth would appear slim. If she looks upon industrial growth solely in terms of national power rather than living standards, she must expect to cope with a refractory population. China must contend with the most dismal of the ancient principles of the "dismal science"—the Malthusian problem. Rapid population growth threatens to keep her *per capita* resources low and to impede the march to national power. In the light of her limited resources, China's recent difficulties, the reduction of her defense budget, and the more peaceful visage that she presents in world affairs may be explicable.

Basic to the study of political economy is the issue of how best to dispose of limited means. If there is one lesson to be taught by economics, it is this reflection of the attempt to come to grips with the fact of scarcity. The "dismal science" has pricked the hopes of many, yet in the current world conflict it gives to us the reassuring note that not everything can go wrong. The resources of our international rivals are not unlimited. In their capacity to do us harm, they must, therefore, be judged on the basis of their capabilities rather than their intentions.

Moreover, if we view the principle of alternative costs in its broadest sense as a law of compensation at work in human affairs, we have developed a framework of analysis capable of more general applicability. Consider, for example, the problem of the possible loss of additional space in Asia to Communism. Would such a loss be disastrous? The Soviets surely recognize as we must, that there are disadvantages as well as advantages in Communist hegemony over additional territory. Communist expansion does imply, to be sure, the loss of whatever resources the area concerned possesses—and in the case of Japan or the littoral of the Persian Gulf, these resources are presently considerable. It also implies the loss of population, but from the strategic point of view (as opposed to the humanitarian one of saving men from the maw of Communism), the significance of population *per se* may easily be overrated. Economically and strategically, populations adequately equipped with resources are invaluable, but a population without resources could simply represent a drain. If such a drain on the Soviet economy were to be established, it would tend to reduce the rate of industrial growth and slow down the advance of the standard of living. This would add to the problems of the Soviet leadership, and at the same time reduce the attractiveness of Communism to others.

One of the chief advantages of the United States *at the present time* in its conflict with the Soviet Union is the much higher level of resources we possess for accomplishing our goals. (In the following chapter, it will be suggested that this advantage is not an absolute one, but rather a relative one that can be overcome by sufficient Soviet determination.) In the nature of Soviet economic development, we may expect that this advantage will slowly disappear. Yet, in the interim, we should devise means of exploiting our position. An armaments race, for example, is far less a burden on the more affluent contestant than it is on the contestant attempting to make do with less. We have tended to concentrate on our difficulties at home, and have ignored the strain on our rivals. The armaments race since the Korean War has, however, damaged the Soviet position in innumerable ways. The post-Korean expansion of Soviet military power was achieved mainly at the expense of the investment component of GNP. The rate of growth was therefore slower than it would otherwise have been. The drastic upheaval in East Europe in 1957, particularly in Poland, was not unrelated to the heavy armaments burdens that the Russians had imposed upon the satellite economies after the outbreak of the Korean War. The disruption of the Polish economy, the diversion of resources from consumption and industrial development, and the ensuing economic distress played no little part in the rise of Gomulka.

At the present time, the development of the submarine-based Polaris missile system creates the possibility of new strains on the Soviet economy. Unless the Soviet leadership is willing to accept the implicit strategic disadvantage, it may now have to devote a sizable proportion of national resources to anti-submarine warfare, which hitherto the Soviet Union has been able to neglect because of its continental position. We need to remember these strains and their consequences. From this standpoint, disarmament would be highly advantageous to the Soviet Union, since it would free resources for other purposes at a time when its economy and those of the satellites have been exhibiting some signs of strain. In this respect, it would not be equally advantageous for the United States, and the price that we demand might be shaped accordingly. We should always be alert to the constraints imposed by limited resources on the opportunities and the policies of our opponents, as well as upon ourselves.

3

ECONOMIC CAPACITY AND NATIONAL POWER

We have already considered the significance of the over-all level of resources that provide a nation with the means (in terms of economic capacity) with which to achieve its strategic and domestic goals. In the present chapter, it is our purpose to examine the limitations of economic capacity as an *index* of national power. The magnitude of present American resources relative to present Soviet resources, it has been suggested, provides us with an advantage in the power struggle. Undoubtedly, this is, in itself, an element of strength. The Russians, in attempting to achieve their purposes with a thinner margin of resources, are under pressure to sacrifice domestic goals in order to accomplish their broad strategic goals. Nevertheless, it has been indicated that the Russians have been impressively efficient in achieving their strategic goals, although at the price of domestic sacrifices. The structure of the Soviet economy has been manipulated so that the objective of national power may be attained, regardless of its impact on consumer well-being. Despite their relatively modest *over-all* level of resources, the Russians have maintained military-force levels that compare not unfavorably with our own, and which in certain sectors of the cold war clearly overshadow the forces that the West can quickly bring to bear. In addition, the Russians have continued to plow back a substantial proportion of national output, thereby achieving an impressive rate of growth. Soviet allocational prowess constitutes, in a sense, an element of Western weakness which is not easily interpretable within the framework of over-all economic capacity.

Economic capacity is an essential ingredient of national power, yet, apparently, there is no simple and obvious relationship between the two. There is a grave danger, however, that we in the West will assume this relationship to be a direct one which can be identified with precision. In a general way, we are all intuitively familiar with the idea that one nation whose margin of resources is greater than another's will possess a sizable advantage in the event of a military encounter. The phrase "economic potential for war" has an insidious appeal; it flows trippingly from the tongue, but the concept itself remains elusive. Any careful analysis of its meaning and of its significance for the formulation of national policy will reveal underlying causes for this elusiveness.

In its relation to national power, economic capacity may be interpreted in two ways: as a doctrine and as an element of strength. In its latter role, the concept has a distinct but limited usefulness in gauging the alignment of power; but, alas, it is in its former role—as a doctrine—that the concept has been popularized. In its most elemental form, the doctrine simply expresses the conviction that economically inferior powers are in no position to throw down the military gauntlet to economically superior powers. During the discussions of the post-Korean reduction in the size of our military establishment, President Eisenhower came close to a perfect expression of this belief: "True security for our country must be founded on a strong and expanding economy readily convertible to the needs of war. . . . We can never be defeated so long as American relative superiority in productive capacity is sustained." [1] Thus, the doctrine expresses the assumption that God is on the side of the strongest battalions, and the latter are sustained through the possession of the most productive factories. By what process of reasoning can such a conviction be reached?

The foundation for the belief is the valid observation that the productive capacity of a nation provides it with the means it may use to attain its national objectives. We have already seen that this is true—but that the distance between potentiality and substance is a long one, and the steps necessary to achieve the goals might not be taken. Economic potential, by itself, is not enough; but in the doctrinal version, the political and strategic questions are simply assumed away.

Generally, in these appraisals of relative power, the nation's economic potential is defined as the maximum output of goods and services during a specified period of time—in other words, the *maximum* gross national product. Allowance is thereby made for expansion of output in wartime through increased employment and reduced leisure. From the useful, if limited, idea of economic potential, it is but one small logical jump to the concept of "economic potential for war" (more familiarly known as the EPW), which has been defined as the nation's economic potential *minus that portion of output which ought to be reserved for civilian usage.* Despite the seeming precision of the definition, EPW is in fact unmeasureable. Plainly, there is no precise way to measure how much output it is socially necessary to divert to civilian usage. The amount will vary in different situations, depending upon the mood and expectations of the populace, the psychological response to international pressures, the demands made on the public, and the willingness of the public to accept sacrifices. By the very logic of alternative cost, ultimately the allocation of resources should reflect any changes in the public's evaluation of the relative importance of the nation's goals.

Values and changes in values that may bring adjustments in appropriate civilian consumption cannot be measured mechanically. In practice, however, certain mechanical rules of thumb are used to specify necessary civilian consumption. In this manner, a residual called "economic potential for war" is obtained, and—despite the amorphous notion, appropriate civilian consumption, and highly debatable assumptions about its size—it is still believed that the residual possesses some absolute validity. It is but one short step from this conclusion to the conviction that, other things being equal, the gross national product or the *per capita* gross national product is a ready index of the degree to which economic capacity may be diverted to war-supporting activities. In practice, some allowance may be made, however, for "dynamic considerations" such as the rate of economic growth, but the upshot of the argument is that ultimately the economic potential for war is the decisive factor.

It will readily be understood that a doctrine stating that the economic war potentials of the several states, measured in accordance with a scale of national production, provide the ultimate determinant of power can be quite comforting to a nation that possesses approximately one-third of the world's productive capacity. It is not entirely a coincidence that the idea has had such wide appeal in the United States, possessor of the pre-eminent economy of the modern world. It provides reassurance that we cannot be defeated, since we are protected by a kind of economic Maginot Line. Those who have studied the military realities of the modern world have long had doubts concerning the degree of reassurance offered to us by the indisputable fact that ours is the world's most powerful economy. Even more suspect is a further amplification of the argument that provides a rationalization for military weakness—to wit, the belief that we cannot *afford* to spend more on defense, since the strength of the American economy is our *first* line of defense; that we must be on guard against the most devilish of Soviet plots, to destroy us by encouraging us to "spend our way into bankruptcy."

Nevertheless, economic power does provide an element of strength, as well as a doctrine of economic determinism. Economists have not been unwilling to emphasize this factor, since it reflects an occupational partiality to the belief that economics is important, and that public attention to national income figures should be strengthened. The danger exists that the public will ignore the qualifications and make something out of the conclusions that, despite their stress on the economic element, the economists never intended. Economic studies can point to few firm conclusions, other than a *rough approximation* of the resources available for war-making activities. Two approaches have been employed in appraising the availability of resources and the role of economic capacity: the economic potential for war (discussed above) and the economic mobilization base.

The economic potential for war. Precise measurement of EPW depends upon assumptions that inevitably are questionable. The notion of maximum national product does make allowance for the drastic change possible in the volume of output between peace and war. In wartime, normally, both the size of the labor force and the length of the work week increase, and in stringent circumstances the workforce may be drastically increased by the absorption of women, the aged, and teen-agers who usually remain outside it. Thus, despite the withdrawal of men by the armed forces, the wartime output may be much greater than that of peacetime, when leisure time is one of the most desirable of consumer goods. In order to estimate the maximum national product, the probable labor force must be multiplied by the anticipated annual output per worker. From the resulting figure, the component for civilian usage must be subtracted; but as has already been suggested, it is impossible to obtain any meaningful estimate, since the amount that must be diverted to civilians will vary, depending on the circumstances.

The concept of economic potential for war[2] has one great strength, and one weakness even more fundamental than the one that has been mentioned. Its great strength lies in its emphasis upon real resources—the labor supply and real output—rather than upon financial resources. The contemporary economic limit on the war-making capacity of industrial states is posed by the scarcity of real resources, rather than by the adequacy of financial organization. In earlier ages, this was not so; the financial resources of the several states could have been decisive. In peacetime, also, the financial capacity of a state is important, since due regard must be given (in the West) to provision of incentives and individual rights, and to distributional justice. In wartime, these issues become subsidiary, and their influence on financial capacity is reduced by patriotism and the willingness of the public to accept conditions that would not be tolerated during times of peace. For the major powers, if the physical resources exist, the financial techniques can probably be devised to extract them from the public. If not, recourse may be had to requisition, or ultimately to directed labor. Thus, the idea of economic potential for war quite properly emphasizes the physical resources, and economists have used the concept to drive home the point that, in modern war, the problem of physical capacity overshadows finance.

On the other hand, relying as it does on GNP statistics, EPW has one overwhelming deficiency. Clearly, before the concept acquires any utility whatsoever, it must take into account the refinements made necessary by the *composition* of the national product and by the *structure* of industry. Some industries are suitable for conversion to war production; others, however, are not. We may beat our plowshares into swords, but we find it difficult to achieve the same results with cosmetics, textiles, or the traditional example, butter. Armament production means heavy industry, so many states are unable to make the choice between guns or butter; only the industrial states possess that choice. A largely agricultural economy, irrespective of its wealth, lacks the industrial facilities to produce the weapons necessary for modern warfare; it can only acquire them from other sources. A highly industrialized nation, such as Great Britain, has a potential far out of proportion to its national product, if—and this is an all-important proviso—it retains access to the food and raw materials necessary to the maintenance of its population and economy.

The root cause of the deficiencies of the EPW approach lies in its intimate association with the national-product account. The latter assumes that the goals of production are consumption and the well-being of the human agents of production. This is a somewhat arbitrary assumption, although it is a reflection of Western social attitudes. If, in a particular state, the purpose of production is assumed to be military effectiveness rather than consumer well-being, then the measurement of output will be judged on criteria other than the conventional ones—the output of hard goods or military hardware, or the capacity that is convertible to the output of military hardware. The conventional measurement of national product is not directly related to such considerations. The composition of national product—and in particular, the industrial component—is far more significant. The growing importance of the structure of the economy may help to explain the decreased weight given to such powers as France and Italy in the twentieth century.

The mobilization base. As we turn toward the analysis of the structure of production, we move from the general and somewhat amorphous notion of potential to a more concrete concept of economic capacity. Instead of using a vague aggregate of national output inclusive of a wide array of heterogeneous goods—many of which are wholly irrelevant to any wartime purpose—we select only those industries which may be considered *strategically* significant. This brings us to the concept of the mobilization base, which is allied to the idea of economic potential for war, but, perhaps, somewhat more meaningful. Actually it may be viewed as the ultimate refinement of the EPW concept, stressing the industrial facilities already in existence, rather than the intangible power represented by over-all resources. The idea of economic potential contains in itself *no hint of the time element*, yet the time element goes to the heart of the relationship between economic capacity and military power. It ignores the degree of readiness of the economy, but the rapidity of conversion is central to the issue of mobilization.

It might be said that the mobilization-base approach views the question of economic capacity positively: What types of production are we likely to need in a possible military encounter, and what facilities do we have presently or readily convertible to provide that output? On the other hand, the EPW approach poses the question of economic capacity negatively: What resources are *not necessary for the civilian sector* and may *eventually* be diverted to supporting war efforts? By concentrating on the here-and-now, the mobilization base is the more cautious approach; it has been defined as: ". . . that capacity available to permit rapid expansion of production, sufficient to meet military, war-supporting, essential civilian, and export requirements in the event of a full-scale war." [3] It may be seen that the mobilization-base concept differs from the EPW concept in three significant ways:

1. It concerns itself with capacity in strategic industries, not with capacity in general.
2. Essential civilian production is viewed as strategic production, not as diversion of resources from the war-making economic capacity.
3. The importance of the time element in the form of readiness or of rapid convertibility is stressed.

In brief, the mobilization-base rationale focuses on this question: How quickly can the sinews of war be provided through the curtailment of non-essential production and the diversion of resources?

Let us briefly review the relative positions of the United States and the U.S.S.R. In providing the instruments of war, the American economy is characterized by some temporary disadvantages and some longer-run advantages. At the present time, the military production of the United States does not seem to be in excess of that of the U.S.S.R.; it is probably somewhat less. Yet, *assuming that we do have time to convert,* our industrial base is far more extensive than that of the U.S.S.R. The Soviet economy is normally on a war or semi-war footing; we possess greater elasticity. Our economy operates on a system of slack, whereas theirs is stretched to the breaking point. At the present time, in most of the essential military-sensitive lines of production, we can outproduce the Soviet Union by two or three to one—and our maximum output is even higher. Currently, a high proportion of our industrial facilities is devoted to the production of consumer goods, such as automobiles, and this proportion could be drastically reduced in the event of war. The output of consumer durables, now running at the rate of $33 billion a year, might be reduced to zero. Much of the capacity devoted to the production of capital goods or non-durable goods is convertible to the needs of war; and in an emergency, the proportion devoted to consumer well-being might be significantly reduced. We thus possess a strategic reserve capacity not available to the U.S.S.R.

With respect to manpower, there exist immense reservoirs in our economy. Some 47 million individuals over the age of 14 are not in the labor force at present. There are 4 million unemployed. For those employed, the hours of work are relatively short, and could be increased by 25 per cent with no undue burden. Some 18 million people are employed in trade or in the service industries, which could be pruned in the event of war. Actually, something over 10 per cent of the GNP is represented by recreation and personal and other services which are highly compressible sectors. Many of the 17 million employed in manufacturing are employed in non-essential production, and would be available for re-absorption upon the conversion of industry. If the mobilization base is satisfactory, there need be no undue concern over the labor picture.[4]

In contrast, Soviet capacity is far more restricted. A very high proportion of total output is *already* devoted to strategic production. There is far less slack available for conversion in trade, services, or non-essential manufactured goods. Only 20 per cent of the population over fourteen years of age is outside the labor force. Almost half of the labor force is absorbed by agricultural production. The non-agricultural labor force, even yet, is smaller than that of the United States, and its productivity is markedly lower, spectacularly so in the consumer-goods sector.

By any standard of measurement, the economic capacity of the United States at the present time is vastly superior to that of the Soviet Union. Our mobilization base, though currently devoted to a much greater degree to civilian purposes than Russia's, is far more expansible. The current advantage enjoyed by the United States is a significant source of strength, and it should not be forgotten in light of subsequent observations. It implies that in any contest between the two nations that is to be decided largely *in terms of material attrition,* the United States is in a position to take advantage of this Soviet handicap. This will remain true in the near future, although recent Soviet growth rates have been sufficiently impressive to cause alarm in Washington. In the longer run, the difference between the two powers in terms of economic capacity must inevitably grow smaller, as the material gap narrows. Economic capacity must be related to some clear purpose, and no purpose would be served for the United States to increase its capacity, merely to stay ahead of the Russians. In the short run, however, the American advantage in economic capacity is manifest.

How important this purely economic advantage is likely to be in the type of struggles in which we might become engaged in the future is another question. Reliance upon the mobilization base has a grave disadvantage in its assumption that there will be time to mobilize. Present military output of the Russians may exceed our own because a higher proportion of their "mobilization base" is already devoted to strategic purposes. During the time lag in which we attempt to bring to bear our superior economic power, many things may happen. Thus, before we find our economic advantages *too* reassuring, we ought to evaluate what role economic strength is likely to play in the contemporary power struggle. Perhaps the most appropriate way of assessing the present-day role of economic power is to start by tracing its historical relationship to national power.

1. THE HISTORICAL ROLE OF ECONOMIC CAPACITY

Historically, the association between power and economic strength is far from clear-cut. To be sure, economic advantages have contributed an element of strength to the dominant power; but all too frequently, this advantage has been offset by counter-vailing advantages accruing to the other side. Moreover, the very complexity of the arrangements of the superior economy has made it more vulnerable to external or internal disruption— an element of weakness. In view of Napoleon's dictum that in war the moral factors are to the physical factors in the ratio of three to one, it would be unwise for us to conclude on the basis of economic logic that our position is anything like impregnable. Nothing could be more reassuring (or dangerous) to a dominant power than to be informed that it simply cannot be displaced by force. In ancient Athens, the good citizens scoffed at Demosthenes' warnings of the threat from the north—the backward Macedonians could hardly hope to conquer an advanced civilization. To the Romans policing the barbarians of the marches, to the Byzantines observing the Muslim horsemen of the desert, to the sixteenth-century Spaniards and the eighteenth-century Frenchmen as they considered their lowly English rivals, there came, no doubt, the soothing voices of "economists" assuring them that, in the end, economic strength would tell.

Commercial eminence and rising standards of living have, on occasion, reflected a decline in the military virtues and in the capacity for resistance, rather than reflecting increased military power. It is interesting to note that the American historian Brooks Adams, in his *Law of Civilization and Decay*, came to conclusions directly opposite to those implicit in the doctrine of economic potential for war. Adams postulated two sorts of men—

one subject to the commercial-rational instinct, the other subject to the military-spiritual instinct. It was the supersession of the military man by the economic man that foretold the doom of civilization—in Greece, Rome, Byzantium, and elsewhere. The rise of a commercial society, with all its centralizing and cheapening tendencies, increased the vulnerability of the society and sapped the will to resist, thus portending a new barbarian age. Of course, it is impossible to discern any general "law" of human development, and few would care to accept Adams' thesis *in toto*, yet what does interest us is the inference that economic potential runs against the grain of military security. Economic plenty, like everything else, can cut two ways.

By vastly increasing the importance of the economic element, the Industrial Revolution has weakened the implications of Adams' hypothesis. The relationship between the economic arts and military potency has changed so drastically that the change is truly a qualitative one. One need think only of the Civil War, the two World Wars, or even the colonial wars. Warfare, between the greater powers, at least, is much more a question of production—more a question of equipment and less one of sheer courage and stealth—than formerly. The issue of mobilization and industrial control becomes fundamental, thus bringing economic potential to the center of the stage. Yet, even in modern times, the decisive elements do not appear to be economic. At the outbreak of World War II, "the British Government based its 'assurance of victory' upon an estimate of the long-run superiority of combined British and French economic resources over enemy resources. 'The Allies,' asserted Mr. Chamberlain, 'are bound to win in the end, and the only question is how long it will take them to achieve their purpose.'"[5] The fall of France upset this placid expectation. Happily, the British were insufficiently convinced of the validity of their previous reasoning, based upon economic resources, to settle for a negotiated peace when they alone faced the Nazi-dominated continent and their own resources had become markedly inferior to those of their foe.

Even in the industrial age, then, economic superiority has not immediately implied military superiority. The Greek defeat of the Italians in the fall of 1940 and the French failure in Indo-China corroborate this observation. Or, to take a case somewhat nearer home, the Chinese, with a national income about 10 per cent of our own, managed to achieve a stalemate in Korea.

Apparently, the applicability of the concept of economic capacity must be carefully qualified. The first qualification concerns the composition of national output: can it be converted to armament production? As has been made clear, the United States has a clear advantage in the fact that so much of its capacity can be converted to the production of military hardware. A second qualification arises from the question of whether a nation has the willingness to translate its economic capacity into military capabilities. There is, at least, some question whether the populations of democratic countries are willing to make the sacrifices that are required, *in time.*

But there is a third qualification—and a far more important one—that we must consider. The impact of economic potential depends upon doctrine and upon timing: will the right amount of strength, of the proper type, be available when it is needed? Unless power and doctrine are properly coordinated, economic capacity may be irrelevant. Thus we come to the necessity of formulating an economic strategy that will be the counterpart of a nation's military strategy.

2. THE ROLE OF ECONOMIC STRATEGY

Intelligent economic strategy is, in itself, a form of economization. If the strategy is effective, maximum results can be obtained by a minimal investment of resources; if it is ineffective, the entire investment of resources may be wasted. Economic strategy must be harmonized not only with a nation's resources and its political objectives, but also with the time requirements for the implementation of predetermined tactics. Moreover, economic strategy cannot be designed by a nation *in vacuo* but must be contrived to parry the thrusts of other nations. In short, economic strategy is but a part of the whole that represents a nation's strategic doctrine. Resources supply the means, but the speed, pace, and weight of the use of those resources depend upon economic strategy.

A concrete illustration may help to indicate the delicate relationship involved. In both World Wars, German military plans were geared to utilize most effectively her limited economic resources. German military strategy accepted the necessity of a quick victory, thus reflecting the inferiority of the resources available to Germany and her allies for a war of long duration. In World War I, command of the seas would make available to the Allies the resources of the world overseas, which would be lost to the Central Powers through the blockade. Quick victory was needed, and German military strategy was formulated accordingly. Implementation of the Schlieffen Plan was to carry the Germans to Paris. Its failure and the stalemate on the Western Front subjected the Central Powers to the incessant pressures of economic warfare, as embodied in the blockade.

In planning for the next war, the strategies of the major powers reflected their previous experiences. It has already been pointed out that the British Government was relying upon a repetition of the techniques of the first war to bring victory. The superiority of Allied resources, in combination with the blockade, was gradually to wear Germany down. As it turned out, this was in a sense what eventually occurred, but there were a few anxious years in between.

Germany was familiar with the painful implications of a protracted war for the belligerent with inferior resources. She based her strategy upon the *blitzkrieg*, a crushing blow to obtain victory. In fact, a modified version of the Schlieffen Plan did achieve the goal of the first war, Paris, but it did not bring victory. Control over the continent reversed the pattern of the first war, and gave the Germans the resources to put the British under pressure. Timely assistance from America, plus the German decision to turn east, permitted the survival of Britain. Until the invasion of Russia, German strategy had been successful, yet the final victory eluded her.

German mobilization plans reflected the strategic bias—victory was to be achieved rapidly with the forces-in-being. The plan was to strike the enemy with the accumulated equipment of war. Hitler had been unwilling in the thirties to restructure the German economy for sustained military production, for that implied several years of heavy investment in capacity with no immediate returns and large sacrifices by the German population. This was the policy of "armament in width" as opposed to "armament in depth," the latter implying a basic restructuring of the economy. Germany's advantage lay in a quick war in which the accumulated production of several years would yield a quick victory.

During the war, the cumulative advantages of armament in depth became apparent. Prior to the war, Britain had tended to view warfare in terms of total commitment, and as an affair of lengthy duration. This was the reverse of the German concept of *blitzkrieg*. Wars were to be won by the gradual application of the pressures of economic superiority. Quite naturally, in Britain's view, mobilization required the restructuring of the economy to a war footing geared to the heavy and sustained flow of war material—in short, armament in depth. After her initial setbacks, the formula began to work. By 1940, Britain's military output exceeded Germany's. It was only in 1942 that the German leaders recognized that the war would be drawn out; military production was sharply increased. But by 1942, Germany was stuck with the policy of armament in width; she could no longer expand her material base, and was forced to make do with existing capacity. Notwithstanding her initial advantages, Germany was little better prepared for war than were the Allies.

Despite the postwar criticism of the policy of armament in width, it was in harmony with Germany's strategic plans, and it did permit the rapid build-up and application of military power. Germany came close to achieving her goals. The assumption of the West was that it would have sufficient time to convert superior resources into military power. After 1942, when the war had become one of attrition, the strategy seemed tenable; but during the first stage of the war, the initial successes suggested the possibility that the Germans would sweep all before them before their opponents could organize an effective defense.

The World Wars thus indicate the need for harmonizing economic and military strategy. A nation's economic resources will influence its military planning, yet, in turn, the military strategy will affect the organization and use of economic resources. Germany staked all on a quick victory. This turned out to be poor strategy. The West assumed that it would have time to mobilize and permitted its forces-in-being to lag behind those of the foe. This turned out to be successful strategy, but frightful risks were run, and conceivably, much of the cost of the war might have been avoided with another strategy.

3. THE PROSPECTS FOR THE FUTURE

Retrospectively, World War II would appear to be an ideal illustration of the influence of economic capacity. It developed into a war of attrition, and ultimately the Axis powers were overwhelmed by the vast output of their rivals. It was the problem of wartime production, and particularly the postwar studies of the relative performance of the American and the German economies, that stimulated interest in the concept of economic capacity. Despite the tenseness of the early days, in the long run, World War II was a triumph of production and logistics. The question we must face is whether or not the *contemporary* American emphasis upon economic capacity is not, in fact, overemphasis—another example of a tendency, not restricted to the military, to refight the last war.

At the present time, the greater capacity of the American economy would provide an immense advantage in the prosecution of war *waged along the same lines as World War II.* In a material war of attrition, we could easily turn out more military hardware than could our rivals, if our production machinery were kept intact. What seems unlikely is that any future enemy is going to be stupid enough to play into our hands, to hit us at our strongest point. With respect to one possible type of future war, the all-out nuclear encounter, the issue would probably be settled in a matter of weeks by the *forces-in-being.* Armament in width would be more important than armament in depth—and economic capacity places no strict limits on armament in width. Although American policy has tended to place great stress upon economic capacity, just what its relevance would be in such a contingency is a grave question. It is debatable whether society, as such, could survive in the event of a nuclear war. It is sometimes suggested that economic potential will determine the recuperative capacity of the society after a nuclear attack. This would appear to be wishful thinking, since a nation's economic potential may be directly related to its vulnerability—in terms of urban concentrations, a complex division of labor and economic interdependence, and the low degree of regional self-sufficiency. Economic potential would then be a key to the barriers to recuperation. Talk of a "broken-back" war (the thrashing about of the contestants after the initial attack), and of economic capacity in determining its victor, would seem to be a not very fruitful form of "whistling in the graveyard." The United States would probably lack the power to exert its influence in the Eastern Hemisphere, and all contestants would be more absorbed in the struggle for sheer survival than they would be in continuing the battle. The upshot is that the role of economic capacity in a nuclear war is rather nebulous. It is doubtful whether it would influence the fighting, which would be settled by the forces-in-being.[6]

It should thankfully be observed that the likelihood of a thermonuclear holocaust appears to be diminishing. Nevertheless, a war of attrition along the lines of World War II also appears unlikely. What does appear likely, as the danger of total war recedes and the nuclear stalemate grows more airtight, is a pattern of diplomatic war, of political wear and tear, of subversion and limited war. As this new pattern of conflict emerges, the possibility of bringing to bear our total power recedes. No single engagement is likely to be sufficiently important to require either power bloc to commit its total strength. Moreover, over-all capacity can cast light only on the strength for general war; it need not apply in specific situations. The essence of limited warfare, however, is its *specificity*—the importance of locale, timing, and circumstance. Over-all strength is outweighed by the peculiar characteristics of the conflict. This throws economic capacity into a new perspective because we are unlikely to pick the spots to start skirmishes. In the brushfires that do "break out," the circumstances are likely to be unfavorable to us—and over-all power may be a secondary matter. The events since World War II, and particularly recent events in the Middle East, suggest that future conflicts may be wholly unlike those of the last war. There are forms of attrition other than material attrition—human attrition in guerilla warfare, for example. Economic capacity diminishes in importance. In such encounters, it is a question of will—of the stubborn capacity to absorb punishment when it is necessary, and to cut one's losses when the goals are not worth the price—that determines the ultimate winner.

In some limited engagements, the ability to impose a heavy strain upon the more limited resources of one's rival is not without significance and cannot be dismissed as trivial. In Korea, this was undoubtedly an advantage for the United States. Nevertheless, although it would be unwise to deprecate unduly the significance of economic capacity, it should be recognized that it is not likely to prove decisive in future conflicts. The limitations of economic capacity ought to be before us always, and we must be on the alert to counteract those exaggerations which in the American environment tend to creep into discussions of the subject. The evidence of many past wars suggests that nations may be able to compensate for economic deficiencies through the ruthless exploitation of inferior resources for strategic purposes. The degree to which economic potential has receded in importance under modern conditions is insufficiently recognized in popular discussion.

Superficially, it might appear that some conflict exists between the skeptical appraisal of economic capacity in the military field and the stress that was placed in the previous chapter upon over-all resources and the rate of growth. If economic expansion is of little strategic significance, why treat over-all resources as so great an advantage? Why worry about growth? Why penalize the present-day consumer in order to spur growth? The answer is fairly simple. It is true that if the growth rate were the crucial factor, we should be making every effort, irrespective of cost, to expand our industrial capacity and to stay ahead of the Russians. This, however, is not the case. Productive capacity exists to serve some purpose—that is, the production of goods for military or consumer uses. There is no purpose in adding to capacity simply to stay ahead. The reason that capacity is significant in the over-all sense today arises not from the strategic element taken by itself, but from the fact that the Russians are attempting to achieve so many objectives with limited resources. They are attempting to catch up with the West industrially, raise living standards, extend aid to associates, and maintain an immense military machine. Limited resources interpose difficulties for them in achieving all of their objectives. In view of the antagonism between the two power blocs, we can draw comfort from the fact that we are in a position to use our present superiority to increase their difficulties in achieving their goals. As the absolute level of Soviet resources increases, the importance of the relative gap will diminish. At the present time, because Soviet aspirations vastly exceed resources, the relative gap between the two power blocs does have considerable importance—but in the over-all sense rather than in a strictly military context.

Moreover, even though economic capacity cannot provide a decisive edge, it should not be forgotten that it possesses some relevance in the strictly military realm, even under present conditions. Additional capacity may permit more rapid conversion of industry in an emergency, since the costs of haste will be more easily borne. A high rate of growth of industrial capacity may also serve as a social emollient—by limiting the need to reduce the standard of living when a resort to force becomes necessary. In a democratic society, these are not negligible considerations. When military expenditures must be rapidly increased, a high growth rate will dampen domestic outcries, because living standards can be maintained—although the higher taxes which become necessary may still constitute a source of resentment.[7]

Finally, it must be remembered that the rate of growth has become a symbol to the underdeveloped nations. If we demonstrate our capacity to maintain high standards of living and, at the same time, a respectable rate of growth, it might conceivably influence some states to refrain from resorting to totalitarian devices which might spur a more rapid rate of growth, but at the price of liberty. To be sure, these are marginal considerations. They suggest that although we should be skeptical of its military significance, we should not go to the opposite extreme of dismissing economic capacity as irrelevant. There is no need to become neurotic over claimed or actual Soviet growth rates, yet, again, we ought not to ignore cavalierly measures that may spur our own rate of growth.

4. SOME FURTHER COMPLEXITIES

Under modern conditions, the role of economic capacity has been transformed. In the over-all sense, the ability to bring pressure to bear upon the narrower resource base of one's rival retains some importance. Even in the strictly military sphere, economic capacity must be considered, but its role is different from the one it played in other major wars of this century. As the danger of general war recedes, the abstract measures of over-all economic capacity have grown correspondingly less significant. In limited war situations, economic capacity may be judged only in the light of the special circumstances of the encounter. The military capabilities of the economy depend upon its specific strengths in satisfying the special needs and characteristics of the engagement rather than upon measures of over-all strength. Over-all economic capacity is an abstraction which avoids specification of the time, space, and purpose of any encounter. In any given situation, these characteristics must be pinned down: at what point in time the encounter occurs, which nations are engaged and which are neutral, and where the fighting is taking place. Even in a total conflict of the World War II variety, these specific characteristics are of importance; but in limited warfare, they completely overshadow the general indicators of economic strength.

Under these conditions, it is erroneous to assume that much significance can be attached to any single indicator of economic capacity. Nevertheless, in the making of intelligence estimates, there still exists a tendency to attempt to develop a single composite figure purporting to represent the economic capabilities of each of the nations for war purposes, through the expedient of assigning weights to various economic aggregates—population, total product, proportion represented by manufacturing, *per capita* income, and so on—and combining them. Such composite figures are misleading, for the weights assigned to the several components should vary depending upon the type and the characteristics of the struggle. In certain encounters, the war-making capabilities of the Canadian economy, for example, would exceed those of the Chinese economy. In other circumstances, the reverse would be true. Composite indicators might suggest that Brazil was more powerful than Australia, but we know that in many types of struggles such a conclusion would be misleading.

In order to consider the role of economic capacity, we must specify the situation in which it will be used. *Within a specified framework,* it is possible to make limited use of some summary economic data—but only within the framework of the problem and against a background of extra-economic aspects. And even against such a background, there is no single summary figure of capabilities, but rather an informed judgment based upon many factors. In the total assessment, such elements as the gross national product, capital stock, population magnitudes, and components may be of slight importance, and there is always a residual of imponderables which are not subject to analysis. Among these imponderables is the domestic political situation—the very manner in which a war comes about may be of decisive importance, or, in the case of limited war, which side has the support of the local populace.

Ultimately, then, under present conditions, there is little value to abstract measures of economic capacity. We can estimate an array of capabilities to accomplish something, somewhere, at some time—not the capacity to do anything, anywhere, at any time. And beyond the array of measurable factors, there is a range of unknowables which can never be dealt with until the die is cast.

The absence of a single criterion of economic capabilities in warfare, in addition to the recognition that economic power only takes form in the context of a specific setting, places a premium upon economic flexibility. The discernment of needs and the suppleness of the economy in responding to those needs may be the keys to economic capabilities. Military effectiveness in the modern world, in itself, is dependent upon the composition of the military forces and their suitability for countering specific threats under a variety of circumstances:

> The ability to wage war cannot be measured in purely quantitative terms. . . . A nation can be adequately prepared to wage one kind of war under one set of circumstances and inadequately prepared to wage another kind of war under a different set of circumstances. The utility of a nation's military power . . . will depend . . . upon its suitability for countering the specific kinds of military threats impinging upon the nation's interests.[8]

Adaptability to specific threats is the price of survival. The rapidity with which a nation can adjust to new requirements may be just as important a part of the mobilization base as the purely quantitative element. In the American case, the movement from time to time from one quarter of the globe to another may cause a drastic change in our production requirements. At one time, we may need to develop capacity in rubber production; at another, the changing international alignments may imply the need to look to oil production; it is not unlikely that some future shift will bring manganese or bauxite or uranium production to the fore. Manifestly, the changeability of circumstances means that there is no final answer to the problem of the mobilization base. At all times, we must remain flexible and be prepared to make good our deficiencies. The process of preparatory adjustment may prove to be expensive; it is, however, necessary.

Perhaps one of the greatest impediments to intelligent economic preparedness for possible international encounters is the idea that there exists a *particular* mobilization base—and that once we have attained that level, we may rest. To be sure, there are certain weaknesses in our economic structure which are perennial and have a permanent part to play in the solution of the problem. Beyond these continuing features, however, there is the area of continuing change, which requires flexibility in the face of the flux of international politics and economic relations in order to maintain a high level of economic readiness. In a sense, over-all capacity may have a role to play in meeting specific requirements by providing buoyancy for the economy and maintaining the morale of the citizenry, whenever quick adjustments become essential.

5. CONCLUDING REMARKS

As a doctrine, economic capacity is the breeding ground of complacency and wishful thinking, and it has not been without influence on American policy. It is based upon the intuition that future wars will be like past wars. Even those who have advocated "massive retaliation" or who have given intellectual assent to the belief that future wars are likely to be limited have frequently boggled at the corollary that, under such circumstances, the influence of economic capacity will be much reduced. As a doctrine, economic capacity exhibits the very type of thinking in military affairs that Clausewitz warned against—the carrying of an abstract principle to its logical conclusion, and then applying the conclusion to reality. Situations of conflict are intermediate states representing divergent tendencies, and in real life logical principles seldom are carried to extremes. In the doctrine of economic capacity, there is little recognition of the fundamental realities of situations of conflict—that there is such a thing as being overextended and that there are limits to the exercise of power. Little recognition is given to the role of moral or political considerations, which ultimately may prove decisive.

It is more difficult to evaluate economic capacity as an element of strength; we must recognize its importance as well as its limitations. The statistics on national income and product, with all their deficiencies and incomparabilities between nations, are probably not too useful in providing an index of a nation's economic capabilities for war. Instead, the significance of the GNP figure, weighted so heavily in favor of consumption, probably lies in the political rather than the economic sphere—in other words, a resilient economy aids in the maintenance of morale. It does provide a very rough guide to the amount of resources that could be released for essential production, but this is only part of the story.

More useful is the idea of the mobilization base—an industrial nucleus which can be rapidly converted to the production of essential military and civilian goods in sufficient volume. It is sound policy to encourage the expansion of those sectors of the economy in which it is anticipated a pinch will be felt in time of war. If this can be achieved by the fostering of, or by restrictions upon, foreign trade, by subsidies, or by accelerated depreciation and tax concessions, it is suitable that parochial interests standing in the way of such policies be overridden.

It should be recognized that there is a cost to maintaining the mobilization base. One disadvantage is that, in the American context, we have attempted to obtain the best of all possible worlds. The mobilization base is a compromise. We wish to have the facilities ready for wartime military and civilian production. However, we do not wish them to stand idle in times of peace, but rather to contribute to higher living standards. The need to convert the dual-purpose industrial facilities from peacetime to wartime production assumes that in an emergency, time will be available to make the transition. The time lag in conversion may be viewed as the weakest element in our economic readiness for war. It is the price we pay for normally having to satisfy the consumer, but it opens the way to initial reverses during war. In light of the changing nature of warfare, and the greater significance of forces-in-being, the price may be one that is too high to pay. In the West, satisfaction of consumption desires has normally had the highest priority, and only war has upset the scale of social priorities. Thus, in peacetime, the endeavor to maintain an adequate military position has continually been impeded. A change in our traditional attitudes seems inevitable, for the military margin for error is gradually but relentlessly narrowing.

Maintenance of an effective mobilization base is probably

more relevant to limited warfare than for general war, which is likely to be nuclear. However, the role of economic capacity is now wholly unlike its role in previous (total) wars. In limited warfare, nations do not bring all of their power to bear, so that sheer productive volume is not decisive. What is important economically is the rapidity with which the economy can adjust to the new demands arising out of the specific situation of the limited war. The speed and effectiveness with which the forces can be mobilized, transported, and supplied may spell the difference between defeat and victory. Under these circumstances, general and abstract indicators of economic capacity are misleading since they imply the power to achieve any goal, any place, any time. The crux of economic power in wars unlike World War II is that power will vary according to the specific context of the encounter, and that power must be weighed in specific terms—to achieve a certain purpose, at a certain place, at a certain time. Over-all economic power may be significant in aiding rapid conversion or in maintaining morale by stimulating economic resiliency, but the decisive element will be supplied by the effectiveness of the application of limited power.

Illustrating this proposition, the superiority of total resources no longer is meaningful in terms of sheer quantities—such as total armaments production, the total number of troops that can be maintained in the field, and so on. *With adequate preparation,* however, superior economic capabilities may permit more rapid mobilization and logistical support of our troops in any limited engagement. This affords an enormous potential advantage. It even suggests the conclusion, wholly at variance with the prevailing climate of opinion, that our greatest relative advantage over the Communist bloc may well be on the ground, based upon quick build-up and effective logistical support.[9]

We must always remember that economic capacity, especially in limited wars, is only permissive. It may imply, as in Korea, that we can bring pressure to bear upon a weaker economy. It should never, however, lead to the assumption that we can predict the final outcome of an encounter—with the expert in economic capacity playing the role of augur. That is a deceptive and dangerous form of economic determinism which is wholly unwarranted in the light of the imponderables involved. Economic capacity may be a necessary, but it can never be a sufficient condition for military security. Lest we miscalculate, we ought to continually call to mind the Biblical injunction that "the race is not to the swift, nor the battle to the strong . . . but time and chance happeneth to them all."

4

PROBLEMS OF ECONOMIC MOBILIZATION

The onset of hostilities or the sudden shift in the international climate that requires intensification of defense preparations imposes a strain on the economy, particularly on the free-market economy. The composition of production must be changed—more stress placed upon military hardware and upon war-sensitive industries, less upon non-essential civilian production. The reorientation of the economy that is required may be so severe that the price system becomes an inadequate instrument to achieve the necessary production shifts, and it may be necessary to utilize a supplementary system of controls to achieve the desired transformation. To these broad problems of adjustment, the term "mobilization" is usually applied. We may define "mobilization" as the process of attaining a higher level of military and other strategic production through the conversion of economic capacity that has hitherto been employed for other, essentially civilian purposes.

Almost any degree of mobilization will impose some strain on the economy, and it will be recognized that the greater the degree of mobilization, the greater will be the strain. The classic examples of mobilization occurred during World War II, which was for most belligerents a total war. For the reasons that have already been developed, it seems unlikely that economic capacity will play the decisive role in future wars that it has in the past. Future wars are likely to be limited; a total war would mean a nuclear war, and the connection between economic capacity and nuclear warfare appears somewhat nebulous. Consequently, the problem of economic mobilization is unlikely to be as severe in future contingencies as it was in World War II. More emphasis will be placed upon advance preparation, and less upon conversion, than was true in the past.

Nevertheless, the topic of economic mobilization remains important. Mobilization strains of World War II were alleviated because we had what was, in some respects, the good fortune to enter the war with a considerable volume of unemployed resources—a consequence of the depression of the thirties. It is unlikely that in any future period of mobilization, the transition will be similarly eased by the existence of a margin of unutilized resources. Although the scope of mobilization may be less extensive in the future, the impact may be disproportionately large. It would be unwise to overemphasize the role of mobilization; this would represent a continuance of the error of preparing for the future in terms of our previous experiences in World War II. On the other hand, we cannot afford to ignore the problems of mobilization: first, because we must be prepared for any contingency; secondly, because some of the techniques of mobilization would be relevant to the reconstruction of society after a nuclear attack; thirdly, because the strains on the economy implicit in limited warfare, though not nearly as severe as those of total war, are not negligible. Any sizable mobilization effort will impose strains on the economy. At some point—and this will be a matter of political judgment—it becomes advisable to develop a system of controls to deal with the tensions that arise.

The issues posed by mobilization may be sorted into two main divisions: the problems of production and the problems of stabilization. Mobilization poses problems of production since it implies a rapid rechanneling of resources to bring about a composition of national output sharply distinct from the old. The free-market mechanism is best suited to handle marginal variations in demand and in output arising from the slow changes in consumer tastes. It may not be either efficient or equitable in achieving large-scale readjustments of production. But mobilization implies large changes, and these are not easily achieved through the market. The market method of achieving the shifts in production would mean the provision of incentives that might drastically and unfairly alter the price structure. The price system is too indirect, too slow, too erratic to achieve the required results promptly, and it may have to be supplemented by a system of direct controls. It is a false issue, however, to argue in terms of controls *or* the price system. Both must be pointing in the right directions. The price system must provide adequate incentives, but after the onset of the mobilization crisis—in an economy in which consumers, producers, and the government are blindly competing for resources which, in the nature of the mobilization goals, must eventually go to the government—an unguided price system may provide incentives that are excessive or confusing to producers. As balance returns to the economy, the price system should be increasingly relied upon. In the short run, however, it must be supplemented. Resources in short supply must be redirected from the production of consumer to the production of war-essential goods. For a brief period, the national economy must be "managed" in order to win the war. The utilization of scarce materials must be coordinated and synchronized in accordance with an over-all plan of production that is devised to extract maximum results from limited resources in satisfying the armed forces, the civilian economy, and the needs of the allies.

In addition, there is likely to be a problem of stabilization. This problem is not distinct, and is associated with that of production particularly when scarce goods are concerned. But there is the more general problem of inflationary pressures. With the diversion of resources to the production of matériel, there is likely to be too much money chasing too few consumer goods, and prices will rise. Whenever mobilization is extensive, any goods can be sold in a free market at higher prices. Half the firms are engaged in production for the government on cost-plus contracts; the rest are selling their output to consumers with swollen incomes. It may, therefore, be necessary to take special steps to prevent inflation. Of course, if there have been

CHART 1
ECONOMIC MOBILIZATION TABLEAU

SITUATION	Increased Preparedness	Limited War	General War	Nuclear War
DEGREE OF MOBILIZATION	Partial Mobilization	Total Mobilization	Total War	

DEGREE OF STRAIN →

Patriotism →

THREE LEVELS OF OPERATION				
SUBSTITUTION				
1. GOVERNMENT FINANCES	Balanced Budget (types of taxes)	Mild Unbalance	Budgetary Disequilibrium	
2. PRICE & MONETARY CONTROLS	No Direct Controls	Voluntary Controls { ? ← Wage Controls ← Price Controls }	Selective Controls	General Price Controls (& Credit Rationing)
3. ALLOCATION OF SUPPLY	Market Mechanism	Voluntary Controls (formal or informal) (Consumer Rationing)	Priorities Allocations Requisition Manpower Direction	

INCREASING SEVERITY (or departure from peacetime practices) →

"NORMALCY"	"DEFENSE ECONOMY"	"WAR ECONOMY"

unemployed resources, the strain will be eased by the re-employment of those resources. At the outset of World War II, widespread unemployment did ease the strain of mobilization, but these circumstances are unlikely to recur, and we shall simply assume in the balance of this discussion that significant unemployment will not exist.

The problem of mobilization is extremely complicated, and a conventional complaint would be that it is far too intricate to be dealt with in a single chapter. We need not worry about the insufficiency of space for two reasons. First, we shall ignore the most confusing element in the picture—that whole range of institutional problems which are industrial in nature—and confine our attention strictly to the general economic aspects. Secondly, I have prepared an oversimplified schematic outline of the mobilization problem, which, following Condorcet, I have dubbed the Economic Mobilization Tableau (Chart 1). It is hoped that the tableau will help to clarify, rather than to obfuscate the subject.

1. THE TECHNIQUES OF MOBILIZATION

At the top of the tableau, I have put various situations imposed by international politics that mold the domestic economic response. These conditions range from increased preparedness, through limited war, to general war. At the extreme right, almost off the tableau, is nuclear war—so placed because, as has already been suggested, it is difficult to discern just what the relationship between nuclear warfare, on the one hand, and economic capacity and mobilization, on the other, would be. Any statement would be purely hypothetical. It is not unlikely that, in the event of nuclear war, there would be a breakdown of all control. Normally, however, international conditions do mold the economic response—requiring varying degrees of mobilization which range from partial to what we conventionally call "total mobilization." Total mobilization in the conventional sense can be surpassed by an even greater national exertion that develops in total war, when all amenities are sacrificed and the one, overriding purpose becomes survival as a political entity.

Perhaps the only modern example of this degree of mobilization occurred in the Soviet Union during World War II.

The attempt of an economy to cope with the strains of mobilization may occur on three levels of operation—government finances, price and monetary controls, and allocation of supply. These are listed in order of increasing severity or, to put it another way, in order of increasing departure from the normal peacetime devices of economic coordination. These different levels of operation may serve, as we shall see, as partial substitutes for one another. The more effective the control is on one level, the less will be the urgency for action on the other levels.

The first level of operation is that of government finances, and it is at this point that the general economic environment in which mobilization takes place is determined. If it is desired to avoid more stringent methods of control, the excessive flow of expenditures which results in the creation of additional purchasing power and a spiraling problem of inflation must be prevented. A minimal requirement for curtailing the growth of over-all expenditures is a budget that is in balance, but if the scope of the mobilization requirements is wide, a balanced budget may be unattainable. Added government expenditures, unmatched by equal revenue increases, do permit the government to obtain a larger portion of national output and to utilize a higher proportion of national resources. As the degree of international strain increases, the government may be forced to resort to an unbalanced budget—first, to a mild unbalance, then to a gross unbalance in which complete disequilibrium exists between receipts and expenditures.

Nevertheless, it must be emphasized that the better the job done by the government on this first level of operation, the less will be the necessity of resorting to more stringent methods of control. The main purpose of taxation under conditions of mobilization is to restrain the growth of total expenditures—and particularly to curtail the expenditures by consumers. Naturally, the issue of the tax *structure* and the relative emphasis on one type of tax as opposed to another limit the effectiveness of taxation in reducing consumption expenditures. Certain taxes—

sales taxes and first-bracket income taxes, for example—are highly effective in reducing consumption, as compared to corporation taxes and a highly progressive income tax. Revenue can most easily and effectively be obtained by these so-called "regressive taxes," yet in the opinion of many people, they are highly unfair because they impose too great a proportion of the total tax load on lower-income groups. The tendency has been to rely to too little extent on the type of taxes that will most effectively restrain consumption expenditures. Such political constraints, of course, reduce the likelihood that budgetary restraint will be sufficiently effective, and therefore that the economy can avoid recourse to other types of controls. Inevitably, the question of equity must be considered in determining the tax structure, but it ought to be weighed in conjunction with the question of efficiency and not to the exclusion of other issues.

The second level of operation is that of price and monetary controls. Such general controls may be applied with varying degrees of intensity, corresponding to the degree of strain imposed on the economy by the international situation, and the degree to which budgetary control is insufficient to offset that pressure. From a condition in which no such controls are required, we may proceed through voluntary controls, selective controls (both on the prices of certain items or on the amount of borrowed money that may be used for particular purposes, especially buying houses or consumer-durable goods), and, finally, general price controls, when virtually all prices are fixed. Under the heading of general controls, we may include credit-rationing programs, under which official approval must be obtained for the type of project for which money is borrowed.

In instituting selective or general controls, the vital question arises whether price controls should precede wage controls, wage controls should precede price controls, or both should be simultaneously applied. In the tableau, this delicate problem is suggested by the arrows leading to a question mark, indicating that it is an open issue as to which takes precedence. In an economy of shortages, wage controls—whether formal or informal—are probably more indispensable in the stabilization problem *per se* than are price controls, since rising costs make price increases unavoidable. Without wage restraint, price control is futile. On the other hand, it is easier to obtain wage restraint voluntarily than it is to restrain price increases by the same means, and price control may be *politically necessary* in order to obtain wage control. The tendency to give priority either to wage control or to price control reflects the fundamental values and the political pressures of the society. It may be observed that in the United States, price control has come first.

The most rigorous level of operation is the third one—that of supply allocation—in which controls are instituted over the flow of resources, especially raw materials and labor. From reliance upon the normal market mechanism to allocate production, one may proceed through over-all controls of increasing vigor—voluntary controls, either formal or informal; a system of priorities; direct allocation of production; requisition; and finally, the ultimate form of control, manpower direction. Rationing of goods for consumers enters into consideration at the point of voluntary control, but will increase in rigor in accordance with the degree of strain on the economy.

The three levels of operation do serve as partial substitutes for each other. It has been noted that if the budgetary situation is good, the nation may get by without any other controls, or perhaps with a limited number of selective price controls. On the other hand, if the budgetary situation is in disequilibrium, it becomes inevitable that stringent price controls, and eventually supply allocations, will have to be used. In addition, control over the flow of matériel may reduce the strain on price control, and will, of course, permit deterioration of the budget situation.

The response on all three levels of operation will be governed by the degree of strain on the economy, as determined by the prevailing international pressures. In the tableau, the degree of strain has been underlined by a heavy arrow indicating that it is the fundamental determinant of the techniques that the government will employ to facilitate mobilization. Not only will additional levels of controls be employed as the strain increases, but as the direction of the arrow suggests, added strains will require resort to more stringent controls. A force operating in the opposite direction to the degree of strain is patriotism (in small letters and underscored by a light arrow pointing to the left). Patriotism may serve as a counterpoise—the greater the degree of patriotism, the less stringent need be the controls; for example, voluntary controls may suffice. As international pressures increase, the importance of patriotism may become ascendant, ameliorating somewhat the underlying stresses of mobilization. But as the lightness of the arrow suggests, patriotism is a rather weak counterpoise. In the face of persistent economic strain, the effect of patriotism tends to be undermined. It cannot be counted upon for more than minor assistance in the long run.

Finally, it may be observed that the farther we move to the right on the tableau, the greater the change in the nature of the economy. With a balanced budget, no controls, and reliance upon the market mechanism, we have a situation best described by that alluring word coined by President Harding, "normalcy." At the opposite end of the spectrum, we have a "war economy," characterized by budgetary disequilibrium and rigorous controls. In between, we have intermediate stages of defense economy, cold-war economy, limited-war economy, and so on. It should be observed that for the Soviet Union, the characteristics of normalcy are those of what we would consider to be a war economy. Structurally, at least, the Soviet economy is permanently on a war footing. Manpower direction in its most extreme form may be used in peacetime. This condition reflects the nature of the Soviet system and the primacy of the overriding purposes of the Soviet state, as opposed to the more individualistic aspirations of the citizenry. This characteristic of Soviet life precludes many of the problems that the American society is forced to face, with its desire to rely upon minimal controls during a period of limited mobilization.

2. THE PROBLEMS OF CONTROL

It is appropriate to indicate the nature of the difficulties that arise when the attempt is made to place controls upon an economy. In theory, controls might appear to be unexcelled devices for achieving both stabilization and the pattern of allocation that the government desires; in practice, however, controls may produce almost as many problems as they solve. It is important to keep the negative aspects in mind, for failure to understand their weaknesses, by leading to excessive reliance upon controls, may be as damaging as the failure to recognize their strengths.

Failure to apprehend the limits of controls has led some persons to believe that controls are sufficient in themselves to permit the government to regulate economic activities in whatever way it desires. At best, such a view is visionary. *Controls do not permit us to dispense with the price mechanism.* Controls serve as a supplement to the price mechanism; they may deflect economic pressures, but cannot reverse them. Consequently, controls must serve to reinforce price incentives, and *vice versa.* Prices must maintain the profitability of desired lines of production and not place unconquerable temptation in the paths of producers to turn their efforts in directions not sanctioned by the controls.

On the other hand, it is equally true that in periods of emergency, controls may be needed to supplement the price system. Without controls, the price system may operate slowly and erratically. Controls assist in bringing about rapid and large-scale changes in the structure of production, for which the price mechanism unassisted is inadequate. It is a false issue to argue in terms of *either* controls *or* the price system. Controls can never do the job alone, to be sure; but *ideologues* of the price system who fail to recognize the distortions of the price structure and the social inequities which may arise in a period of rapid economic transition will tend to resist the introduction of controls, even when the case for them is overpowering.

Controls are merely temporary devices to achieve immediate goals. They cannot serve as permanent regulators. The pressures that controls are designed to contain continue to build up until the controls bend or break. The effectiveness of controls is greatest in the short run, and after initial successes the system breaks down. Unless the difficulties of controls are kept in mind, these devices will not be used with maximum effectiveness. In enumerating the difficulties of controls, we shall concentrate on the question of price controls for several reasons: because price controls most simply exemplify the general economic problems posed by controls; because it permits us to avoid the most intricate problems of supply allocation; and because price controls, as an intermediate weapon in mobilization, cover that range of problems which is likely to engage us in cold or tepid wars. Many of the observations on the dilemmas arising under price controls may, however, be applied by extension to the more complicated problems of matériel controls.

Let us recapitulate the type of situation in which price controls become essential. The economy is faced with the dangers of excessive expenditures, which give rise to a vicious circle of inflationary movements. As the government spends money, it causes incomes to expand; with larger incomes, consumers will want to spend more and demand increases; with higher demand, prices will rise; as prices rise and profits increase, the demand for labor increases, pushing up wage rates. This leads to further increases in incomes, still higher demand, and so on. As prices rise, the government must increase its own expenditures, thus adding to the upward spiral. The purpose of controls is to break into this circle and to prevent or bring to a halt the rise in prices, for inflation is highly inequitable, breaks down morale, reduces the usefulness of monetary calculations, and thereby impedes intelligent decision-making.

It is the budgetary situation that provides the key to the need for control. In principle, in coping with the continual pressure of government expenditures, the budget should be a tight one. If taxes and revenues are sufficiently high, then there need not be excessive demand, and the need for direct controls is alleviated. But it is difficult to tax sufficiently. As has been suggested, the most effective and remunerative taxes are considered either inequitable or politically unwise. In a complex social order, each social group attempts to foist the tax burden off onto the rest of society. Since each group is likely to be effective in protecting its own "rights," the usual outcome has been a compromise on the lowest common denominator of the fiscal system— to wit, insufficient taxation to limit purchasing power. As government spending rises, a surplus should be attained in the budget, but we have never been willing to tax ourselves sufficiently merely to avoid inflation. The best that we have been able to obtain is a rough balance between receipts and expenditures—but this is a minimal goal if we are to avoid gross inflationary pressures.

Whenever the budget situation gets out of hand, then we must turn to direct controls to sterilize the excessive purchasing power that has been created. Otherwise, inflationary pressures will spill over into rising prices, and consequently distort productive efforts. Controls are essential under such conditions to deflect the excessive purchasing power from the market place, with its disruptive repercussions on the war effort. But the controls themselves will set in operation a chain of forces, which we will analyze under five separate headings: reliance upon selective controls, the amplification of controls, the impact on big business and small business, wages and prices, and the problem of enforcement.

Can we avoid general control and rely upon selective controls? Selective controls (or even weaker, voluntary controls) will serve only as the most temporary expedients. The only situation in which selective controls may work will be one in which merely a temporary shortage of a few critical materials is anticipated. A few controls at critical points may suffice if supply is expected to catch up with demand soon. Of course, the over-all situation must be in balance, for controls can be applied sparingly only when total expenditures are kept within the capacity of the economy to supply goods. The budgetary situation must be "satisfactory" to prevent the generation of added purchasing power. Otherwise, the controls will tend either to spread or to break down, as prices in the uncontrolled sectors rise. If, for example, we were to attempt to control the price of steel in an emergency, it would mean that wages in the steel industry would be held down. As prices and wages rose in other industries, both the real pay and the relative pay of steelworkers would fall. The employees would become disgruntled; the union would be restive; and the firms in the industry would discover that they were hard put to recruit and to retain their labor force. Many employees would quit in order to get higher-paying jobs elsewhere. To encourage steel production, wages and prices in steel would then be eased. Thus we can see that selective controls can only cope with temporary difficulties, when the over-all supply situation is good and pressures are concentrated at a few critical points rather than being general.

The amplification of controls. Under any circumstances, controls will tend to spread, but this is particularly true when demand is excessive. The cumulative tendencies, so frequently at work in economic matters, are rarely seen more clearly than in this issue of controls. The spreading of controls is similar to the ripples that emerge from the point at which a pebble is thrown into the water. The law of extension of controls is most dramatically illustrated when, in the face of excessive demand, one starts with the notion that controls will be used only for "essential" production. Resources tend to be attracted from the controlled industry to the uncontrolled under such circumstances, and in order to prevent the diversion of resources, controls must be extended all along the line.

We may cite the difficulties of the British Labor Government just after the war. It was forced to cope with what was termed an "empty economy"—that is, high demand accompanied by low peacetime production. In order to speed recovery and social reform, it was determined that necessary production should be encouraged and controls should be retained. But strict controls in the "productive" industries, with excessive purchasing power in the hands of consumers, led to a diversion of energies to the most profitable lines of occupation—the uncontrolled areas. The entertainment industry, for example, flourished and could afford to entice managerial and other personnel from the controlled industries. The result was the expansion of dog racing, book-making, and other lesser and greater forms of vice to which the British are addicted. In other words, controls led to the expansion of what the government considered to be the "parasitical" industries—those they had intended to encourage least. Naturally, the demand arose for expanded controls to prevent this cancerous growth.

The differential in the impact on big and small business. The subject of the divergent impact of controls on big and on small business is more closely related to the tendency for controls to proliferate than might be apparent at the outset. It is the small-business sector of the economy, in which controls are most difficult to implement, to which resources are attracted unless stopped by supply allocation, and toward which both the wrath and the ingenuity of the control administrators is directed. Effectiveness of control is in conflict with the competitive ideal.

The competitive ideal envisages an industry composed of thousands of producers, dealing with many buyers, so that no single firm on either side of the market is able to influence the price. In the United States, however, the number of firms in many industries is quite small, and their size is quite large. A small number of large firms implies the existence of market power, which public policy has generally attempted to limit by strengthening competitive forces. Yet, during periods of mobilization, it is extremely easy to impose controls on a small number of large and prominent firms; it is difficult to do the same with thousands of small and virtually anonymous producers. Despite the allure of the competitive ideal, those charged with the responsibility for controlling prices prefer to deal with those industries in which monopolistic elements are strong, and at the same time express their helplessness and disgust in dealing with the "old-fashioned" industries in which competition remains powerful and the market mechanism is fully operative. It is more pleasant and more efficient to give orders to three aluminum producers or six automobile manufacturers than to thousands of saw-mill operators, who are likely to violate controls with impunity. This tendency toward the lopsidedness of controls—effective in coping with big business, less effective in coping with small business—has its ironical aspects, as can easily be imagined.

Oscillating government attitudes toward the market in the thirties and forties illustrate the varying attractiveness of monopolistic and competitive forces as policy objectives change. After the demise of the early New Deal attempts to cartelize industry, the government changed its policy to one of fostering competition. Toward the end of the thirties, the Roosevelt Administration accepted the theory that the recession of 1937 had been caused by monopolistic big-business concerns which "administered" their prices. Small businesses whose prices were determined by market forces—and, in addition, the consumer, the employee, and society at large—were viewed as the hapless victims of the monopolists. Yet, a few short years later, in wartime, the same Administration had sharply revised its position. Big businesses were proving cooperative and amenable to control, but small firms—for much the same reasons that they had been hailed a few short years previously—were now seen to be obstructive, uncooperative, and, in fact, unpatriotic. It is understandable why those who are most enthusiastic about price control have the greatest praise for industries with a few sellers, and the harshest words for the "chaos" of small business.

It is in the agricultural sector that these oscillating responses are most sharply demonstrated. In the thirties, the agricultural economy was viewed as "the football of industry"; the hapless farmer deserved sympathy and public support. But in the forties, the farmer became a "profiteer." It was always difficult, for example, to deal with the problem of meat, and it will be recalled that, eventually, wartime price controls were abolished because of the meat question. Since there were countless producers, it was impossible to make controls effective. The big packers, who were carefully supervised, found it increasingly difficult to purchase cattle. Local slaughterhouses found controls a boon, for an increasing stream of cattle came in their direction, since they were less fussy about price regulations. There is a story of a price administrator attending a cattle auction in Texas toward the end of the war. To his great chagrin, he noticed that the bids were markedly in excess of the ceilings. "How come," he said, turning to his neighbor, "no one is paying attention to the price regulations?" "Oh," replied the Texan, "you mean that there OPA; we never had that down here."

Wages and prices. The problem of coordinating wages and prices is fully as intricate as that of obtaining the proper results from both the big-business and the small-business sectors. As has been suggested previously, whether a society is readier to impose wage controls or price controls, and which it is readier to enforce, will reflect the nature of the society. It is notable that the Emergency Price Control Act of 1942 made no mention of wage controls. President Roosevelt had stated that the nation could rely upon the voluntary cooperation of labor organizations; and it should be mentioned here that labor's record during the war was rather good. At the time of the establishment of price controls, the only vigorous observations on the subject of *need* for wage controls came from the farm organizations—less because they desired wage controls than because they wished to attack the proposed scheme of price control.[1]

In the United States, wage control certainly does not take precedence over price control; yet, in order for price control to be effective, costs must be held down. There must, therefore, be some kind of restraint on wage increases. In a democracy, wage and price controls would appear to be mutually dependent. Yet, in a democracy, seasoned politicians will be sensitive to the desire to avoid wage control, and lack of wage restraint will undermine price control. Our experience of 1945–1946 tends to confirm this observation. In November, 1945, President Truman lifted the restraints on wages, although he desired to preserve price control. In the throes of reconversion, with productivity reduced and profits low, some of the unions conceived the idea that take-home pay should be maintained—that is, that the workers should receive fifty-two hours' pay, despite the reduction of the work week to forty hours. In their quest for higher wages, the unions received considerable support from the Administration. Irrespective of the official position that price control should be retained, when the first round of wage increases took place in the winter of 1946, price control was dead, although it took the meat crisis of the following summer to scuttle the system entirely. We shall note later, when we appraise the Korean War experience, that much the same thing reoccurred.

The difficulties of obtaining effective wage control, even when the labor organizations lend their support, should not be overlooked. In a mobilized economy, demand and profit margins are generally high; markets are assured. Employers will attempt to pirate each other's labor. They will push up wage rates in order to attract additional labor and to retain their own working forces. This phenomenon is sometimes referred to as the "wage slide." Even when the wage structure is controlled, wages can be raised without changing the wage structure—by upgrading jobs and men. During World War II, despite wage restraint, average wage rates gradually drifted upward. In the long run, the upward drift of wages may prove embarrassing to unions that are not obtaining for their membership all that the market is willing to give. The unions may be embarrassed into making wage demands and strike threats. Thus, even under the most favorable political circumstances, preventing a rise in costs in the face of a labor shortage is a very ticklish problem.

Enforcement. It is time to make a few observations on the delicate problem of enforcement, which, sad as it may seem, goes to the root of the difficulties of maintaining controls. Only when patriotic fervor is at its height are controls likely to be self-enforcing and the violator an object of public scorn. Controls are irritants, however, and irritation dissolves the patriotic glow. Consequently, the controls are self-enforcing for only a brief period, and then the desire to evade grows. Mild penalties are not likely to deter violators, but stiffer penalties are not likely to be enforced. Thus, stringent and enduring controls usually lead to a flourishing black market, and public opinion will probably condone the violator while condemning the enforcing agency.

As a general rule, it may be suggested that as soon as controls are established, the pressures build up to break them down. There are various technical reasons for this deterioration stemming from the dynamism of the price mechanism. We need not go any further into these reasons, except to say that the price structure must be volatile to reflect changing cost and demand conditions, and even bureaucratic price fixing must inevitably make adjustments that break the stabilization policies. It has been observed that a general freeze is soon followed by a thaw; that was our experience during the war.

Beyond the technical difficulties, there is a deep-seated conflict that arises between the desire for controls (stabilization) and the desire for greater production. Business firms operate for profits and will generally respond to profit opportunities. If prices are not favorable, certain types of essential production will be curtailed, and capacity converted to other uses. In the event of a conflict between greater production and price stability, stabilization is forced to yield. The price administrators will be forced to compromise—that is, retreat—in their dealings with persistent producer groups. It becomes necessary to raise prices progressively on essential items, regardless of the impact on stability. In World War II, for example, a shortage of dowels occurred at one point. Mills had found it profitable to make broomsticks, on which the profit margin was more favorable. The OPA raised prices on doweling; but then the broomsticks disappeared from production, and it was necessary to increase the price of broomsticks.

Discussion of enforcement and of productive expediency brings us back to our initial observations. Unless a condition of generally excessive demand can be avoided, there is little hope of preventing severe restriction of the market mechanism. But direct controls are not effective in the long run, and the market opportunities have a way of creeping back in and forcing concessions. It is desirable and, in the long run, essential to avoid excessive demand by proper budgetary action; otherwise, controls become more severe, and yet, at the same time, begin to break down.

Demanding too much of controls is similar to the overloading of any economic device, leading to frustration of designs. One of our most distinguished economists has touched upon the heart of the issue by raising this question: What is it that economists should economize?[2] His conclusion: they should economize on the need for love. Wise public policy will not tempt men by creating a wide discrepancy between what a man should do and what it is in his interest to do. We must always make use of the strongest of human drives, if not the noblest—and the most persistent of impulses is, of course, self-interest. Controls are relatively weak instruments if we put too much temptation in the paths of men. If we desire to avoid black markets, gray markets, and the like—if we wish to channel the bulk of human energies into productive effort—we should seek to avoid economic conditions in which the law stands starkly in opposition to the interests and the desires of the majority of the populace. Stamped upon the package of economic controls should stand the label "handle with care."

3. SOME SPECIAL PROBLEMS OF SUPPLY ALLOCATIONS

In analyzing controls, it is useful to concentrate upon price controls at the outset rather than supply allocations, because the apparatus for the control of prices is far less complicated. However, quantities produced and prices are closely interlocked, and an understanding of the difficulties of price controls provides an insight into the similar but far more intricate problems of supply allocation. Shortages on the supply side will be reflected in price pressures, and all that has been said already about the difficulties of price controls will apply to supply allocations as well. There are, however, special aspects in the attempt to allocate supplies that should be touched upon here. Supply allocation is the most stringent type of control used in mobilization drives, and it cannot be predicted in advance whether the degree of pressure will be severe enough to force the society to have recourse to them. If only a few bottlenecks exist, and the general supply situation is good, it will be possible to avoid over-all supply allocations, as it was during the Korean War. If limited war is to be the pattern in the future, with the corollary that centralized management of the nation's economy is a thing of the past, we may be able to cope with mobilization strains by price controls and, perhaps, some allocative controls of an informal nature on the few critical materials.

In World War II, it was necessary, however, to develop an over-all system of supply allocations. In general, whenever there is marked excess of potential demand over supply, it will be necessary to channel vital materials *directly* into war industries, and away from civilian markets in which adequate demand exists for all possible production. In fact, in severe shortages, it becomes necessary to allocate scarce materials among the several war industries. The first problem may be avoided by sufficiently severe taxation; the latter may only be avoided if the international situation permits.

To put the problem another way, if the pressures are severe enough, centralized coordination and synchronization of productive effort must be attempted. The two major problems in mobilization are stabilization and production. Stabilization may be achieved without centralized allocation of resources, but as the production problem comes more to the fore, allocation becomes essential. The allocation of supply can be a particularly intricate problem because it requires more than the immediate allocation of raw materials for prevailing patterns of production: it requires the allocation of materials for the production of capital goods that will be necessary for *future* production patterns. Thus the allocating authority is faced with the necessity of determining the time and pace of capital construction, which implies forecasting the future needs and equipment of both the armed forces and civilian economy.

Two approaches to the problem are conceivable—the halfway approach and the "whole-hog" approach. Both were attempted by the War Production Board, which was established by executive order shortly after Pearl Harbor and absorbed the previously existing agencies, the Office of Production Management and the Supply Priorities and Allocation Board. In the halfway approach, the controlling agency makes no attempt to direct the actual flow of resources, but instead attempts to control the demand for them through the issuance of priorities. Priority orders are qualitative; those with a triple-A rating, for example, may "bump" those with a double-A rating. They are likely to be issued in excess—and the value of any particular rating is likely to depreciate over time. Since they are issued without consideration of the supplies available, they are, at best, mere "hunting licenses" carrying no guarantee that the necessary supplies will be forthcoming. Moreover, even if a producer can obtain one necessary commodity, there is no assurance that he will obtain the others.

Whenever true shortages exist, the halfway approach will give way to the whole-hog approach. The controlling agency will develop a plan for assuring that those who need supplies will receive them. It will limit allocations within the range made permissible by available supplies, and will channel the materials to producers in accordance with an over-all plan for national production. But the transition to centralized coordination of production has deeper implications. Control over production implies control over national strategy. In allocating materials directly, the controlling agency holds the power to determine what proportion of national effort will be devoted to the support of allies, to the civilian economy, and to the military services. The power to control national policy is not lightly surrendered nor easily retained. During the war, it was the feeling in the armed forces that the civilians in the WPB had too much influence in determining which of the various needs of the armed forces were to be met. The civilians held that war was too important to be left to the generals, that the services could not appreciate the needs of civilians, nor were they inclined to recognize the desirability of aiding allies. As a matter of fact, one of the reasons for the earlier decision to create the Supply Priorities and Allocation Board as a policy group superimposed on the Office of Production Management was that the latter had been too inclined to accept military judgments and disinclined to give extensive aid to the Soviet Union. Creation of SPAB, composed of individuals more sympathetic to the Administration's policies, permitted effective support of the Administration's desire to aid the U.S.S.R.

After creation of the WPB, power to control national production and policy was too great to be lodged permanently in an administrative agency. Rather than serving as the *decision-making body* with respect to production alternatives, the WPB became largely an *information center* responsible for the accomplishment of policy decisions made at higher levels of government. The WPB became an instrument of coordination, lacking the power to initiate decisions. Even this authority appeared excessive to interested parties, and gradually the over-all coordinating discretion of the WPB was watered down through the introduction of overlapping boards and with the emergence of "czars" to control the allocation of specific commodities; thus we had a "food czar," a "rubber czar," and so on. The emergence of the czars did not alter the nature of the problem of allocation, and it merely weakened centralized coordination. The purpose of the czars was to satisfy the complaints of interested groups who felt themselves ill-used by the WPB. The czars were supposed to reassess and readjust productive requirements. Administrative reorganization did nothing to change the nature of the problem; all it did was to point to the inevitable dissatisfactions which arise under mobilization controls.

The conflict between the achievement of centralized allocation of resources and the necessity for allaying dissatisfactions by permitting centrifugal tendencies to lower the efficiency of use of resources is best illustrated by the issue of labor direction. Manpower direction or the allocation of labor represents the ultimate in both supply allocation and in mobilization controls generally. In contrast to materials controls, in which the quality of the product is unlikely to be changed significantly, labor direction may mean a notable change in the nature of the resources. Compulsory services, as opposed to voluntary services, especially when they appear to be based upon erratic standards, may mean a decline of morale, effort, and output—and may, therefore, be self-defeating. In coping with the labor market during wartime, society must choose between the advantages of maximum mobility through manpower direction and the advantages of voluntary movement through industrial decentralization. As displayed in Chart 2, there are two direct advantages of manpower direction. First, we attain rapid movement of resources to the most necessary jobs, without waiting for the slow process of inducement to operate. Secondly, we attain true price stability by achieving stabilization of costs. To combine the extremes of mobility and stability in the absence of direction is a formidable task.

The disadvantages of manpower direction are grave. First, there exists the constitutional and moral question regarding to what degree the state has the power to tamper with what are normally regarded as private liberties. Secondly, high mobility, when achieved by government edict, may not accomplish its purposes and may result, instead, in reduced economic efficiency. The advantages of industrial decentralization are simply the reverse of the disadvantages of manpower direction. If we attempt to induce the movement of labor through manipulation of the wage structure, voluntary cooperation of the human factors of production may be obtained. The use of economic incentives provides for high morale and high productivity. Most individuals find suitable jobs, and mobility is sufficiently high to

CHART 2

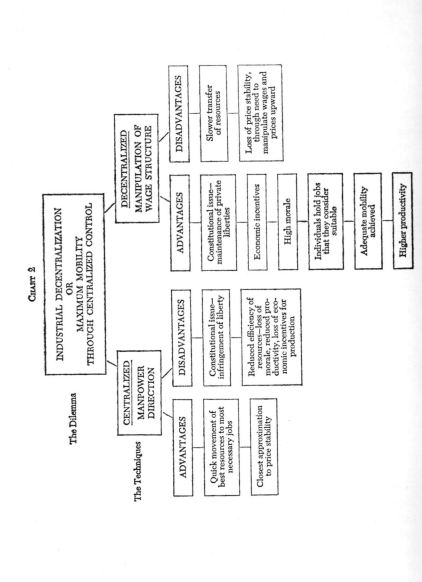

The Dilemma

INDUSTRIAL DECENTRALIZATION
OR
MAXIMUM MOBILITY
THROUGH CENTRALIZED CONTROL

The Techniques

CENTRALIZED
MANPOWER
DIRECTION

DECENTRALIZED
MANIPULATION OF
WAGE STRUCTURE

ADVANTAGES

Quick movement of
best resources to most
necessary jobs

Closest approximation
to price stability

DISADVANTAGES

Constitutional issue—
infringement of liberty

Reduced efficiency of
resources—loss of
morale, reduced pro-
ductivity, loss of eco-
nomic incentives for
production

ADVANTAGES

Constitutional issue—
maintenance of private
liberties

Economic incentives

High morale

Individuals hold jobs
that they consider
suitable

Adequate mobility
achieved

Higher productivity

DISADVANTAGES

Slower transfer
of resources

Loss of price stability,
through need to
manipulate wages and
prices upward

achieve the nation's purposes, without recourse to the debilitating instrument of direction. At the same time, the Constitutional and moral issue of the infringement of private liberties is not permitted to arise, with its creation of unease of conscience in the body politic. Real output and what we may call "effective mobility" may be greater if we rely on voluntarism and the manipulation of wages.

It must be observed, however, that achieving stabilization will be practically impossible when manipulation of wages is the instrument for achieving labor mobility. Wages will be under constant upward pressure because of the wage slide—that is, the upgrading of both jobs and men that permits the raising of wage rates without affecting the wage structure. Stability and efficiency may be in conflict, and under such circumstances stabilization will yield. Yet, for those in the armed forces, the observation of the wage slide, while their own pay remains fixed and low, may be an embittering experience.

In World War II, our method of allocating labor was through the centralized manipulation of the wage structure by the War Labor Board. The Board recognized "essentiality" of the output of a particular industry as a justification for increased wages. Elsewhere, the Board attempted to resist wage increases, but not at the expense of morale. When pressure became unbearable, a cost-of-living adjustment might be granted. Otherwise, the policy was a sympathetic deferral of requests. President Roosevelt's handling of the labor problem was a masterpiece of political discernment. The unions were cajoled into *voluntarily* giving a no-strike pledge. In treating labor's complaints, which in the nature of the circumstances could not be satisfied, the President temporized, sympathized, and deliberated; he might agree to investigate, and in the end make some small but satisfying concession. Morale remained high. It was a tribute to the decentralized approach, and, all in all, the wage slide was not unendurable. It may be doubted that equally satisfactory results could have been achieved through compulsory techniques. Although it is necessary to restrain the increase in wages to achieve stabilization, in labor matters the old adage that "you can catch more flies with honey than you can with salt" is frequently illustrated.

But the objectives of the government must be clear, and the techniques of cajolery must be *honestly* employed. As we shall see, during the Korean War these requirements were more honored in the breach.

Finally, it must be reiterated that controls are essentially expedients. In this respect, supply allocations do not differ from direct controls over prices. Emergency management of the nation's economy may be necessary on a short-run basis to achieve production adjustments. It must, however, be temporary management, and controls must be increasingly dispensed with as the adjustments are achieved. The economy can be controlled through a period of disequilibrium with remarkable efficiency, considering the pressures at work. Direct controls do not, however, constitute an enduring framework. The passage of time permits cynicism to develop and human ingenuity to devise techniques of evasion of controls. Not only does this process lead to the erosion of controls, but it undermines the fundamental morality of the citizenry upon which society, in the final analysis, is based.

4. THE KOREAN WAR: A CASE STUDY

To illustrate the problem of administering controls, I should like to discuss the history of our mobilization efforts during the Korean War. This will be a useful exercise, since the Korean War episode illustrates some of the gravest weaknesses of a system of controls in a democracy. But it is also important for another reason, since it represents the kind of emergency with which we are most likely to be confronted in this long-range and enduring conflict posed by the hostility of the Communist world. We face a period of cold war, interspersed with brush fires or tepid wars, *not requiring total mobilization*. The Korean War was not deemed significant enough to force the several economic groups that make up our society to sacrifice their own ambitions for the national interest, as they had in World War II. Neither was it sufficient to suppress the prevailing mood of "politics as usual." For the general public, the war seemed to be more an irritant than a struggle in which it was completely absorbed. Yet it imposed an immediate strain upon the economy which had to be dealt with. What were the results?

The Defense Production Act of 1950 was written as the first blare of the bugles died away. Though surely not above criticism, it was a well-conceived bit of legislation incorporating much valuable experience from World War II. It gave important powers to the President, and encouraged rapid and controlled mobilization. Yet, in the years that followed, crippling amendments were to chip away at this edifice. Erosional forces are, of course, always at work at controls. What is surprising in the Korean case is the speed of the process and the lack of resistance to dismantlement.

It was provided in the original Act that price controls could be instituted either generally or for individual commodities or services, in case the President found that the price might otherwise rise "unreasonably" and that such an increase would "materially affect the cost of living or the national defense." Whenever ceilings were individually imposed, the Act required that wages be stabilized in that industry—and, of course, whenever prices were controlled generally, that wages in general be stabilized. The Act encouraged the President to seek voluntary cooperation from business, agriculture, and labor in order to maintain price stability. It permitted controls to be imposed on agricultural prices, more or less when parity had been reached.

By comparison to the jerry-built structure of World War II, the framework for control was soundly constructed. The budgetary picture was excellent, suggesting that any shortages which developed would prove to be temporary. In view of this fact, the Administration wisely decided to rely upon selective controls. The Office of Price Stabilization established maximum prices for essential commodities, and the presumption was that wages would be stabilized.

The scheme might have worked had the climate of labor-management relations been similar to what it had been at the outset of World War II, or if collective-bargaining agreements had contained the same kind of terms that they had prior to 1948. But both the climate and the agreements had changed.

On the part of management, hostility to unions was much diminished. In order to obtain industrial peace, corporations were willing, even eager, to grant wage increases, if they were offset by price increases. Labor organizations had emerged from the underdog role. In World War II, they had been willing to settle for union security clauses and for an expansion of employment from depression conditions. Now they were less willing to tolerate a decline in the living standards of the membership because of rises in the cost of living, and were correspondingly more aggressive in presenting wage demands.

Moreover, after 1948, new features began to appear in union contracts. In particular, the use of the cost-of-living or "escalator" clause was widespread. In addition, a few contracts included the so-called "annual improvement factor"—providing for an annual boost in hourly wages of about five cents an hour. The issue facing the Administration was clear-cut: if the new contracts *that provided automatically for wage increases* were permitted to stand, the stabilization program would be undermined. For one thing, if wages were advanced along with the cost of living, production costs would rise, thus squeezing profits and leading to price adjustments. For another, if some groups of employees were automatically to receive higher wages, it would discriminate against those unions which did not have contracts including automatic adjustment features. Those labor organizations could not afford to sit idly by while their members were inequitably treated and their real wages fell in relation to the others. It would not be long before cost-of-living adjustments would have to be provided all around.

The first blow against the stabilization program came in the form of a decision by the Wage Stabilization Board in the fall of 1950. The Board held that the implementation of the cost-of-living adjustments in existing contracts would not be considered inconsistent with the program of wage stabilization. In the long run, this action implied that other employee groups would receive similar adjustments on grounds of equity. Subsequent action by the Board confirmed the view that the *national pattern* of wage increases would be based upon the settlements that the most powerful unions had been able to obtain. For this

reason, the WSB was facetiously referred to as the "wage stimulation board" or the "wage ratchet board." It has been argued
that the proper function for the Board was not to seek stabilization, but to seek settlements to conflicts, and that effective
stabilization policies had to be politically negotiated at a higher
level. If this view is accepted, it is apparent that the Administration did not feel its position was sufficiently strong to oppose
powerful labor organizations on this point. There is little doubt
that the actions of the Board were *inconsistent with the stabilization goal*, and that its policies tended to *push up* wage rates.[3]
Despite the improvement of the provisions of the 1950 Act, as
compared with the Price Control Act of 1942, *in reality* the
program of wage stabilization was weaker and was rapidly
undermined. This suggests the conclusion that in matters of wage
restraint, voluntarism accompanied by the intent to hold the
line may be a more effective method of procedure than is statu-
tory enactment of limits. More fundamentally, it raises the
question whether democratic governments, except in rare instances, are willing to stabilize wage rates effectively.

A second blow at price stabilization was struck by the passage
of the so-called Capehart Amendment to the Defense Production Act. This amendment provided protection for previously
existing profit margins, by requiring that the Office of Price
Stabilization make compensatory price adjustments whenever the
costs of producers were increased. No doubt, in an economic
system that relies upon the price mechanism, it is necessary
to provide *some* flexibility for price adjustments in the face of
cost rises, but there is little justification for guaranteeing *full*
protection under *all* circumstances. The Amendment illustrates
the weakening of Congressional resolve.[4] Whatever the justification in special cases, the over-all impact of the amendment was
to weaken further the system of stabilization.

The troubles came to a head in the steel strike of 1952. The
steelworkers, who had been watching the pay of the auto
workers climb automatically in accordance with their collective-
bargaining agreement, demanded a healthy wage increase to
compensate them for advances in the cost of living. The President's fact-finding commission recommended a wage increase

which not only brought the steelworkers in line with other unions but pushed them somewhere out in front. The President threw his weight behind the proposed settlement, although it undercut the stabilization program. The OPS, under the Capehart Amendment, offered the steel industry a price increase of three dollars a ton, which the industry rejected, demanding five dollars a ton. At the expiration of the contract, the President seized the steel mills—an action later held unconstitutional, and certainly a precipitate one, since he had available legal devices for maintaining steel production. In the end, the industry got its price, the union got its increase, and the stabilization program was scuttled with the approval of the Administration and the WSB.[5]

Let us examine the end result of the stabilization program. Labor was given assurance, in the cost-of-living adjustments, that the burden of war would not affect its standard of living, and it was guaranteed wage increases. Business concerns were guaranteed against reduced profit margins by the Capehart Amendment, which made price adjustments mandatory. The farmer was automatically protected by the parity formula, which provided for price increases whenever the cost of things he bought increased. All great social groups, with the obvious exception of salaried workers and pensioners, were guaranteed protection though the mechanism of price and wage advances. All of this was supposedly consistent with a program of stabilization. In actuality, *the net effect of these provisions was not merely to make inflation permissible, but to make it mandatory,* in case there was any decline in living standards not caused by taxation.[6] It was not a very encouraging demonstration of democracy at work.

The reason that inflation did not become a cumulative upward movement was the excellent budgetary position, which resulted from prompt and responsible action in raising taxes. The absorption of purchasing power through higher taxation prevented demand and total expenditures from getting out of hand, and brought the inflation to a halt after a brief and relatively moderate increase in prices. However, had the emergency been greater, and a reduction in living standards been necessary, inflation would have been required by law through the continuous escalation of wages and prices—and the legal systematization of the vicious circle of inflation.

This melancholy little episode raises a number of searching questions. Can democratic governments, responsive to the will and the whims of the populace, take the proper steps in meeting emergencies? No system of controls that is merely irritating without being effective—and those were the conditions in the Korean War—is likely to command much public support. Yet, in the years ahead, in view of our enduring struggle with the Communist world, it is not unlikely that we will have to face several emergencies similar to the one posed by the Korean War. Such engagements, however, although they require quick and effective action, seem to be too pallid to arouse massive public support, and to persuade various social groups to sacrifice their own special interests for the national welfare. On the contrary, these emergencies, by bringing pressure to bear upon the standard of living, may simply intensify the squabbling among the social groups.

I have already mentioned that so-called "economic laws" do not interpose any serious barrier to meeting the requirements of defense; rather, it is a question of will, of the capacity to absorb punishment and to make sacrifices. In the long-term struggle, the issue of rapid and effective mobilization in limited warfare goes to the heart of the question of whether or not democratic societies can have the will and the capacity to meet the challenge. As a case study, the Korean War seems to point to the unhappy conclusion that democratic governments are, in practice, likely to yield to each pressure group in turn— with inflation as the end result. If this process of piecemeal capitulation is permitted to rot out the core of stabilization programs, except in the direst emergencies, we have something to be concerned about, indeed.

5

BUDGETARY PLANNING

Up to this point, the problem of resource allocation has been treated largely in real terms. From time to time, however, allusions have been made to the financial mechanisms by means of which the desired allocation of resources is achieved. Such considerations lead quite naturally to the topic of budgetary planning, which is inextricably bound up with the main question of resource allocation. For the appropriate sectors of the economy, the government's budget should be viewed as *the financial counterpart of the real allocation of resources.* Under free enterprise, the allocation of resources will reflect the pattern of total spending; and the budget, which reveals the planned division of resources as between the public and private sectors, and the allocation of resources among the several programs of the government, helps to indicate that pattern. (In a controlled economy, of course, the imprint of the budget goes much deeper.) The budget will detail the financial mechanisms by which transfer of resources to the state may be accomplished, in addition to indicating the broad division of resources. Under free enterprise, the budget shows the portion of resources that the citizenry has jointly determined to appropriate to the state for collective purposes, and the distinction between the calculus of satisfaction in the governmental and in the private sectors cannot be forgotten. In the two sectors, attaining maximum returns from given resources implies different things, and it is only in the governmental sector that we may consider the best usage of resources in terms of the social interest. In the private sector, best usage simply implies the sum of individual satisfactions.

It is not surprising that the epithet "dull" is frequently applied to budgetary discussions. Reading the President's budget, a document of some 1,200 tightly packed pages, or the Congressional hearings on the budget, which will run to 25,000 pages of rather discursive testimony, may not be an enlivening experience. Yet, to the initiated, the budget can be a dramatic document representing, as it does, the financial embodiment of national policy. The budget may be viewed merely as a dull collection of figures, or it may be viewed as a comprehensive plan for the achievement of the nation's objectives. Quite naturally, if one views the budget in the latter sense, it is likely to prove somewhat more enticing. William Ewart Gladstone, who did more to make budgets best sellers than any other finance minister in history, took this attitude toward budgets: "Budgets are not merely matters of arithmetic, but in a thousand ways go to the root of prosperity of individuals, and relations of classes, and the strength of kingdoms."[1] The budgets of Gladstone's day were, of course, vastly simpler than our present budgets, with the incredible multiplicity of activities carried on by the modern state; and Gladstone's budgetary goal was retrenchment, which added a certain zest to a series of budgets, since one might hope that they would progressively shrink. Yet his passionate interest in budgets was more than the musty statistical curiosity of the dry technician; rather, it was a reflection of his overriding concern for the *structure and direction of society*. It raises a standard for our own day, for unless we are better able to perceive the connection between finance and policy, we will be doomed to make inadequate use of our total resources. What is worse, we will find that our aspirations, our policies, and our achievements bear little relation to each other; and in the present era, the margin for error is slim.

Our examination of the budget can be most conveniently divided under four general headings: the development and the purposes of budgets; present procedures in the United States; budgetary complications of recent years; and some comments on possible improvements of American budgetary practices.

1. THE DEVELOPMENT AND PURPOSES OF BUDGETS

Of the many purposes for which a budget is formulated, the earliest to develop was its function as a *vehicle of control.* Since the time of the Magna Carta, the privilege of financial control of the executive has gradually been asserted—first by the barons-in-chief of the realm, then by corporations and other privileged groups, and finally by the populace at large. In the long contest for dominance between Parliament and Crown, the issue of financial control of the executive by the representatives of the people became the ultimate weapon and objective in the struggle. It is essential to remember this background in considering the significance of the Constitutional provision that "no money shall be drawn from the treasury, but in consequence of appropriations made by law." In this era of frequently expressed impatience with the delays and the irritations of Congressional deliberations, it must be emphasized that Congressional control of the power of the purse is a dearly purchased right and is, perhaps, the fundamental bulwark of our liberties.

It is proper to stress the Constitutional aspect of the budget; however, it has important technical features as well. In view of the Constitutional proviso, some cynical wag has observed that "a budget is simply a device for securing money from a legislature." It is not unreasonable, however, to entertain higher aspirations. In serving as a vehicle of control, the budget should, ideally speaking, serve as a complete harness for *all* the activities of the government. In fulfilling this role, the budget should embody that division of resources between the public and private sectors which will best attain the nation's goals, and should indicate the most suitable allocation of the public resources among the several programs of the government. At the same time, the budget should promote maximum efficiency in the use of resources in the public sector, thus minimizing the need to divert resources to the government or maximizing the results

achieved with a given volume of resources. Therefore, technically speaking, the budget serves two interrelated but sharply
distinguishable purposes: to establish public policy in the form
of government programs, and to achieve efficiency and economy[2]
in the administration of those programs. The distinction between
these two aspects of budgets is of fundamental importance.
The failure to keep them separate is, as we shall see later, a basic
structural weakness in our budgetary thinking.

A convenient fiction has helped to imbed in our attitude the
confusion between the program and efficiency aspects of the
budget, and to perpetuate a vision of the budget expert as a
neutral technician perfecting the financial mechanism that will
carry out *established policy* as economically as possible. The
heart of the fiction lies in the belief that the Congress sets policy
unambiguously; thus the role of the administrator is simply
to provide the financial skeleton for basic legislation. Even in
the less complicated days of the nineteenth century, the reality
was somewhat different from the fiction. But the rise of the
executive power in the twentieth century, the role of the President's budget, and the complex network of formal and informal
relationships among the President, the Congress, the Bureau of
the Budget, and the several departments and agencies have
turned the once-useful fiction into a myth. Still, it is perpetuated
and continues to haunt our budgetary procedures. The Congress,
secure in its belief that the basic legislation has established
policy, may view its annual consideration of the budget formulated by the experts simply from the standpoint of assuring
the most economical attainment of legislative goals. Thus policy
formulation, which is so intimately connected with the appropriation levels, may slip into organizational limbo and finally
be unconsciously seized by the Bureau of the Budget—the one
organization that, in theory, should be concerned with economy
and efficiency, and should be divorced entirely from policy
formulation (the direction given to the Bureau by its first
head, General Charles G. Dawes, after its establishment in 1921).

From the standpoint of budgetary considerations, the formulation of policy should possess certain characteristics. In its most
concrete form, policy determination consists of decisions as to

which programs will be supported and what amount of resources will be devoted to the programs, individually and over-all. In principle, this should imply the simultaneous consideration of *total* receipts and *total* expenditures, in order to determine the appropriate diversion of resources to the public sector. Concurrently, a comprehensive consideration of all the programs of the government should be attempted, with estimates of the costs and the benefits of each, in order to ensure that when the final decisions are made, the most beneficial programs will be the ones to survive.

In formal economic jargon, all programs should be weighed at the margin to ensure that the additional satisfaction (the marginal utility) of the last dollar spent on each program equals the additional satisfaction of the last dollar expenditure in the other programs. At the same time, the marginal social benefits provided by the last dollar's worth of government expenditure should be adjusted so that it is equal to the marginal social sacrifice (of private goods), as represented by the final demand upon the taxpayers. Such is the implication for public finance of the traditional marginalist analysis of the allocation problem.[3] Critics of this approach have sharply questioned the applicability of marginal-utility concepts, particularly with reference to strategic decisions, and have jocularly hinted that the total utility of marginal utility is approximately zero. With respect to the actual measurement of utility, one can readily accept the strictures of the critics. There is no objective criterion for evaluating the benefits of government programs, as there is in the market place. There exists no unit of comparison; one is attempting to weigh incomparables, and that requires judgment rather than measurement.[4] It is difficult to judge programs until they have been tried. Moreover, many programs are characterized by "indivisibilities"—that is, they cannot be varied by small amounts at the margin—and therefore, the government may be forced to concentrate on certain programs to the exclusion of others.

Nevertheless, it is true that marginalism lies at the heart of economic analysis. Although the reasoning is purely formal and cannot be "quantified" in actual cases, we ought always keep its implications in mind. Marginal analysis points to the need for continual reassessment of the pattern of expenditure *at the margin,* rather than being beguiled by arguments concerning the over-all "necessity" of a particular program. Expenditures should be judged comparatively, on the basis of alternative cost. The process of budget determination is essentially one of balancing satisfactions and dissatisfactions, and of achieving equivalent satisfaction in the final dollar's expenditures on all programs. Even though the costs and benefits of programs cannot be objectively measured, marginal analysis does provide guidelines for decision making.

The actual characteristics of budget formulation in the United States, however, bear little resemblance to the ideal pattern we have postulated. Congress has never considered revenues and appropriations at the same time. The Appropriations Committee of the House of Representatives has only the most informal relations with the Committee on Ways and Means; appropriations are determined without simultaneous consideration of the revenue side. The President's budget message makes only the briefest and most indirect references to taxation. In addition, government programs are considered individually, so that no scale of priorities can be established.

There are those who look back upon the uncomplicated budgeting of the nineteenth century as a golden age of sensible budget practices. Nothing could be further from the truth. In the nineteenth century, and until the Budget and Accounting Act of 1921, there was no budget at all in the United States. For a considerable period, the Appropriations Committee, with whatever unifying tendencies it provides, existed in name only— since it had been rendered ineffective at the close of the century. Government departments in the "good old days" established relations with the appropriate legislative committees of Congress, each of which suggested appropriations in its own realm, without consideration of the appropriations demanded by other committees. As can be imagined, this arrangement provided an incentive for spending. One observer described the practices of this period in the following manner: "Thus it came about that instead of one road into the Treasury—and that a thorny one—

there were seven or eight primrose paths and 'as many byroads as there were members of the appropriations committees.'"[5] Moreover, the Congress had no need to consider over-all expenditures. For considerable periods of the century, revenues were excessive—embarrassingly so, because they were the fruit of the protective tariff—and unless ways could be found to spend the revenues, the unwanted result might be a lowering of the protective tariff walls. Thus spending was encouraged, and spending programs were not subjected to any rigorous analysis of the costs and the benefits. Obviously, the essential features of efficient budgeting were lacking: there was no comprehensive consideration of the whole budget, with one program weighed against another, nor was there measurement of the total costs of expenditures in terms of taxation. Such a background provides a poor heritage for budgetary planning in our more complicated age.

2.   CONTEMPORARY PROCEDURES IN THE UNITED STATES

The budget cycle in the United States consists of four stages: (1) the preparation and presentation of the President's budget, (2) Congressional consideration and authorization, (3) budget execution, and (4) review. This cycle takes between two and three years to complete. Some fifteen months prior to the start of the fiscal years for which planning is in progress, the Bureau of the Budget will begin its preliminary studies of the amounts that the executive departments and agencies will need to continue their operations in that fiscal year. When the preliminary soundings have been made, the Bureau puts them together for the first look at the over-all budget position. After conferring with the President, at which time the major spending programs are approved, the Bureau sends back to the departments preliminary figures which represent *targets* for final expenditures. On the basis of the target figures, the final estimates are then prepared by the departments and are subjected to the scrutiny of the budget examiners, who make their recommendations on these requests directly to the Bureau's director. In the latter part of the fall, the director's review gives the opportunity to the departments to appeal for reconsideration of the Bureau's decision—and also an opportunity for a committee to survey the Bureau's own procedures. Subsequently, the President's budget is prepared at the end of the year and is sent to the Congress in January.

The main instrument of Congressional consideration is the Appropriations Committee of the House of Representatives. The Committee is divided into a number of subcommittees, each concerned with a particular government department or division. It is quite natural that a group of men familiar with a particular division of the executive branch will be inclined to take a parochial interest in its welfare. This is especially true for the subcommittees dealing with departments, like Agriculture and Interior, that touch upon sectional interests. Ordinarily, therefore, the subcommittees do not tamper significantly with the estimates in the President's budget; a cut of as much as 5 per cent is rare. Occasionally, the so-called "meat axe" will be wielded to indicate widespread dissatisfaction with a particular budget. In the 1958 budget, for example, this occurred in the case of appropriations for the United States Information Agency. On rare occasions, the Congress will launch an economization drive, and then only a few programs will be secure. It should be noted, however, that budget cuts made under such circumstances may be token ones for publicity purposes, and will often be made good at a later date by deficiency appropriations.[6]

Usually, the full Appropriations Committee will accept the recommendations of its subcommittees, and it is relatively rare that the House as a whole will differ with the findings of the Appropriations Committee. The Senate, which gets into the consideration at a much later date, has little time for study, and remains as a kind of court of last resort for executive departments that wish to protest the decisions of the House.

As a general rule, Congressmen recognize their own limitations in appraising the national security program. They are aware that they are in a poor position to criticize military policy and expenditures. They have other pressing duties, and on any particular issue, they are highly dependent upon the technical staffs of the committees. Usually, unless a program appears particularly suspicious, the Congress will be satisfied to make a token cut, to assert its control over the purse strings, but will go along with the program of the executive. This inability to take issue with the major elements of the President's program means that the lengthy hearings are concerned largely with trivia—the price of shoes, autos, or rifles, whatever item in the budget the questioner is sufficiently familiar with to challenge. As a result, the net effect of the questioning is to attack the problem of the economical and efficient operation of the department concerned rather than to cast light upon the policy issues, as such.

In making its appropriations, Congress allots sums in the appropriation bills under separate titles. The degree of flexibility varies. If the number of titles is small, considerable discretionary power is left to the spending agency, since transfers are permitted *within* appropriation titles. Transfers are not, however, generally permitted *among* appropriation titles. Though Congress has the power to authorize such transfer, it is usually reluctant to do so. The Congress varies in its attitude toward detailed appropriations, sometimes requiring more detail, sometimes less. Although the insistence upon detail may be an encumbrance in spending and may prove irksome, when Congress does get into an economy mood, it is likely that its cuts will fall on the broadest aggregates, rather than on the detailed requests.

The last two stages of the budget cycle, subsequent to the passage of the appropriation acts, may be touched upon briefly. Though Congress appropriates funds directly to the spending department, the latter, in order to secure the release of funds, must apply to the Bureau of the Budget. The plan of release, accepted by the Bureau, is known as "apportionment"; it permits the Bureau to control the rate of spending. The Bureau may also establish reserves—and this means that at the end of the year, if the funds have not been spent, they may not become available to the department at all. Thus, even in the stage of budget execution, the administrative arm of the President may maintain control over the spending that the Congress has authorized. From time to time, the impounding of funds by the Bureau has provoked severe criticism in Congress and movements to

strip this power away from the Bureau—movements that have
been unsuccessful thus far.[7]

The final stage of the budget cycle, the review, consists largely
of an audit by the General Accounting Office to ensure that
expenditures have been made in accordance with law. The
emphasis of the review is, therefore, legal rather than a retro-
spective analysis of the wisdom of the government's policies
or the efficiency of its operations. In the audit, the possibility of
unauthorized expenditure is checked. So long as expenditures
have been confined to those authorized within the several titles
in the appropriation acts, no question is raised concerning the
possibility of improving the performance of the government.

The crucial position of the Bureau of the Budget in this cycle
should be noted. It stands between the President and the operating departments—setting spending goals, screening requests,
and etching the outlines of the President's budget. Moreover,
the Bureau stands between the Congress and the operating departments, and (presumably, with the approval of the President)
may impound funds authorized by Congress. It is important to
recognize that the main cuts in departmental requests are normally made by the *executive* rather than the *legislative* branch.
And it is the Bureau that wields the axe during the period in
which the President's budget is drawn up. Naturally, regardless
of their private and parochial misgivings, the operating departments must go along with the President's decisions.

3. BUDGETARY PROBLEMS OF RECENT YEARS

The aftermath of World War II has ushered in a condition
that is essentially new. With respect to budgetary practices, the
international exigencies of the cold war have precluded a return
to the *status quo ante*. Prior to the postwar era, a sharp anti-
thesis had characterized the American attitude toward the logic
of the budget during times of peace and war. In peacetime, the
strictly delimited portion of economic activity carried on by the
government was to represent a small proportion of total output,
managed as economically as possible. In wartime, on the other
hand, all restraints were removed. Ultimately, the military lead-

ers determined the size of the budget, and they could have virtually anything they demanded, with no consideration as to cost.

These sharply antithetical approaches to peace and war have, perforce, faded in the light of the changed international position of the United States. For the first time in our history, we have had to cope with the necessity of reconciling large peacetime budgets based upon heavy military expenditures with the traditional budgetary problems of cost-consciousness and limited means. In so many ways, our traditional attitudes and arrangements are now unsuitable, and we must make the painful process of adjustment. Two major adjustments have been required of the public at large, and a lesser adjustment of military men.

First, the public has had to accept an enormous expansion of the government's relative share of economic activity, with all that is implied—a series of record peacetime budgets, expenditures *and taxes* that remain high. From the traditional standpoint of the appropriate scope of government activity, the change has been drastic. Yet, under the circumstances, there has been no alternative, and for some the adjustment has been hard. The traditional business attitude has tended toward the belief that the government exists mainly to create an environment in which private economic activity may be carried on. *Any* government intervention, regulation, or taxation tends to inhibit incentives and production; a *significant* growth of the government's role might provoke an economic breakdown.

Consequently, throughout the postwar period, warnings have regularly been sounded: how long can this go on? The continued growth of national output has not deterred the dire prophecies. It is argued that we must reduce the size of the government, that both taxes and expenditures must be cut back to a "reasonable" level.[8] A sound economy, it is argued, is the nation's first line of defense; the Russians want to force us to "spend our way into bankruptcy." The heart of the controversy seems to be the allegation that we are spending more than we can "afford," a statement that can evoke a sympathetic response in view of man's reluctance to pay taxes.

How much, then, can we afford to spend? On this issue, the views of the professional and the lay economist seem to diverge. The lay preconception that the present level of expenditures constitutes an intolerable burden finds little support among professional economists. Whatever the case against certain categories of government expenditures, and there are powerful arguments to be heard, it is fallacious to argue, under the present circumstances, against present levels or higher future levels of government expenditures on the grounds that we cannot afford them. However, since the solemn prediction by a prominent businessman or politician that we are on the road to financial ruin carries far more weight than does the professional opinion of economists, we have unfortunately as a nation developed a chronic neurosis on the subject of the capacity of our economy, and the symptoms intermittently become acute.

As has been suggested previously, the immediate limits on our spending capacity are political rather than economic in nature. There is nothing in our present situation that would preclude very much expanded government spending—provided, and this is the crucial political question, we have public determination to bear the increased costs and a willingness to accept a broadly based tax structure. Although economic limits do exist (when incentives or morale are so affected that production begins to diminish), we have not, as yet, begun to infringe on those limits. It may be that it would be unwise to increase taxes too precipitately. Nevertheless, with the weapons at our command to bring down the prices of military hardware—that is, by giving preferential tax treatment to firms producing military goods, by ceasing to use military expenditures as an expensive method of bolstering local economies, and so on—we could, without substantial difficulty, double the amount of military protection we are receiving, even without doubling military expenditures. To put the problem another way, it would not be difficult, economically speaking, to increase the military budget to, say, $70 billion.

On the other hand, the anxiety that has been expressed by the traditionalists concerning the *relationship* between receipts and expenditures is valid, and this is the kernel of truth in the argument over the nation's fiscal capacity. The over-all budgetary condition cannot be permitted to deteriorate in the long run, but this is once again a political question concerning the willingness of the public to bear taxation. There are times, of course, when expenditures need not be limited by receipts. During depressions, when resources are idle, expenditures may exceed receipts by a substantial amount, and this procedure—expansionary fiscal policy—is quite proper. During periods of extreme emergency, likewise, the budgetary situation may be permitted to deteriorate, and expenditures may sharply exceed receipts, as in World War II. But such behavior is proper only during emergencies. Normally, the budget should be approximately in balance. We cannot bear *sizable* deficits, year after year, without grave inflationary consequences. Normally, we must tax ourselves sufficiently to pay for expenditures, even if this means higher taxes. There is a sharp difference, however, between observing that there is strong political resistance to higher taxes in a democracy and stating that, economically, we cannot afford greater expenditures.

Periodically, we have succumbed to the notion that we are spending more than we can afford. During such periods, we shave expenditures and, at the same time, force objectives. Subsequently, a dramatic event, such as Korea or Sputnik, reawakens us to the power of our foes, and we begin to rebuild. Our policy thus oscillates between budget cutting and the recognition of the costs of our international objectives. This is the second major adjustment required of the public at large.

It should be emphasized that the great waves of budget cutting in the United States since World War II have been carried out by *the executive branch,* through the instrumentality of the Bureau of the Budget. It has been the Bureau rather than the Congress that has reduced the requests of the spending departments. It may be that these slashes were made in response to an anticipated mood in Congress, but the final responsibility was the executive's,[9] and did reflect a sincere conviction concerning the desirability, if not the necessity, of budget reduction.

During the Truman Administration, the slashes were deep. As Arthur Smithies has put it in his study of the budgetary process:

> There was a strong conviction, shared by the President, most of the Congress, the Cabinet, and the business community, that it was imperative to reduce the budget total to some figure that was "tolerable." During the entire discussion no one produced any definition of "tolerable," and it rested on no economic analysis worthy of the name. But the combination of intuitions and prejudices of those in authority produced the conviction that $40 billion of expenditures was definitely too high.[10]

Thus it came about, in the course of this process, that the director of the Bureau of the Budget indirectly became the architect of the nation's military and foreign policies. For the fiscal year 1951, for example, the Bureau set a tentative ceiling of $12 billion for military expenditures. This limit simply evaporated after the outbreak of the Korean War. In the peak year, fiscal 1953, expenditures on the military functions of the Department of Defense reached almost $44 billion.

Since 1953, expenditures have been declining, particularly with the unveiling of the "new look" in fiscal 1955. Under the Eisenhower Administration, the cuts have been made not in the name of "reducing the budget to tolerable proportions," but in the name of "maintaining a sound economy." The essence of the decisions has been similar to those prior to the Korean War. Our tendency has been to create "fat" years and "lean" years. During the lean years, sacrifices are made on the altar of economy; then, after an alarming international incident, we begin to spend again, perhaps at an excessive rate. In the campaign of 1952, Mr. Eisenhower deplored the tendency of military budgets toward "feast or famine," and urged the *consistent* maintenance of a high level of military preparedness. The original theory of the Administration was probably a sound one. Despite expectations to the contrary, the Administration did not permit the post-Sputnik anxiety over Soviet missile development to inaugurate a new cycle of military spending. The grave question that critics continue to raise, however, is whether the present levels of spending are *adequate* to achieve our strategic objectives.

Some types of military spending are still declining. The most recent wave of reductions in military forces started as the result of the Administration's decision to hold military spending in fiscal 1958 at an arbitrary level of $38 billion, a consequence of the economy drive engendered by the acrimonious debate over the budget early in 1957. The cutbacks started that summer were intensified, as far as conventional forces were concerned, by the decision after the Russians launched Sputnik to concentrate a higher proportion of total spending on missile development. The process was continued in the budget for fiscal 1959, which called for a further reduction of manpower. Despite Congressional protest and appropriations sufficient to maintain its strength, the Army was scheduled to shrink to 870,000 men organized in 14 divisions (down from the post-Korean peak of 27 divisions). The Navy lost 103 ships from its active fleet, and the number of air wings, including both tactical and strategic strength, was reduced from 127 to 103. This pattern has been roughly maintained in the 1960 budget. Air Force appropriations are being reduced, but the Army will be maintained at 14 understrength divisions. Plainly, the Administration has not been panicked into excessive expenditures.

Military spending has risen modestly to approximately $41 billion, but it should be recognized that the effectiveness of a dollar's expenditure on defense has steadily declined. The continued inflation and the rapidly rising cost of military equipment have meant that the real military power purchased by fixed dollar outlays is falling. In 1957, Secretary Wilson himself testified that defense dollars would then purchase only 88 per cent of what they did in 1954,[11] and he indicated that in real terms, budgetary requests were considerably lower than they had been. Personnel costs, moreover, are now rising sharply. In order to maintain the real level of appropriations, the amount must rise in dollar terms each year. Seemingly, one of the ways that we reduce effective demand in the United States is to permit the erosion of the purchasing power of government outlays, including military outlays, which are fixed in absolute terms. Yet, in considering military spending, we tend to ignore the rise in prices.

Why has the budgetary record been so spotty since World War II? We have had violent oscillation in military spending and drastic cuts carried out by the Bureau of the Budget in the name of economy. We ignore the impact of inflation on the effectiveness of appropriations.

The basic flaw in our budgetary planning has been *too narrow a concept of budgeting*. The connection between finance and policy has been inadequately recognized. The conventional assumption has been that the Bureau of the Budget is concerned solely with efficiency—and that the efficiency concept, attempting to implement set government programs as "economically" as possible, constitutes the heart of budgeting. The fiction has been maintained that the Congress sets policy, and that the Bureau merely sees to it that the programs are carried out economically. The perpetuation of the fiction has permitted the Bureau to invade, perhaps unwittingly, the sphere of policy formation, which is reserved for the Congress or the President. In the name of efficiency or economy, the Bureau makes cuts, which, in effect, alter the scope and the emphasis of the government's programs.

It should be recalled that the Bureau was designed as a special instrumentality. Under General Dawes, its goal was a simple one: the attainment of economy and efficiency through centralized control and coordination of government departments and agencies. It needs to be recognized that this goal has never been achieved. The Bureau has not been singularly effective in forcing the departments to operate more economically; that depends on efficient management. The departments have resisted the attempt to impose efficiency from above; improved management has had to come from within the agency itself. Thus the impact of the Bureau has been to affect the size of programs and alter the nature of policies, since significant savings are not obtainable via the "economy" route. But the rectifications wrought in policies have rarely been given adequate consideration by the responsible parties.

120   THE POLITICAL ECONOMY OF NATIONAL SECURITY

Surely, we must recognize in the back of our minds that when we "boil the fat out of the military budget," as in 1949, or "get a bigger bang for a buck," as in 1955, we are doing something different from economizing with no loss of efficiency. We are changing the whole complexion of our military policy and, therefore, our foreign policy as well. Yet our present institutional arrangements do nothing to clarify the distinction between economy and policy change. What we intuitively recognize is blurred by our present process of budget making.

The time has come for us to alter our institutional arrangements developed in a less complex age. A mechanism is needed to help us distinguish between the *alternative* concepts of budgeting. Either a new agency should be established to analyze the policy implications of different levels of appropriations, or else the Budget Bureau should be given the additional responsibility to see that appropriations are *sufficient* to achieve the policies enunciated by Congress. The Bureau of the Budget is properly the servant of policy rather than its master. Appropriately, the Bureau should recognize its dual obligation: on the one hand, it bears a responsibility to the general taxpayer to see to it that goals are achieved at low cost;[12] but on the other hand, it bears a responsibility both to the government and to the public to see that policy objectives are fulfilled. Our administrative structure needs to be varied so that the latter responsibility is clearly recognized, so that we no longer can mask changes in policy under the heading of "economization."

A third adjustment is required in order to complete the transition to a state of perennially high military budgets. This adjustment is less pressing, less vital than the first two, and this is fortunate, since this adjustment is less likely to be achieved in the near future than are the first two. It requires no less than a change in attitude toward spending on the part of American military officers.

It is painful to officers to remind them of the widely held impression that military men lack a sense of cost-consciousness, that they are, in fact, impervious to the concept. Some justification for this notion does, however, exist. In constructing tables of organization and equipment, for example, no consideration is given to cost. The very suggestion that cost should be considered would be rejected with horror as corrupting military judgment and tampering with the effectiveness of the armed forces. Those charged with the responsibility for constructing the TOE's are not the least concerned with the dollar, but rather with the best technical means for achieving the goal in question. Cheaper construction or substitutes, which might mean that more divisions, for example, could be provided with the same expenditure, are not considered. Similarly, in the procurement of military hardware, it is asserted that the specifications often include expensive but superfluous devices. Engineers have questioned, and military men have confirmed, this tendency toward gadgetry.[13]

The relationship between cost and volume is easily ignored when functional aspects of procurement policies are considered alone. The Army, in designing the specifications for the M-48 tank, was faced with the problem of whether the transmission system should make use of an automatic or manual (conventional) shift. The Army chose the automatic shift. The problem of increased fuel consumption, which limited the range of the tank—a not unimportant feature—was considered. Some thought was given to the risk of breakdown because of the intricacy of the mechanism, and also to weight and space problems. The final decision, seemingly, was based on the hypothesis that the boys in the service should not be deprived of the benefits of the rising American standard of living, whether or not this reduced the range of the equipment. At no point was the question of expense considered—and the possibility that higher costs might mean a reduced number of tanks.

To make decisions from what is referred to as a "purely military point of view" is both incomplete and deceptive. It hides from consideration the fact that the real choice may be, for example, between a small number of expensive but technically appealing aircraft and a much larger number of inexpensive ones. There is no question but that the technical aspect of these questions must ultimately be settled by military men. At the same time, it is true that awareness of cost and of budgetary limitation ought to be one of several principal considerations at the time that the decisions are made. Recognition of the cost question involved will help to reduce the frightful gap between what the armed forces say they need to meet our commitments and what they get. It would end that anomalous situation, arising from divergent attitudes toward the budgetary process, when military men sheepishly assert that they will try to "make do," although they clearly consider the specified appropriations inadequate, while Administration officials make dogmatic statements about the economic burdensomeness of military expenditures, and justify cuts as necessary to protect economic solvency. Budgets are limited. Inevitably, they are subject to political accommodations. When organization and equipment are being determined, this fact needs to be kept in mind. The military man must indicate to the troubled civilian, who eventually must cut the requests to fit the means, what the alternatives are, his scale of priorities, where money may be saved, and so on. If he fails to do this, and insists instead that "everything is necessary," then, when the appropriations are determined, the entire brunt of economization falls on the number of fighting units. It is desirable that force objectives and their costs be considered jointly, rather than the force objectives being surreptitiously abandoned when the cost is made known.

With the passage of time, the degree of cost-consciousness, in the sense of weighing alternatives, is likely to rise. Much of the present attitude of the military springs from the cycles of lean and fat years with which they have traditionally lived. If the outlook is hopeless in the lean years, and if there are no limits in the fat years, the only course of action is to set one's standards as high as possible and wait for the return of the fat years. Efficiency in lean years does not result in greater military strength, but only in further cuts. Squirrel-like tendencies toward hoarding are encouraged. Ideally, a budget should encourage efficient management—by shaking up the thinking of administrators and forcing them to consider their organization and costs. The American budgetary tradition has put the incentives in other directions as far as the military services are concerned. Although the sole desideratum was economization, budgetary practices actually put a premium on inefficient planning. We may hope for a change for the better.

4. THE ROAD TO IMPROVEMENT

There are several areas in which improvement in our budgeting procedures may be sought and achieved. Perhaps most important is the need to emphasize the role of policy formation. Though in the long run it may be possible to integrate the conflicting budgetary concepts of efficiency and public policy, in the short run we must recognize the conflict between the alternative concepts. Temporarily, it may be necessary to downgrade the narrower concept of efficiency. This concept has blurred the connection between finance and policy and has encouraged the view that the budget is an unromantic statement, rather than being the financial embodiment of public policy. It has permitted the Bureau of the Budget to formulate policy (partly, perhaps, with the connivance of Congress, which has on occasion sought to avoid responsibility, and has been willing to see its policies undermined if money could be saved). For the future, the distinction between policy and economy should be drawn as sharply as possible, and the importance of the former underlined. In view of the national emergency created by the cold war and foreign-policy considerations, the criterion of resource allocation that will satisfy the claims of policy is of far greater importance than efficient administration, *per se*. A small degree of waste is of less importance than the losses that could accrue from improper policies.

The policy alternatives implicit in the budget ought to be more widely discussed, and in this respect Congressional deliberation has left much to be desired. The fault, however, is not all with Congress. The form of the budget is hardly conducive to enthusiasm. The method of presentation could be improved, so as to encourage Congress to take its proper interest in policy. Budgetary requests should be framed in terms of policy goals, which would permit Congress to discuss the implications intelligently, rather than to carp about trivia. Something has been achieved along this line with the development of the so-called "performance budget," perhaps more appropriately referred to as a "program budget." [14] Instead of enumerating total purchases of nuts and bolts, shoes, typewriters and paper, the budget may outline the purpose for which expenditures will be made—maintaining such and so many air groups or divisions, building air bases or multi-purpose dams. This may make the budget a simpler but more useful document, since it encourages Congress to play its proper role. Since the passage of the National Security Act of 1949, the Department of Defense has been required to submit a program budget. The Hoover Commission has endorsed the idea, and Congress itself has encouraged further experimentation with program budgeting in other departments. It does provide a more useful framework for program evaluation, and has at least partially filled the policy vacuum into which the Bureau of the Budget has tended to be drawn.

Certain valid criticisms have been made of program budgeting. Essentially, they may be classified in two broad groups: program budgets have been submitted to Congress in such form that Congress cannot approach any single individual who has responsibility for the program; and the material submitted in support of the program budgets has in many instances been so scanty that Congress has been unable to evaluate adequately either the goals or the efficiency. Neither of these criticisms, to be sure, applies to program budgeting in general, but only to the types of budgets that have been submitted to Congress. The use of program budgets does not preclude the inclusion of the traditional line-item information, but merely helps to present this information in a more useful and understandable manner. If programs do not conform to the administrative hierarchy, it raises the question of whether executive departments should not be reorganized along more functional lines. Though the criticisms do indicate the difficulties in the way of radical change, they should not discourage continued effort to discover ways of clarifying the policy objectives embodied in the budget.

The efficiency aspect of the budget will not and ought not be ignored, but it should be recognized that economy and efficiency are difficult to impose from above, and must come ultimately from within the departments. Congress has its role to play in this matter. It should, of course, encourage efficient administration, and may intervene when obvious mismanagement occurs. But it ought also to recognize that effective administration normally comes from within, and legislative querulousness, whatever its merits under certain circumstances, is no substitute for good administrators. We ought also remember that affluence has dulled the American sense of economy, and that we cannot expect governmental departments to be significantly more efficient than other bureaucratic organizations, including our great corporations and charitable institutions.

The problem of policy formulation and budgetary planning has been intensified in the last decade by an increased rate of change—in military technology, in the geographical areas of conflict, in the methods and the possible types of warfare. Whereas, in the past, policy might have remained relatively static, in the modern world it must keep abreast of changing conditions. In the past, the implications of increased military expenditures were relatively straightforward; today, the composition of expenditures is infinitely complex. If dangers are pressing, a policy of immediate preparedness is dictated, yet the policy of immediate preparedness is terribly expensive in terms of cost, manpower, and political union. In addition, it is likely to cause a reduced allocation of resources for research and development in military technology that could produce important advances, both strategically and psychologically. For long-run preparedness, the structure of defense (and of expenditures) is apt to differ quite sharply from that when the pressures are immediate. The needs differ, and consequently the allocational pattern will change. In view of the fact that neither type of preparedness can be ignored, the structure of the budget will need to be varied from time to time to reflect changes in the pattern of pressures.

This might require a speeding-up of certain stages of the budget cycle and a greater flexibility in expenditures subsequent to the appropriation of funds. Little has been done to shorten the preparatory period in budget formation, although the requests for the Department of Defense are the last to be considered prior to the submitting of the President's budget in January. Greater flexibility is possible through increased use of contingency funds and of the discretionary power to transfer appropriations from "less promising" to "more promising" categories. In proposing Pentagon reorganization in 1958, the President urged that the Secretary of Defense be given virtually unlimited power to transfer appropriations as he saw fit. Such power would undoubtedly provide the flexibility that is required, but in view of the long historical struggle for the right of the representatives of the public to control public expenditures, the proposal in question may have been too drastic. In any event, the Administration subsequently withdrew its request.

Budgetary flexibility can, of course, only be based upon mental flexibility. The process of change is disruptive; changes may be so steady and imperceptible that they go unrecognized, or they may be so great that although they are recognized, they are not believable. For either reason, it is difficult to adjust to change. Without the test of war, in a period of rapid military change it is difficult for the military authorities to know just what their goals should be or how to evaluate the new techniques. For this reason, those closest to the day-by-day operations may be insufficiently detached to make the soundest decisions. It may well be, for example, that civilians are better suited to make the broader evaluations of military techniques, since they are less inhibited by tradition.

Administrative flexibility may require greater suppleness in personnel procedures. Civil Service procedures designed for a different purpose in a different age may actually hamper intelligent and efficient administration. Here, too, greater flexibility is required. It may be inefficient use of scarce resources to force a trained technician to perform routine administrative functions. Yet, in order to pay enough to retain the services of certain individuals, we give them a Civil Service rating that requires them to perform administrative duties for which they may not be particularly well suited. Moreover, rapid change may result in "personnel obsolescence," and the finding of make-work jobs for bureaucratic driftwood who might be well able to perform a useful service elsewhere in the government, if Civil Service regulations permitted his transfer.

There are other improvements that would be desirable. In principle, consideration of the budget should be less fragmented than it is at present. The costs and benefits of one program as against other programs should be more carefully weighed in light of the total means available. In post-Sputnik discussions and in his proposals for the 1959 budget, the President did urge Congress to take a "new look" at our domestic programs, in view of the increasing international pressures. It must be recognized that certain expenditures—interest payments, veterans' benefits, grants-in-aid to the states, and agricultural supports—which are fixed by statute or contract are relatively untouchable. Although, such programs ought to be periodically scrutinized by Congress and their merits weighed in light of changing needs, circumstances, and means, this may be too much to hope for, since the political strength implicit in the establishment of a permanent program carries with it the hint that the program would not be altered in the event of an annual review. At some point in the budgeting process, however, Congress should be forced to consider simultaneously the relationship between over-all expenditures and receipts, instead of lightly entering into expenditure commitments without adequate consideration of the ultimate cost to the taxpayer. At the present time, at no point are the revenue and expenditure sides of the budget considered, except in a somewhat offhand way in the President's budget. If the decision makers were forced to consider the means available, it would result in more rational construction of the budget and more effective use of the taxpayer's dollar.

Finally, the nation must recognize how extensive is its economic capacity. In peacetime, the main barrier to increased government expenditure is the great reluctance to sacrifice additional consumer goods, which is not so strong in wartime. Aside from this understandable reluctance, the chief impediment has been the traditional American attitude toward government expenditures and budgetary efficiency. *The ultimate test of the efficiency of an economy is the test of survival.* The survival of our society as we know it is at stake. In dealing with this crisis, we will be governed either by a permanent sense of urgency or by intermittent panics. Our commitments are great, to be sure, but there can be no real question that we must shoulder the financial burdens involved. Timidity concerning what the economy can tolerate leads us into the most expensive path of being "penny-wise, pound-foolish." It has led in the immediate past to inadequate spending along traditional lines, to the gutting of conventional armaments, and to the reckless rivalry among the services to come within the charmed circle of strategic retaliatory capabilities, the only sure source of funds. It has led to the cutting of our strategic doctrine—not to fit our means, but to fit the expediencies of political budgeting. We do, indeed, need that "permanent sense of urgency"; whether we obtain it or not will immediately be reflected in the budget, the embodiment of public policy.

6

THE ROLE OF INTERNATIONAL TRADE

Rare are the economies that can be islands unto themselves; rarer still are those which can be both self-sufficient and prosperous. Since few economies are self-contained, in order to appreciate fully the implications for national security of economic pressures, we must widen our sights and study the national economy in its international role. The most significant of the external economic relations of a nation are its commercial relations. In international trade, the economic and strategic elements are inextricably intertwined. Traditionally, the main arguments for international trade were the economic ones; the strategic implications were largely ignored. In recent years, however, the strategic elements in trade have come to outweigh the economic, at least for the so-called "superpowers." One thing that must be understood is the need for consistency between a nation's strategic goals and its commercial policies. The commercial relations between nations are the ones that most affect the well-being of the populace. If they are awry, they will inevitably affect the political connections.

The subject of trade will be treated here under four main headings: the economic implications of trade, the strategic implications of trade, American commercial policy, and the role of trade in American foreign policy.

1. THE ECONOMIC IMPLICATIONS OF TRADE

Study of the economic implications of trade was the principal goal of the theory of international trade. Basically, the theory represented an extension on the international scene of the principles of allocation developed for the domestic economy; it was, so to speak, simply the principle of alternative cost "writ large." Each nation was faced with the fact of scarcity—the fact of limited resources to achieve unlimited ends. What could be more reasonable than to apply the principles of economical allocation of resources internationally, as well as domestically? Each nation could conserve its own scarce resources by avoiding production of those commodities for which the relative costs were quite high, and by concentrating resources on the production of those commodities for which relative costs were quite low. The high-cost commodities could be obtained from other nations where the relative costs were low. All nations, even those with an *absolute* advantage in the production of several commodities, would benefit by concentrating upon the commodities in which their relative advantage was greatest, and would obtain more of the other commodities through indirect production—that is, by trading with other nations, sending to them the product each produced most efficiently and obtaining in return those products each produced less efficiently. All the economic resources in the world economy would be used in those activities for which they were best suited; and consequently, trade would encourage greater efficiency and greater real output. All countries would benefit from an international division of labor.

It is not surprising that the theory of international trade was developed in the nineteenth century—an era of relative tranquility, astonishingly lacking in national rivalries, which accepted as axiomatic the view that the primary economic goal was to enhance the material well-being of the individual consumer. The essence of the theory was that free trade would contribute to that end, since all nations would benefit if each specialized in that type of production in which it possessed a comparative advantage and traded with others for the additional supplies required. It will be recognized that the theory was based upon an assumption of natural harmony among nations and peoples which was tenable, perhaps, until the breakdown of the balance of power at the time of World War I. There can be little doubt that—from the cosmopolitan view, and aside from the relative benefits to be enjoyed by the several nations—an absence of restrictions on trade would provide the greatest availability of goods at the lowest prices to the world's population, and thus provide for maximum material welfare and maximum consumer satisfaction.

It is true that, in a certain sense, the goal of the early classical thinkers was national advantage. In fact, nations do benefit to a marked degree from *relatively* free trade. But the argument for *completely* free trade has always been a cosmopolitan one. Increasingly, qualifications to the free-trade argument have been accepted. Though *all* nations might be better off under free trade, *individual* nations might benefit by restrictions imposed upon trade. Even in the nineteenth century, objections were framed to the idea of free trade in the name of national interests, producer interests, and non-economic interests. Only Great Britain, among the major powers, accepted the logic of the classical economists and instituted free trade. Since the only restriction upon trade came traditionally in the form of the tariff, the arguments in behalf of tariffs are worthy of note. Many of these arguments were wholly erroneous and were designed simply for propagandistic purposes, but there were several that had validity: the defense argument, the infant-industry argument, the vested-interest argument, the retaliatory tariff to extract concessions, the revenue tariff, and the use of the tariff to improve the terms of trade.

All of these arguments have a certain theoretical validity in carefully specified circumstances. But although the circumstances may, in fact, be rare, the arguments are, nevertheless, used generally. Some of the arguments have now become or are becoming obsolete in the United States, but they are clung to tenaciously. A major argument in behalf of the revenue tariff, for example, was based upon the administrative ease of external, as opposed to internal, taxation in earlier eras; but now both forms of taxation are equally feasible, administratively speaking. Moreover, in order to obtain revenue, tariff schedules ought to be moderate; yet somehow, in practice, tariff proponents have demanded prohibitive schedules.

In the light of the strength and dominant position of the American economy, we need no longer concern ourselves with the use of tariffs to extract concessions through the threat of retaliation; nor need we attempt to improve our terms of trade with other nations. The very fact that the United States has felt obliged to extend considerable assistance abroad suggests that we consider our terms of trade "too favorable." Tariff protection, to paraphrase Bismarck, is necessary only for the weak. Finally, it must be observed that the argument for the infant industry—representing, in a sense, the bellwether of protectionism—no longer applies to the United States. At one time, it could be argued that the tender shoots of American industry needed protection temporarily from foreign competition, so that the long-run comparative advantage of such industries would be permitted to appear. Now, however, American industry consists of brawling giants, rather than squalling infants, although the giants do occasionally squall like infants for protection. Implicit in the argument is the belief that as an industry grows and prospers, it will be able to dispense with protection. Historically, we may observe, it has been no easy task to withdraw tariff protection, once granted.

At the present time, in regard to the American economy, it would appear that the only relevant issues are raised by the defense and the vested-interest arguments. Certain industries have long been recognized as contributing to national security; Adam Smith himself mentioned the merchant marine. Even if it were cheaper to use the services of foreign states, it might be argued that it is necessary to protect from foreign competition an industry that produces a commodity or service that is indispensable in time of war. "Defense," said Adam Smith, "is more important than opulence." It certainly may be argued that in the modern world there are many industries that are vital to national security and ought to be protected.

The vested-interest argument, on the other hand, holds that

we ought to protect and maintain full utilization of available personnel and capital equipment in certain industries and regions, to avoid suffering a drain on the nation's resources in the form of reduced production, unemployment compensation, and psychological *malaise.* Essentially, this argument emphasizes the *distribution* of income rather than its *production.* It is also concerned with the difficulty of transferring resources from less productive to more productive industries. Adam Smith was concerned that the too-abrupt removal of tariff protection would destroy capital, and argued, therefore, for gradual tariff reduction. In our more specialized, less flexible economies of modern times, the problem of vested interests and their possible destruc· tion through tariff reduction poses a difficult question, to which we must return later.

In the United States in the nineteenth century, commercial policy was protectionist in design, based largely on the need to help the infant industries. The advantages of protection were held to be more appealing than were the advantages of free trade. It is most important to emphasize that, at the time, *protectionism was in harmony with our strategic position,* based on continental isolation and a desire to avoid entangling alliances. But isolation was never complete, and trade has been one of the "entanglements" that has from time to time threatened our continental security. It is notable that the last great menace of foreign intervention in American affairs—that of British intervention in behalf of the Confederacy during the Civil War—arose in no small degree from the fact of raw-material starvation in the Lancashire cotton mills, a consequence of the snapping of the normal ties of trade. From time to time, the United States has been drawn into wars originating in Europe because of the ties of commerce and the interference with seaborne trade. American involvement in both the War of 1812 and World War I may be explained in large part in this manner. Obviously, international commerce is fraught with power implications. During the era of continental isolation, the typical American response to the power implications of trade was to avoid them. The policy answer came in the form of embargo acts to prevent America's involvement, even indirectly, in foreign quarrels. Thus we had Jefferson's Embargo Act of 1807 and the neutrality legislation of 1935–1937. The latter reflected the disillusionment with American entry into World War I. In the twenties and thirties, there was a widespread belief that American involvement had been brought about by the lure of trade and the machinations of the "merchants of death." This attitude suffuses the writings of the noted historian Charles Beard, for example.

During the nineteenth century, the American people were willing to forgo many of the advantages of international trade. We were willing to hide behind tariff walls—and until the change in our international financial position, which occurred during World War I, the only cost of this policy was the loss of the benefits of trade. With the wide variety of resources to be developed on this continent, the loss may have been relatively modest over-all, and there were compensating benefits. Since 1920, however, our commercial policy has been irrational. During World War I, the international financial status of the United States shifted from that of net debtor to net creditor. Prior to the war, the United States could expect to export more than it imported in order to service or amortize its debt. After the war, it was necessary to *import* a considerable volume of goods simply to permit others to service or repay their debts to us. Under the changed financial relationships, in order to maintain a substantial export trade, it became necessary to have a trade policy sufficiently liberal to permit a substantial volume of imports. In the absence of the willingness to import, an export trade may be maintained through heavy and sustained lending (that is, the export of capital). Since 1920, we have failed to supply foreigners with sufficient dollars through either loans or purchases of their goods to maintain existing export markets. Yet, at the same time, we have been unwilling to relinquish these markets. Periodically, we have been driven to emergency measures to augment the supply of dollars, since we have been unwilling to supply dollars through normal channels.

Not long after our commercial policies became economically irrational, they became strategically irrational as well. A policy of continental isolation might be considered by some to be defensible as late as the fall of France in 1940, when it became clear that friendly powers could not survive without our assistance. Conceivably, isolation could be defended until the advent of the atomic age. It is clearly out of date in the present context of world politics. To be sure, it would be possible for the United States to disregard the economic issues posed by international trade; we can no longer, however, ignore its strategic implications.

2. THE STRATEGIC IMPLICATIONS OF TRADE

Inevitably, trade is fraught with strategic implications. The strategic position of any power will be sensitive to any change in the network of trade relationships. In the nineteenth century, this aspect could be ignored, but *in the present era,* as far as the United States is concerned, the central issue with respect to trade is how it affects the relative power positions of the several national states. Some nations have been provided with the sinews of war through trade. At the same time, a nation dependent upon foreign supplies is at a disadvantage if its normal trading channels can be interrupted. Even a state that is pacifically inclined may be subjected to pressures, since the well-being of its population might be affected by an alteration of trade relations. The existence of a significant volume of trade provides one state with a weapon for influencing—either explicitly or tacitly—the policies of another power.

The elements of power embodied in trade are subdivided into two types, which may be referred to as the "supply effect" and the "influence effect." [1] The supply effect, in itself, has two aspects—one connected with the total supply or real income, the other with the supply of specific, vital commodities. In the first place, international trade is the route by which certain nations, rich in some resources but poor in others, have achieved opulence—and opulence, as Bentham observed in opposition to Adam Smith, is necessary to defense. By participating in trade, a nation may sharply raise its total and *per capita* income, and thus may provide that margin of resources which is essential to national power. Unless there exists a disposable margin, a nation is unable to allocate sufficient resources to provide itself with the instruments of security. In modern terms, trade adds to a nation's economic potential for war by enlarging its national product. Nations possessing so narrow a resource base as those of Great Britain or Japan might never have risen to great power, were it not for the possibility of increasing productivity and making the most efficient use of limited resources through trade. On the other hand, relatively self-sufficient powers like the United States and the Soviet Union will not benefit from trade to the same extent. Moreover, it must always be remembered that increased economic potential, in itself, is only permissive of national power, and after a certain point has been reached in terms of resources, it may count for less in this era than do will and determination.

But the supply effect has a second aspect relating to the provision of specific strategic commodities essential to national power. By furnishing a critical material, trade may directly augment a nation's power by providing the sinews of war. Through commerce, then, a nation's relative power may be sharply increased; yet, dependence upon foreign supplies opens the nation to the risk of interdiction during war. Britain's control of trade routes, for example, long posed a threat to any potential rival; yet, on the other hand, her dependence upon overseas supplies meant that she herself could be threatened, as she was by submarine warfare in both World Wars. The supply effect, it will be seen, is simply the converse of the defense argument for protection. The former states that vital supplies may be obtained by trade; the latter accepts this, but insists that the risk of interdiction is so great that it is preferable to supply the necessary materials domestically. Clearly, the decision as to whether or not to rely upon foreign sources of supply will be based upon the nation's over-all strategic objectives.

The second element of power implicit in trade is the influence effect. It is far more subtle and indirect than the first. More frequently than not, it operates on the side of demand rather than supply, making use of the instrument of massive buying power. Just the merest hint, the most delicate blackmail, may convince a nation that an important market may be lost unless it follows a suitable foreign policy. Obviously, it is the smaller states, most dependent upon trade, which will be most subject to pressure. In its operation, so subtle a tool as the influence effect is by no means confined to the suggestion that markets may be lost. It may operate on the supply side as well. When nations are as dependent on a major power for the maintenance of their industrial machines as the satellites are on the Soviet Union, the slowing down in the delivery of spare parts and replacements may be sufficient to eliminate any deviant tendencies in their external relations. Or a nation may be subject to the threat of the loss of oil or steel, and may adjust its attitudes accordingly.

A major power may use trade as a weapon of economic penetration. By bringing about a condition of mutual dependence through trade, a state may forge an instrument to influence the policies of other states. From the strategic point of view, it is desirable to bring about a condition in which severance of the trading connection would be more damaging to the trading partner than to oneself. Plainly, a condition of asymmetrical dependence may most easily be achieved by great industrial nations in dealing with small primary producers of raw materials who are largely dependent upon the sale of one crop or commodity. Trade binds together national policies through ties of mutual interest and the fear of dislocation. It can be seen that the supply effect and the influence effect may, to some extent, be in conflict. The harder the bargain that is driven by an industrial power in obtaining needed supplies, the less likely is it that the particular market involved will be viewed by the supplying nation with the mixture of affection and apprehension that maximizes the influence effect.

A type of trade that is particularly potent in terms of the application of power is transit trade. In this case, both the buyer and the seller may be threatened with a loss of trade; yet the nation that severs the trade is likely to have relatively little at stake. The disproportionately large strategic power of transit nations is a critical issue at the present time in the Middle East. Syria and Egypt (now joined in the United Arab Republic) are astride the oil transit routes and are therefore in a position to threaten both the oil-producing countries of the Middle East and the oil-consuming nations of Western Europe at relatively little cost to themselves.

In fact, trade and its strategic implications have been at the root of much of the recent conflict in the Middle East, including the Suez crisis of 1956.[2] It is probably unnecessary to point out the desirability of avoiding the domination of one's source of vital supplies by one's enemies. It is essentially on grounds of avoiding excessive dependence on a threatened source that the defense argument sanctions interference with the trading channels that supply maximum normal (that is, economic) benefits, making use of tariffs, quotas, or subsidies in order to achieve this objective. The very threat to oil supplies precipitated the Suez crisis. The issue was not an economic one, for there is no doubt of the Arab desire to continue to sell oil. Instead, it was a politico-economic issue; the threat of domination of a vital source of supply by a potential enemy was considered intolerable. It might well be argued that the present power structure in the Middle East is particularly unfavorable to Western interests. Hostile as it is to both the West and the oil-producing nations of the area, the stake of the United Arab Republic in the continuance of normal trade is relatively small. It is arguable that if Colonel Nasser dominated the oil-producing areas in the Arab world, his greatly expanded stake in peaceful relations with the West would modify his attitude of truculence, and might make him more amenable to reason (or susceptible to pressure).

A word might be added about the much-discussed but little-understood subject of economic warfare. Quite obviously, much of the substantive content of economic warfare is based upon the strategic implications of trade. But economic warfare is a much weaker weapon than is generally realized. Use of the weapon blunts its cutting edge. If, for example, we ban the export of certain strategic goods to the Sino-Soviet bloc, we merely encourage them to develop alternative sources of supply, usually domestic sources. On the other hand, the bloc economies might be temporarily hampered. It has been argued that the embargo on oil has substantially restricted Chinese industrial development. There is, however, no suitable *long-range* pattern of economic warfare. It is essentially *ad hoc*, based upon temporary advantages, and cannot be used to achieve anything other than immediate purposes. Many economies are relatively impervious to economic pressures. Surprisingly, this has been true for subsistence economies, which have been protected by their own backwardness. In implementing economic warfare against Mossadegh's Iran, and more recently against Nasser's Egypt, some Western observers have been astonished by the powers of resistance of these economies. They have been protected by the low levels of living and the lack of industrial development. The phenomenon has been put in the facetious terms of this rhetorical question: How can you bring pressure to bear when an economy is already prostrate? One ought not to generalize about the uses of economic warfare, except to say that it is a short-range weapon, based upon the circumstances existing at a fixed point in time.

It would be folly to ignore the strategic possibilities inherent in trade. It was an illusion of those nineteenth-century thinkers who developed the theory of international trade that the power implications of trade might be overridden. They assumed that men were essentially pacific and interested almost exclusively in economic well-being. It was therefore postulated that a harmony of interest existed among nations, and that this underlying harmony might be fostered by trade. In a famous passage, John Stuart Mill observed: "It is commerce which is rapidly rendering war obsolete by strengthening and multiplying the personal interests which are in natural opposition to it." The hopes of the nineteenth century have been crushed by the realities of the twentieth. It may also be added—and twentieth-century observers have increasingly recognized this—that rather than always assuaging frictions, as the classicists anticipated, trade itself has been one of the great causes of international friction. Lord Keynes, in direct opposition to the classical position, once argued in behalf of increased self-sufficiency on the grounds that it would reduce the antagonisms induced by excessive interdependence, and thereby further the cause of peace.[3] Power implications are inherent in trade. They may be ignored, but, nevertheless, they exist. The postulate of harmony merely glossed over the inherent power possibilities, and the development of political controls over trade in the twentieth century has simply made overt what had hitherto been tacit.

3.   AMERICAN COMMERCIAL POLICY

The U.S. tariff barriers of the nineteenth century culminated in the Smoot-Hawley Tariff of 1930, passed during the depression to protect American jobs from foreign competition. From the standpoint of our own export trade, the Smoot-Hawley Tariff was unwise and undoubtedly intensified international financial difficulties, since it increased the difficulties of our debtors in finding dollars with which to service their debts to us. Accompanied as it was with the complete cessation of the extending of dollar loans, it helped bring international commerce to the meager levels that prevailed during the thirties. Many different arguments had been advanced to defend tariffs during the era of protection—some tenable, most fallacious. Increasingly after 1920, the valid ones became obsolescent in view of our desire to maintain our export trade. But by and large, the American people were willing to forgo some of the material advantages that might be obtained through an international division of labor in which we would specialize in the production of those commodities for which we possessed the greatest comparative advantage. The price we paid was the uneconomical use of scarce resources for the production of commodities that we could have imported more cheaply. But our resources were many and varied, and our losses were relatively small; there were compensating advantages, both non-economic and in terms of industrial growth. We were rich; we had a continent's resources to exploit, and so whatever the loss through the impeding of trade, we felt we could afford it. Most important, also, is the fact that the policy of tariff production was in harmony with the strategic doctrine of isolation.

The passage of the Trade Agreements Acts in 1934 represented the end of an era. Since that time, the pressure has been in the direction of lowering tariff walls. Sometimes, as at the present, the pressure has waned, but there has been no strong tendency to rebuild tariff walls. Under the Trade Agreements Act and its extensions, the President has had authority to negotiate with other nations in order to achieve mutual concessions in removal of trade restrictions. Such concessions have been applied to other countries under the "most-favored-nation" principle. Since 1947, when the General Agreement on Tariffs and Trade (GATT) was signed, the previously existing bilateral relationships have been extended into multilateral ones. Through GATT, the United States has trading agreements with thirty-three other countries.

Increasingly, the nation has come to recognize some essential truths of commercial policy. One is that unless a nation is willing to purchase goods from others, it will be unable to sell any goods to them. Another is that certain foreign countries are dependent upon trade for survival. Unless they trade with us, they may be tempted to trade with somebody else—and if the somebody else were the Soviet bloc, it could easily lead to *excessive* dependence upon our rivals. A third truth that has come to be recognized increasingly is that there is little point in wasting scarce resources to produce a commodity if it can be imported more cheaply. International specialization can provide lower prices for consumers and higher real incomes for most citizens. Under the Eisenhower Administration, the traditional Republican goal of higher tariffs has been abandoned, and, at least in the abstract, the Administration has spoken warmly in favor of further trade liberalization. The newer attitudes were subsumed under the polemical slogan of "trade, not aid."

In formulating commercial policy at the present time, however, we are troubled by a legacy of problem industries that cannot survive without tariff protection. Such industries are the consequence both of the earlier impeding of the flow of trade through tariff barriers and of the continually increasing cost advantages of foreign producers due to the rise in the American wage scale. Yet these problem industries have been placed under competitive pressure in an era when the advantages to the United States of more liberalized trade have been stressed more and more. Under the circumstances, those branches of industry which have sought protection have been faced with the need for a new propaganda argument. The older protectionist arguments—building domestic industries, the so-called "scientific tariff," the pauper-labor argument, and so on—have gradually lost their appeal. The chief argument against trade liberalization today that possesses wide appeal is the one for defense. In addition, the vested-interest argument in the form of "jobs lost through foreign competition" excites some sympathy, but its acceptance is not so widespread.

The problem of these vulnerable industries presents a dilemma. On the one hand, if imports are to be expanded, they should be expanded in those industries in which the American competitive position is weakest. On the other hand, a painful adjustment is required of certain groups, an adjustment that falls with particular force on specific industries and regions. Naturally, the affected regions and industries resent fiercely the suggestion that their interests should be sacrificed for broader national purposes. It is a justifiable cause for concern that the economy of the South or of New England may be disrupted by trade. The problem of the vulnerable industries poses a question to which there exists no clear-cut solution on abstract grounds. The present uneasy compromise solution is supplied by the so-called "escape-clause" procedures. Under present legislation, the Tariff Commission is obliged to conduct an escape-clause investigation upon the request of a domestic industry. If the Commission discovers that imports are occurring in such volume "as to cause or threaten to cause serious injury to domestic producers," it is required to report such a situation to the President, and recommend adjustments in the tariff. The President may then accept, reject, or modify the Commission's findings. The procedures are considered by advocates of a liberal trade policy to be an unwarranted concession to the protectionists, whereas the latter regard the procedures as a mere sop, giving far from adequate protection to deserving interests.

The vested-interest argument is, however, far less effective in winning public support than is the defense argument. With the declining effectiveness of other appeals, it is quite natural for an industry, in presenting its arguments to the public, the Congress, or the Tariff Commission, to attempt to come in under the national-security umbrella. Briefly, the essence of the defense argument is as follows: if a certain industry is vital to national security, and even if the nation lacks a comparative advantage in that type of production, it is desirable to ensure a market for domestic producers by granting protection. In this manner, domestic sources of supply will be built up. Obviously, the commodity or service must be a vital one, and domestic sources must be *inadequate for wartime purposes*. The stronger the danger of interruption of supply during wartime, the greater the force of the argument. Some industries immediately spring to mind as possible recipients of tariff support on these grounds: synthetic rubber, the merchant marine, chemicals, perhaps aluminum and watch manufacturing. Even the tuna-fish industry has argued, with the support of the Navy, that it is affected by national-security considerations, since it provides auxiliary vessels in wartime. But some of the contentions have been close to absurd. The lace manufacturers have claimed defense status because they produce military mosquito nets; the glove manufacturers because they produce soldiers' gloves; the cutlery manufacturers because they produce machetes. "In the name of defense, the dairy lobby succeeded in restricting imports of foreign cheese . . . and the lead-pencil producers claimed defense status simply because pencils were 'indispensable.'" [4] To illustrate the popularity of the defense argument among industries seeking protection, we may cite the testimony of a spokesman for the Schiffli Lace and Embroidery Manufacturing Association before the House Ways and Means Committee:

> It is important to remember, however, that in a time of national insecurity and peril, it was the one and only industry the United States military forces could turn to for the manufacture of all shoulder patches and insignia . . . considered vitally necessary for the morale of our soldiers and sailors . . . no industry capable of producing such a valuable military commodity should be allowed . . . to wither and become extinct because of the lowering of tariff rates.[5]

This little excerpt suggests how widespread in American industry is the altruistic concern for national security and for the well-being of the members of the armed forces. For some, it may be that it also illustrates the strong tendency for vested interests to wrap themselves in the flag and to present private concerns as a part of the national interest. In that case, it tends to corroborate an initial supposition that any claim that tariff protection is necessary for defense purposes must be carefully scrutinized.

In its place, the defense argument for protection has a certain validity. In view of the contemporary American goal of maintaining a free-world anti-Communist coalition, its applicability to American policy *at the present time* is more in dispute—a point we will return to later. For the present, let us examine the strengths and the limitations of the defense argument:

The chief purpose of tariff protection in the case of defense-sensitive industries is to add to what we earlier called the "mobilization base" of the economy. The reason for augmenting the domestic mobilization base is fear that foreign sources of supply are *likely* to be interrupted in time of war. We desire to decrease our dependence on trade over which we have little control. Yet, it must be remembered that severance of trading links reduces the dependence of others, as well as ourselves, upon trade; therefore, it may add little to our relative strength. Certain of the industries making the most substantial contribution to our mobilization base are export-oriented. Among them are automobiles and agricultural implements, chemicals, and machinery of all descriptions. By building up the export market, therefore, we bring about the expansion of such industries and thereby add to our mobilization base. Since it is necessary to purchase foreign goods in order to export, foreign trade may, in fact, add more to our mobilization base than the impeding of trade. Manifestly, the defense argument cannot be mechanically applied, but will depend upon the circumstances and, most important of all, upon the nation's strategic doctrine.

Those are some of the reasons for skepticism toward the ease of applicability of the defense argument. Now, what specific examples of the application of the doctrine can be cited? Under the law as amended in 1955, the Director of the Office of Defense Mobilization, "whenever he has reason to believe that any article is being imported into the United States in such quantities as to threaten to impair the national security, he shall so advise the President, and if the President agrees that there is reason for such belief, the President shall cause an immediate investigation to be made to determine the facts." If the investigation demonstrates that there is a threat, the President is free to take whatever action he deems necessary.[6]

Even in 1954, before the passage of the national-security amendment to the Trade Agreements Act, the government had acted to increase the duty on watches in the interests of national defense. In an escape-clause case, the President cited national security as a reason for acceding to an increase in the tariff.[7] The cause for protection of the watch industry is quite complex, and there is no need to go into the details, although it might be noted that the Department of Defense reached opposite conclusions concerning the essentiality of the watch industry to national security. Domestically, there was strong protest over the decision; in Switzerland, there was anger; and in Europe, there was general alarm, perhaps unjustified, that the United States was reverting to outright protectionism.

An even more complicated decision occurred in the summer of 1957; it was concerned with a most important commodity in international commerce and with one of the two major commodity imports into the United States. A special Cabinet Committee, organized after notification by the Director of the ODM, reported that crude-oil imports, then running at almost a million barrels a day in the area east of the Rockies, threatened to impair national security. In August, the President requested the major oil companies who do the importing to reduce imports "voluntarily" to 755,700 barrels a day—a cut of a little more than 20 per cent—and to set an importation limit at 12 per cent of U.S. petroleum production outside the Pacific Coast area. In December, the government cancelled the West Coast exemption from the voluntary restrictions, and ordered a 37 per cent reduction in imports, over vehement Canadian protests. In March of 1958, the allowed imports east of the Rockies were cut back further to 711,000 barrels a day starting April 1, and, at the same time, petroleum products were put back under the "Buy American" Act, requiring the government to purchase only from domestic sources for domestic use. At the same time, purchases from non-compliers with the "voluntary" program among American concerns were prohibited.[8]

American petroleum output has been running at the rate of approximately 2.4 billion barrels a year—almost 50 per cent of the world output, outside the Soviet bloc. Simultaneously, we have been consuming some 55 per cent of the free world's oil output. At the present rate of production, our proven oil reserves—a little more than 30 billion barrels—would last almost thirteen years. At the rate of consumption prevailing when the controls went into effect, our present domestic oil reserves would be exhausted in a decade. Our own proven oil reserves constitute only 15 per cent of the present free-world estimates of about 207 billion barrels.

As a matter of simple arithmetic, it would seem that if the United States were to consume 55 per cent of the world's oil production, and rely primarily upon its own reserves, our reserves would soon be depleted. On what grounds, then, did the President take the action? It was his desire to build up a "thriving oil industry." The Cabinet Committee had been concerned about the gap between exploration and production. Oil reserves are not static. It was hoped that the assurance of a domestic market would provide a stimulus for the industry to go out and discover additional reserves. This was the reasoning behind the decision; its wisdom has been questioned.

The rationale for limiting imports is to add to the industrial mobilization base, and the reasoning is clearly applicable in the case of the development of manufacturing facilities. But oil is a *wasting asset*: the more that is taken out of the ground, the less there will be left to exploit. It becomes increasingly more expensive to discover and to produce additional oil as the more accessible deposits are drained off. In the United States, wells are now drilled to an average depth of more than 4,000 feet. More than 40 per cent of wells drilled produce dry holes. Today, the number of barrels of oil added per foot of hole drilled has fallen to thirteen. These are some of the reasons why domestic costs have risen, and why it was considered necessary to provide more incentive for domestic producers. But clearly, under these circumstances, the applicability of the mobilization-base concept in an issue of this kind, which involves wasting assets, is questionable. Cost conditions in the Middle East, for example, offer a vivid contrast, illustrating the price we are paying for relying on domestic sources. In the Saudi Arabian fields, there are only 154 wells producing an average of 8,650 barrels per day; in the United States, there are almost 600,000 wells producing an average of 13 barrels a day. Even the best American wells can efficiently produce only about 1,500 barrels a day, and such wells are relatively rare. Virtually no dry holes are drilled in the Saudi Arabian field. The costs of extraction, consequently, are but a small fraction of American costs—and despite transportation and tariffs, oil brought here from the Middle East can be sold at a much lower price than can domestically produced oil. Oil fields in the United States are more difficult to find, smaller, and less accessible than in the Middle East. To a lesser degree, this comparison holds true also in regard to Venezuela. The question is to what degree we can make use of cheap foreign sources without endangering national security.

Manifestly, in the event of war, we would not find all of our present consumption of oil to be essential. Much of it is luxury consumption, and this raises the question of whether it is wise policy to go to the trouble of proving up expensive and vital oil reserves merely to see these reserves go through the engines of America's sixty-odd million automobiles. In the peak year of World War II, the armed forces purchased less than 600 million barrels of oil, and that was a war of material attrition. In the event of a crisis, we might be able to get by with something like half our present production. Foreign sources would remain open to us; if they did not, our range of military operations and, therefore, our oil requirements would be considerably more restricted than at present. Oil is, to be sure, a resource vital to our national security, but does not that imply that we ought to conserve it rather than to waste it? The implication of the President's argument is that it is a menace to our security if our rate of production slips to a mere 40 per cent of the world's total. It is to be noted that the President's Materials Policy Commission in 1952 reached diametrically opposite conclusions, suggesting that we increase our utilization of foreign sources.[9]

Maximum present security is achieved at the cost of greater risk in the future. Husbanding of our oil resources is in order, and the present system is ill-suited to meet our needs. Surely the problem of conserving oil for a moment of crisis is not too deep for the ingenuity of an Administration that designed the soil bank. We might well develop an oil bank—paying bounties for discovery, and impounding the oil by capping the wells until it is needed. Subsidies might be paid to maintain the production of the so-called "stripper wells," in the face of foreign competition.

Other issues may be raised with respect to the decision: Is it implied that all oil imports are a similar threat to national security—that oil shipped from Tampico is to be distinguished sharply from that shipped from Galveston, and regarded, instead, as the strategic equivalent of that shipped from the Middle East? Are the Caribbean and the Canadian basins outside our security area, and is it, therefore, a matter of indifference whether or not other oil resources in the Western Hemisphere are developed?[10] Is this not a direct reversal of the Administration's original "trade, not aid" doctrine? Does it not worsen our strategic position by embittering relations with other oil-producing states, particularly those Middle Eastern nations which we are simultaneously attempting to aid and to cultivate? Can it be true that our neighbor to the north—with whom we are associated in the North American Air Defense Command, through whose territories runs the Distant Early Warning (DEW) Line, with whom we are allied in NATO—is so unreliable a source of petroleum as to constitute a strategic threat? If so, why do we not carry the policy to its logical conclusion and protect ourselves against dependence on Canadian sources of uranium and other materials?

To ask these questions is to answer them. The Venezuelan protest that, for purposes of national security, all hemispheric resources should be treated as a unit simply missed the point. The government had determined to protect an important group of domestic producers. But if protection of an interest group was the goal, why go through the routine of an ODM national-security investigation, when the escape-clause process was created precisely for this purpose? Why be sanctimonious when it achieves nothing? Others can see through the dissembling. If we are determined to protect domestic interest groups, let us plainly state so. That much, other nations can understand, even if they dislike it, but sanctimoniousness and the gratuitous implication that foreign sources are unreliable simply add insult to injury.

In a democracy, decisions result from an alignment of pressure groups. Behind public policy, we may observe the operations of the affected parties. The domestic oil producers are one of the most powerful of domestic interest groups—so powerful, in fact, that they are rarely used as a political target, indicating a sure sign of strength. Deeply entrenched in both major political parties, they wield tremendous power in Congress, and are not without power in dealing with its leadership. As has been suggested, it is, indeed, a ticklish question in determining to what degree domestic groups should be protected, and inevitably there will be compromise. Nevertheless, it is ironical to observe glaring protectionism operating under the aegis of national-security procedures. Perhaps, in the end, this decision will do little harm. Decision makers may not be consciously biased. The issues are complex—diversion of resources as opposed to dependence on foreign sources. But unless the public is ever alert to the role of pressure groups, decisions on public policy will simply reflect the pattern of pressures.

4. THE ROLE OF TRADE IN AMERICAN FOREIGN POLICY

How, then, should our commercial policy be related to our foreign policy? In order to attack the problem, we need to dispose of some deadwood. State Department propaganda in behalf of the reciprocal-trade-agreements program notwithstanding, the United States is not now a "have-not" nation, absolutely dependent upon foreign sources for essential commodities. The United States could pursue a policy of autarky. The concept of the have-not nation depends to a large extent on price ratios.

It is not a geologic concept, but an economic concept stating that at present prices, some domestic resources are uneconomical to work, and that certain substitutes give less satisfactory performance. It does not imply an absolute shortage. To be sure, it may be desirable to take advantage of the relative cheapness of certain raw materials produced overseas, but we ought to remember two things. First, if we wished to supply ourselves from Western Hemisphere or even North American sources, we could, provided we were willing to pay the added costs of diverting additional real resources for the purpose of achieving self-sufficiency. The price is the reduction of real national income. Secondly, part of the reason for the high relative cost of extraction in the United States results from high labor cost; this is something different from what one may call the "high physical cost" of inaccessible deposits. This relative financial cost could change, in the event that foreign labor cost creeps upward.

In the event of the United States being forced back into a "fortress America," we would be able to get by on the basis of this continent's resources. We would have to pay a higher price, but there would be no absolute shortage. With modern technology, we could find substitutes or more expensive processes for obtaining what we want. Steel and magnesium could replace aluminum, manganese could be eliminated from alloy steel, and so on. For confirmation, all one need do is to consider with what success the Germans utilized technology to maintain an impressive war machine, despite a drastically restricted raw-material base. Limited as were the Germans' raw-material supplies in absolute terms, at no time were they critically short though restricted to the sources on the European continent.

We could, to be sure, be self-sufficient if we were willing to pay the costs, but that does not imply it would be sound strategy. George Kennan once observed that "the problem of dealing with international Communism . . . is largely a matter of what we do in our relations with the non-Communist world." [11] In those relations, trade has a distinct—perhaps an indispensable—role to play. In the nineteenth century, our national strategy was based upon continental isolation, and, under those circumstances, the impeding of trade through the protective tariff was not inconsistent with our national purposes. In the mid-twentieth century, our national objective has become opposition to the further expansion of the Sino-Soviet bloc. Our role, as leader, is to hold together a coalition of non-Communist powers, differing greatly in aspirations and in strength. In holding together this coalition, trade has a vital role to play. *The counterpart of global defense is global trade.* Ideological bonds with foreign powers are potent, but they are even more potent when the nations concerned are linked together by mutual interests, and when such relations are economically beneficial to us.

Yet our foreign policy seems to be based partly on an autarkic concept: the idea that we must produce all we need at home. We state that we must prevent the further expansion of the Sino-Soviet bloc; yet our policy seems to be based upon the supposition that, in the event of war, all the rest of the world will be lost to us as a source of supply. Clearly, this would be untrue in the case of limited war. Although the pattern of nuclear war is unclear, it is probable that a wide dispersal of the coalition's resources would best ensure survival in the event of an attack, and, in addition, such a dispersal would tend to discourage an attack. If, however, we refuse to trade with other nations, we undermine our own long-run purposes by encouraging the drift to Communism. We must recognize that autarkic policies are consistent with a strategic doctrine based upon "fortress America." They are inconsistent with the goal of maintaining a world-wide coalition of non-Communist powers. Now, some schizoid tendencies in our policies may be unavoidable. For reasons that will be developed at the end of this chapter, they may even be desirable to some extent, particularly in the case of trade. But if we wish to maintain our coalition, we must do what we can to strengthen it—and not act as though foreign supplies are unacceptable because they are likely to be lost in wartime.

Let us bind up the coalition with the ties of trade. Trade is an ideal instrument, since it generally contributes to an all-round increase in real income. It is an instrument that should be uniquely accessible to the West. The Soviet Union tends to be autarkic: first, because collectivist planning comports ill with external trade, since control over foreign prices and production cannot be brought within the plan; secondly, because the pathological suspicion of external hostility has precluded normal ties, except in conditions of subservience. Up to the present, no power has established independent, profitable, permanent, and extensive trade with the Soviet Union. Seemingly, autarky is a permanent feature of Soviet thought; external economic linkage has been limited largely to the Communist bloc.[12]

The total trade of the Soviet Union is small. Either because of fear for their security, or because they refuse, on ideological grounds, to rely upon regions not subject to their political authority, the Russians have refrained from extensive trade with countries other than their own satellites. The present leadership has, to be sure, introduced more flexibility in the approach to autarky, but the basic pattern remains unchanged. When the Russians do trade with countries outside their orbit, it is likely to be with smaller states like Egypt or Burma, where political advantages can be gained. The flow of goods is a secondary consideration. The Soviet Union does not seek *extensive* trade with powerful partners, such as unsovietized Germany or Japan. Yet, there is a myth prevailing in Western-oriented industrial countries that to the east lie markets (or, in the case of Japan, to the west in Communist China). The Soviet bloc is anxious to build up its own industry. If it desires to import, it is to import capital goods and not consumer goods. The Chinese, for example, have no intention of providing the Japanese with a market similar to the one that existed when Japan was the dominant power in the region. Despite the hopes of the Japanese and others, trade with the Communist bloc ultimately offers relatively little in terms of total volume.

Some of the smaller nations have also learned that the lure of a Soviet market is not quite so appealing as it may appear at first thought. The Russians wish to avoid dependence on foreign sources, particularly those that might be interrupted in time of war. Relations with the smaller countries have had political rather than economic objectives. Egyptian cotton sent to Russia has been dropped upon West German markets at low prices

thus damaging the local markets for Egyptian cotton. The same
has been true of Burmese rice. Soviet trade, up to the present
time, at least, has been more of a come-on device to cause dissension in the non-Soviet world than a device to create firm
associations through the exchange of goods. Thus, in certain
circumstances, it may be desirable to permit members of the
Western coalition to see for themselves the limits of the market
in the Soviet camp.

That this is not always wise, particularly when the nation
in question is one of the smaller ones, may be illustrated by
the following modern Icelandic saga. In 1956, the Tariff Commission received an escape-clause petition from the domestic
ground-fish industry, and upon investigation discovered that it
was suffering grievous injury from imports. Some hardship was
occurring in the fishing ports. Some of the people of New
England were disturbed; their representatives in Congress were
definitely disturbed. It was a clear-cut case for tariff protection
on the basis of a threatened vested interest. President Eisenhower, in December, 1946, rejected the findings of the Tariff
Commission and decided against raising the tariff on imported
ground-fish fillets. In the previous week, the Icelandic Government had decided to permit American forces to remain in Iceland. The earlier decision had been based upon the expectation
of the forthcoming action by the President. Iceland must export
in order to survive; her main export is fish. In 1955, the British
began to exclude Icelandic fish as a result of a dispute over
the extent of Icelandic coastal waters. The Russians began to
buy fish. By the end of 1956, they were buying 35 per cent of
Iceland's fish. Their influence rose, and there came the threats
about American bases. Then came the President's decision, pre-
ceded by the Hungarian episode, which helped persuade the Icelandic Government (a coalition which includes Communists) to
permit us to stay on. This saga provides an excellent illustration
of the importance of fish to American security, of the role of
trade in achieving a world-wide defensive coalition, and of the
problems that arise when it is necessary to sacrifice a domestic
interest group to security considerations.

In view of our strategic objectives, there is little question as to what our trade policy should be. However, because of the burdens placed upon the affected domestic interest groups, protection must be regarded as something more than "infantile escapism," as George Kennan has called it. Nevertheless, strategic considerations ought to take precedence, and trade is an excellent device for winning friends and influencing people. Our policies should be based upon two principles: first, in the contemporary setting, the influence effect is more important than the supply effect; secondly, it is, nevertheless, desirable to have *alternative sources of essential production* out of the reach of the Russians. These principles are in mild conflict, but the emphasis on the former and the characteristics of the latter would mean that the strategy of coalition should carry the nation further along the road away from protection.

Certain states must export. We should tie them to us by providing them with a non-Soviet source of livelihood, which may prevent their turning to Communism in despair. Trade may be more important than ideology, and in this respect we have an important advantage over the Soviet bloc, which, because of its autarkic tendencies, will only enter into limited trading arrangements with nations that are not subservient. Take the case of Japan. With a narrow resource base, Japan is a highly industrialized country, dependent upon foreign sources for the raw materials that she processes into finished goods. Roughly 80 per cent of Japan's imports are raw materials. Unless she acquires foreign exchange through export, the Japanese standard of living would collapse. Yet, in the West, Japanese goods are subject to discriminatory treatment.

The American interest in the viability of the Japanese economy is obvious. Yet, some years ago when American textile producers were under pressure from Japanese competition, the Administration persuaded the Japanese to limit the volume of their exports to the United States "voluntarily." It is clear that if we are to have restrictions on trade, it is preferable for American consumers to have restrictions by way of price (that is, tariffs) rather than in the form of quantity restrictions, since the former leave them liberty of choice. It is unclear whether such action represents an appropriate exercise of executive power. It is unclear what is meant by "voluntary" restriction. Finally, the action that the United States took is manifestly in conflict with our obligations to Japan in terms of the spirit, if not the letter, of GATT. Aside from the economic and legal questions involved, the decision was foolhardy on strategic grounds. In 1957, to take a typical year, Japan exported to the United States $600 million worth of goods, and imported $1.6 billion worth from us. For some years, expenditures by the armed forces in Japan and auxiliary assistance have helped to bridge the gap. With the departure of American troops, though, one source of foreign exchange is waning. Japan must find markets, yet her exports are only 75 per cent of the prewar level, and her population has increased by 30 per cent. The case for liberalization of Western trade with Japan is clear-cut. Here, the first principle is dominant.

But, what about our second goal—of providing alternative sources of supply, out of Soviet reach, which would provide for our minimal needs in emergencies? The economic and strategic advantages of increased trade cannot be permitted to override the disadvantages of vulnerability. The case of oil is, perhaps, the most important one, and may serve to illustrate the principles involved. The West should continue to draw upon the cheap resources of the Middle East. But Western Hemisphere resources should be maintained at a level that could satisfy our minimal needs if necessary. It would be beneficial if Western Europe had alternative sources, and the opportunities in Canada—particularly for Britain—are impressive. There are at least 50 billion barrels of oil in the sedimentary basin in Canada. In addition, the Athabasca oil sands in Alberta contain an estimated 200-300 billion barrels of recoverable oil. A joint American-Canadian *scientific* endeavor to uncover an economical process for extracting oil from the Athabasca sands might be a wise investment against a possible day of reckoning for the West. It would be wise policy, in general, for the United States to devote some resources for research and development in alternative sources of supply. In the event of an emergency, and if parts of the world are cut off, we must be prepared to make use of many substitutes. On the other hand, to resort to alternative sources in advance would be both highly expensive and politically self-defeating. Perhaps the best approach is the preparation of plans for emergency use—new techniques, more tankers, and new sources of supply.

We may take advantage of the opportunities open to the West through trade, without running the risk of overdependence upon menaced sources of supply. Let us recognize the inherent power potentialities of trade, which do stand in stark contrast to the assumptions of harmony in the nineteenth-century theory. A policy of economic autarky on the part of the United States is not consistent with a policy of maintaining a world-wide coalition. The economic counterpart of global defense, as we have previously observed, is global trade. The tendency to pervert national-security measures to protectionist ends must be firmly resisted. International trade has been referred to as "a peaceful means of economic penetration" and also as a "bloodless revolution." The West must make this power work in its own behalf by cementing together the free-world coalition through trade, thereby denying to the Russians this particular route to a bloodless revolution.[13]

7

SOVIET ECONOMIC GROWTH

In recent years, the subject of economic growth has become most fashionable for the purpose of analyzing international power tendencies. Few are the popular journals that do not contain an article by some pundit pointing out the dire consequences that will follow for the West—first, if the Soviet Union continues to grow rapidly, or second, if the underdeveloped areas do not. Since the subject divides so neatly into these two categories, we will follow the conventional practice here, reserving this chapter for an analysis of growth trends in the Soviet Union and the comparative American performance, about which we have heard in recent years so many alarming statements. In the following two chapters, we will examine the economic and political implications of growth in the underdeveloped areas.

Comparing Soviet and American growth trends is a treacherous undertaking. The goals and the structures of the two economies differ, and by varying the sectors selected for comparison, different and seemingly conflicting conclusions may be reached with respect to the over-all performances. The present-day habit is to study industrial growth—partly because of strategic interest, partly because of statistical ease. For certain purposes, studying industrial growth alone is perfectly appropriate, but since both agriculture and the service industries are neglected in such studies, they should not be taken as representative of over-all economic performance. Since economic growth has become so important in the propagandistic sense, it is desirable occasionally to remind ourselves and observers in other countries of the limited inferences that may be drawn from studies of industrial production alone.

In the earlier analysis of resource allocation, it was pointed out that a controlled economy may have certain advantages over a free-enterprise economy in stimulating industrial growth which follow from the centralized control over the allocative process. First, the rate of capital formation may be controlled by holding down the level of domestic consumption; secondly, investment may be directed into those basic industries which are particularly conducive to the expansion of industrial production, irrespective of consumers' desires or the impact upon the standard of living. Whether growth of industrial capacity in this manner should be referred to as "economic growth" is a debatable question. Conventionally, in the West, it has been assumed that the function of industrial capacity is to serve consumer welfare. Since this function of industrial expansion has largely been disregarded in the Soviet Union, ought we use the phrase "economic growth" in our Western meaning of the term? The distinction is not an unimportant one, since in the underdeveloped areas the difference between industrial expansion for its own sake and for contribution to living standards has not been clearly discerned.

Nevertheless, although economic growth means different things under the two systems, and although the Soviet Union has economic objectives that differ from those paramount in the West, it is possible to compare the changes in physical production with no regard to the purpose it serves. Properly understood, the meaning of industrial production is relatively clear. The same is not true, however, for measures of total output. It will be recalled that a question has already been raised with respect to the meaningfulness of the concept of gross national product in a controlled system in which prices do not reflect costs. On a more general level, the very significance of intercountry comparisons of gross national product was questioned. Although some estimates of the relative changes in national product may be made, it should be understood that they are far more nebulous in meaning than measures of physical production. Consequently, for purposes of comparison between the Soviet Union and the United States, measures of national product ought to be viewed with a high degree of skepticism.

We will attack the problem of Soviet economic growth in four main areas: the record and its interpretation, extrapolation or retardation, the long-run prospects, and speculation concerning a Soviet business cycle.

1. THE RECORD AND ITS INTERPRETATION

In appraising the Soviet record, it should be observed at the outset that the nonspecialist must proceed with caution in venturing to discuss a topic about which the experts have not ceased to argue. The purpose of this section must be, therefore, to indicate the main characteristics of Soviet growth, to outline the disputes that have been engendered, and to hint at a *possible* resolution of these disputes rather than to reach any definitive conclusions. Our first task is to examine industrial production, about which most of the controversy has raged; then to turn to other types of production, particularly agricultural, concerning which more definite comments may be made; and then to attempt to appraise the over-all picture of Soviet economic growth.

For the past three decades, the main Soviet ambition in the economic field has been to expand industrial production. It is no great overstatement that the ethos of the Soviet system has been based upon Stalin's injunction that the fundamental task of the Soviet Union was *to catch up to and surpass the advanced capitalist countries in terms of* per capita *industrial production.* That great drive toward industrialization was launched with the commencement of the First Five-Year Plan in 1928. After a decade of internal unrest, political conflict, and lagging production, Stalin turned to the technique of state stimulation of industrial production in order to close the gap with the West. Since 1928, the growth of Soviet industrial production has been both rapid and impressive. In Table I, the production figures for a number of representative industrial commodities have been listed for four years—1928, the start of the First Five-Year Plan; 1937, the end of the Second Five-Year Plan (the last completed before the war); and 1950 and 1955, the boundary years for the Fifth Five-Year Plan. In addition, the *goals* have been listed for both the Sixth Five-Year Plan, abandoned soon after its inception because of economic difficulties, and the new Seven-Year Plan, announced by Khrushchev in November, 1958, and intended as a replacement for the Sixth Five-Year Plan. Close inspection of the target figures will reveal that the annual growth rates projected under the new plan are lower than under its predecessor, though this evidence of retardation has been partially hidden by pushing the target year further into the future.[1] Our present purpose, however, is to examine not future goals but the actual production record. Cursory examination of the figures in Table I will suggest that during the first two five-year plans, the rate of growth in those basic industries in which the Soviet Union was concentrating her efforts was enormous in relative terms. On the other hand, the rate of growth in the traditional industries producing consumer goods, such as cotton textiles and leather footwear, was quite modest indeed. In the earlier years, the over-all index of industrial growth was heavily weighted by these less rapidly growing traditional industries, which in that era bulked much larger in the structure of Soviet industry. Nevertheless, the average rate of industrial growth was quite rapid. After 1937, however, it slowed quite perceptibly as a result of the rearmament drive. Then came the onslaught of World War II, with its widespread devastation. The immediate postwar period was one of rebuilding, under Stalin's iron hand. In the table, it may be seen that new progress had been made in the Fifth Five-Year Plan (1950–1955), particularly in the basic industries, but the rate of growth in these industries was substantially less than it had been at the outset of industrialization. In appraising Soviet industrial expansion, we shall concentrate on this last period, since it is the most recent and at the same time illustrates the major problems of interpretation.

The official Soviet index states that for the period 1950-1955, the rate of growth of industrial production was 13.1 per cent a year. All Western observers are agreed that the Soviet claim

TABLE I

SELECTED PRODUCTION STATISTICS FOR MAJOR INDUSTRIAL COMMODITIES,
SOVIET RUSSIA–1928, 1937, 1950, 1955, 1960 (Plan), 1965 (Plan)

Commodity	1928	1937	1950	1955	1960 (Plan)[a]	1965 (Plan)[b]
Steel (million tons)	4.3	17.7	27.3	45.3	68.3	86-91
Coal (million tons)[c]	35.5	128.0	261.1	391.1	593.0	596-609
Electric power (billion kwh)	5.0	36.2	91.2	170.1	320.0	500-520
Cotton fabrics (million meters)	2,678.0	3,448.0	3,899.0	5,904.0	7,270.0	7,700-8,000
Cement (thousand tons)	1,850.0	5,454.0	10,194.0	22,484.0	55,000.0	n.a.
Oil (million tons)	11.6	28.5	37.9	70.8	135.0	230-240
Paper (thousand tons)	284.0	832.0	1,193.0	1,864.0	2,722.0	3,500
Leather footwear (million pairs)[d]	58.0	182.9	203.4	274.4	455.0	515
Tractor production (thousands)	1.3	51.0	108.8	163.4	322.0	n.a.
Motor vehicles	.7	n.a.	362.9	445.3	650.0	750-856

Source: *The National Economy of the USSR: A Statistical Compilation*, issued by the Central Statistical Administration Council of Ministers USSR (Moscow: State Statistical Publishing House, 1956); for targets of the Seven-Year Plan, "Khrushchev's Theses on the Seven-Year Plan–I," in *The Current Digest of the Soviet Press*, vol. X, no. 47, December 31, 1958.

[a] Goals of the Sixth Five-Year Plan, announced at the Twentieth Party Congress, February, 1956. Plan scrapped January, 1957, after preliminary announcements in December, 1956.

[b] Goals announced at plenary session of the Central Committee of the Communist Party, November, 1958. The new Seven-Year Plan (1958-1965) serves as a replacement for the lapsed Sixth Five-Year Plan.

[c] Includes lignite, which has increased from 4 per cent of total production in 1928 to 30 per cent today. Calorific content has declined 12 per cent.

[d] The 1928 figure is low, since it does not include private (nonfactory) production.

is overstated; they differ, however, with respect to the degree of overstatement. In general, composite averages issued by the Soviet, unlike the individual statistics, are regarded as unreliable. As a rule, the individual commodity statistics are accurate—if they are regarded as sufficiently unfavorable, they are not reported rather than being distorted. Most American and Western observers have credited the Russians with a growth rate of between 10 and 11 per cent for the period. Though this is considerably below their claimed growth rate, it should be realized that a steady growth rate of 10 per cent a year would *double output every seven years*. Such estimates have caused widespread alarm in Washington. It has been stated, for example, that Soviet industrial growth has been twice as rapid as American growth. If these estimates are accurate, and if such growth rates continue into the future, then the Soviet Union will have reached *present* American levels of industrial production within a decade. For this reason, it has been argued that the United States must take steps to speed up its own rate of industrial expansion.

In the United States, however, observers have been by no means unanimous in their conclusions. There exist both high-estimate and low-estimate schools. At the present time, the former is the dominant group and has been, in large degree, responsible for the attitude of pessimism expressed in Washington on the subject. Study of the figures in Table I will reveal that over the period of the plan, production of the basic commodities increased by at least 50 per cent, but did not double. The consumer-goods industries exhibited a somewhat lower rate of growth. One American expert, Gregory Grossman, of the University of California, has suggested that such figures are broadly representative of Soviet growth trends in the Fifth Five-Year Plan—8.5-13.5 per cent for the basic industries, and 5-10 per cent for typical consumer-goods industries. He has concluded that the over-all rate of increase seems to be roughly 10-11 per cent per year.[2]

The views of the majority have been challenged in recent years by a small but forceful low-estimate school which maintains that the official Soviet indexes have been even more exaggerated than the high-estimate school has recognized. The most intensive study of the Soviet economy to date, a National Bureau of Economic Research project directed by G. Warren Nutter, still in process of completion, has come to much more modest conclusions. The choice of weights is of vital importance in determining the size of any composite average representing growth rates. The Nutter study, using 1955 Soviet prices as weights, points to a rate of growth of 7.7 per cent for the period of the Fifth Five-Year Plan.[3] Thus, there is a considerable disparity in the estimates, ranging from 7.7 per cent to 11 per cent.

It is well to recognize that statistical analysis can never reach definitive conclusions with respect to Soviet growth. Not all of the necessary information is available. Indexes depend upon the selection of data and of weights, and in every case it is inevitable that these will be influenced to some degree by the underlying assumptions of the investigator. It should be noted, however, that in recent years the National Bureau study has been the only comprehensive survey to be made, and until its figures have been challenged in detail, it must be accorded respect. The views of the high-estimate school have been more impressionistic with respect to the most recent period and have been based upon perspectives developed in earlier studies. There are several technical reasons for believing that the results of the high-estimate school may be biased upward. For one thing, the statistics measure *gross* production at all stages of industry. This implies that any disintegration of industry (that is, increased specialization), by adding more stages to production, will increase the figure for industrial output. Moreover, the figure for gross production may overstate the rate of increase because of encroachment on the household sector by the organized sector of industry. Thirdly, the tendency to introduce new production with implicit fixed-price weights has tended to push the index upward.

On the other hand, there are reasons for believing that the National Bureau index might exhibit a downward bias. The nature of the statistics that are available makes it impossible to include some of the more rapidly growing new industries—for example, electronics or rockets and missiles.[4] Another and unavoidable difficulty is the one discussed in Chapter II: Soviet prices are designed to encourage expansion of the heavy industries; prices of industrial goods are manipulated downward, whereas prices of consumer goods are manipulated upward. Therefore, the use of Soviet prices as weights may tend to understate growth by reducing the weights for just that range of industries in which growth is most rapid.

Unhappily, until the experts reach a greater degree of agreement, the nonspecialist will remain in a quandary. He must hazard a guess, but this is almost a case of *lèse-majesté*. A seemingly reasonable, but cowardly, judgment would be to assume that the results lie somewhere in between—let us say, a growth rate of 8-9 per cent. This would imply that the Soviet growth rate in the recent past has been both quite high and substantially in excess of that of the United States. On the other hand, it would mean that the high-estimate school has been somewhat too pessimistic regarding the position of the West. It would be inaccurate to assume that the industrial expansion in the Soviet Union has been proceeding at twice the American rate, or that Soviet industrial output will double every seven years. Consequently, it would take a longer period of time for Soviet industrial production to reach *present* American levels than is currently believed in Washington.

Let us turn now from industrial production to over-all economic growth and to the non-industrial sectors of the Soviet economy. It has already been emphasized that estimates of the rate of *economic* growth are somewhat less meaningful in the Soviet case than are those for the rate of *industrial* growth. It is desirable, however, to make some such appraisal. Since the stimulation of industrial production has been the main economic purpose of the Soviet state, it is to be expected that the comparative performance of the Soviet economy will be at its best in the industrial sector, and that the rate of over-all economic growth will be markedly lower than the rate of industrial growth. This is, in fact, the case. Growth of the non-industrial sectors—in particular, the service trades and agriculture, the latter being notoriously the "Achilles heel" of the Soviet economy—has been quite modest by American standards. The figures on the service industries are scattered and not particularly helpful. We do know that medical services and education have been very markedly improved. These are the prize Soviet exhibits outside the industrial sector, but most of the consumer-oriented services have been correspondingly neglected. We do not know the number of barber shops, dry-cleaning establishments, or service stations, but we can be fairly certain that growth, if any, has been at a low rate, hardly comparing with industrial growth.

The record of Soviet agriculture has been most inauspicious—partly as a result of an unfavorable resource base, partly as a result of the single-minded concentration upon industry, and partly due to the deficiencies of the chosen method of agricultural organization. Collectivization has inhibited the initiative of the agricultural population. Soviet statistics have sought to disguise the relative failure in agriculture. For many years, it was the practice to report biological yield rather than barn yield—that is, a mechanical estimate of the amount of crops planted rather than the amount actually harvested. This practice has been abandoned, and production has since been reported as percentages of production in 1950, but the volume figures have not been released. A single statistic that suggests the failure of Soviet ambitions is the estimate for Soviet grain production in 1957 (admittedly, a drought year)—102 million metric tons. This was lower than the target for 1933 in the First Five-Year Plan (106 million metric tons), despite the territorial expansion of the Soviet Union westward. Except for the crop years 1956 and 1958, Soviet grain production has been no greater than that of the prewar year 1937.

Much of Khrushchev's energies, it has already been noted, have been used in an attempt to bring about an improvement in Soviet agriculture. He has promised a vast improvement in the Soviet diet, and in order to end the stagnation in agriculture, he has been willing to provide greater incentives for the peasantry. Prices have been raised, and compulsory deliveries to the state reduced. The decision has also been taken to abolish the Stalinist vehicle of control over the collectives, the machine tractor stations, and to sell these tractors to the collectives (a rather unorthodox step, since it implies private property in the means of production). It has been hoped that these measures will raise output. In addition, Khrushchev has launched the virgin-lands program and the corn program, but in these endeavors the Soviets must struggle with an unyielding nature.

As compared to the United States, the agricultural-resource base of the Soviet Union is extremely weak. Despite the immensity of the Soviet land mass, larger than the entire North American continent, much of this vast expanse is useless for agricultural purposes, consisting as it does of tundra, scrub conifer forest, semi-arid steppe, and desert. More than 40 per cent of the total is underlaid by permafrost; no more than 10-15 per cent of it can be considered tillable. What is arable suffers from a short growing season and low rainfall, a consequence of the continentality of the Russian climate. Agricultural production is generally limited to a belt known as the "fertile triangle," stretching from the western frontiers and tapering until it reaches its eastern apex at Lake Baikal. The term "fertile" should not be misconstrued; the best Russian land is equivalent to that in the Dakotas and in the Canadian prairie provinces. There is nothing in the Soviet Union at all comparable to the American Corn Belt or the lower Mississippi Valley.

The land being brought into cultivation under the virgin-lands program is distinctly inferior to abandoned lands in New England and the American plains. Plowing up this marginal land is a venture fraught with risk—under cultivation, the soil moisture diminishes, and the structure of the soil deteriorates. Some of the land had previously been tilled and abandoned. Although good harvests were obtained in 1956 and, again, in 1958, 1957 was a drought year; the harvest was poor, and the soil began to blow. On such lands, returns can be obtained periodically, but only at high cost.

The corn program is another dramatic attempt to increase agricultural output. The Russians have increased corn acreage from 11 million to 40 million acres, and have attempted to introduce hybrid corn. But Soviet agricultural science has lagged under the baleful influence of Lysenko, and even in the best of circumstances, the expectations of what hybrid corn could accomplish under Soviet climatic conditions have been greatly inflated. In the United States, the use of hybrid corn has been most successful in raising output in the humid areas; output has failed to rise proportionately in the more arid areas like the Dakotas, which provide the closest American counterpart to Soviet agricultural conditions. The Soviet growing season is short, and the corn will have to be harvested for silage before it has fully matured. The Soviets have failed to concentrate corn production in the most suitable climatic areas, but have scattered it all over the fertile triangle. Under the best of circumstances, yields will remain low in relation to the American levels, and the variability of rainfall implies the risk of crop failure. Under Russian conditions, the corn program is no panacea.

Soviet agricultural prospects are clearly less favorable than are industrial prospects. Agriculture labors under an immense natural handicap. It still absorbs some 40 per cent of the labor force, as opposed to 10 per cent in the United States. In time, Khrushchev's rash promise to raise meat production to American levels by 1960 or 1961 could be fulfilled, if the Russians are willing to invest the resources. But with so shaky an agricultural-resource base, it will prove quite costly. If the Russians were rational economic men, they would raise consumption levels in the Soviet Union by extensive international trade, by exporting manufactured goods and importing foodstuffs. But the autarkic drives in the Soviet Union are such that dependence upon foreign sources would be intolerable.

The new agricultural emphasis is highly significant in terms of over-all Soviet growth. Increasing peasant compensation implies more consumer goods, less resources for heavy industry. Emphasis upon agriculture in the face of heavy natural handicaps means a heavy drain on Soviet resources for the next decade, at least. The final outcome is difficult to predict. Conceivably, the development of drought-resistant, quick-growing hybrids could help. Whether such hybrids can or will be developed is a grave question. In any event, improvement of Soviet agriculture will be a long uphill struggle, which inevitably will have repercussions on the other sectors of the Soviet economy.

Measures of the growth of Soviet gross national product are necessarily imprecise. We have seen, however, that half of the Soviet economy, the industrial sector, may have been growing at a rate of 8-9 per cent during the period of 1950-1955; the balance of the Soviet economy at a rate of 1-2 per cent. Thus a convenient estimate for the growth of total output would be 5 per cent a year. Though it is clear that Soviet industrial output has grown at a pace substantially greater than that in the United States, it is generally agreed that Soviet gross national product has grown only slightly more rapidly, if at all. The fact that Soviet agriculture still absorbs 40 per cent of the labor force and produces only 28 per cent of the national product is highly significant.[5] We should not allow the rapid pace of Soviet industrial development to deceive us with respect to the over-all performance.

These observations permit us to view in proper perspective the fears currently expressed in Washington. At the moment, we are living in the midst of a "wake up, America" campaign; and as a result, the performance of the Soviet economy has been exaggerated, that of the West belittled. It is implied that somehow the Soviet system is more efficient than our own. The Director of the Central Intelligence Agency asserted in a recent speech that, between 1957 and 1958, Soviet industry grew by 11 per cent.[6] This is the *Soviet figure;* in view of the recent sharp reduction in the Soviet growth rate, 7 per cent is probably a more accurate estimate. It is true that Soviet industrial rates have been substantially greater than our own, and probably will continue to be. This should not, however, be taken to mean that the Soviet economic system is more efficient than our own. The Russians have demonstrated a capacity to hold down consumption and to plow back a considerable proportion of the national product into industrial investment. In view of the high rates of saving and of capital formation, Soviet *net* investment in industry is probably proceeding at more than twice the American rate. In view of this fact, there is nothing particularly surprising or "efficient" about the Soviet industrial growth rate surpassing our own. Industrial growth in the Soviet Union is an end in itself; it has not been reflected in living standards. American living standards are still rising more rapidly than Soviet living standards—in absolute, if not in relative, terms. When we consider economic growth, apart from the strategic importance of heavy industry, this is the comparison that we should bear in mind. It is also the one that we should invite the underdeveloped countries to consider.

2. EXTRAPOLATION OR RETARDATION?

Soviet industrial expansion has been proceeding at a pace substantially greater than our own. If it continues to grow rapidly, the relative gap between American and Soviet production will gradually narrow. Relative industrial capacities of the major powers are not without their strategic implications, although it has been emphasized earlier that the significance of this comparison has been greatly exaggerated, as a result of viewing possible military encounters in the future in terms of our experiences in the two World Wars. Nevertheless, it is of some importance to consider how rapidly the gap will be diminished. This question will take us into the realm of prophecy, and will depend upon whether we may extrapolate Soviet industrial growth at the present rate, or whether we may expect substantial retardation of the rate of growth.

There is but one major reason to anticipate that past Soviet industrial growth trends may be extrapolated into the future. It is, however, a powerful one. The Soviet economy is not governed by market forces, but is centrally controlled. In planning for the expansion of industrial facilities, the Soviet leaders do not have to worry about whether the expanded output made possible by these new facilities will actually be utilized. The Soviet leaders, in other words, need not concern themselves with demand; if expansion of industry is desired, they may order it forthwith. If it can be anticipated that the government will attempt to maintain or even to increase the rate of capital formation, and if it possesses the political freedom to do so, there is no logical reason why the rate of industrial growth cannot remain high. A second, but rather unlikely, possibility also could stimulate the rate of growth: if the Russians were willing to make extensive use of international trade, and to use industry as a method of obtaining expensive agricultural products elsewhere, the rate of industrial growth could be spurred by specialization. In view of Soviet autarkic tendencies, this possibility may be discounted.

On the other hand, there are a number of weighty reasons for expecting a gradual slackening in the rate of growth. These factors may be summarized under four major groupings: (1) resources, (2) investment policies, (3) the growth of amenities, and (4) external relations.

Resources. The population of the Soviet Union has barely increased from its level at the time of the German onslaught. What has been responsible for this stagnation is hard to say—underestimated war losses, postwar starvation, possibly mass liquidations. In any event, the 1957 announcement by the government that the Soviet population was only 200.2 million was greeted with amazement by Western population experts who had thought the population at least 10 per cent greater. The reported crude birth rate in the Soviet Union is about the same as the American; nevertheless, the Soviets face a short-run labor pinch. The German invasion had a particularly devastating impact upon the birth cohorts of 1940-1945; high mortality and low reproduction rates in wartime were responsible. These are the cohorts now entering the labor force and attaining the age of reproduction. By contrast, in the United States, population has grown by 30 per cent, or 40 million, since 1940. The low birth cohorts of the thirties have been absorbed in the labor force, and the high birth cohorts of the forties and fifties will soon be entering both the labor force and the age of reproduction. Consequently, the short-run labor picture is more favorable in the United States. For the first time in its history, the Soviet Union may be facing a sizable shortage of labor.

Much of the growth of Soviet productivity in the past has resulted from the shifting of labor from low-productivity agriculture to higher-productivity industries. But the pool of surplus low-productivity labor in agriculture has now been sharply reduced, particularly if the Russians are determined to increase agricultural output. Much of the present agricultural labor force consists of women, youths, and old people. The opportunity for growth through the freeing of labor from agriculture is therefore much diminished, considering what it has been in the past.

In addition, there is some evidence that costs of raw-material extraction are increasing. The growing proportion of lignite in total coal production, for example, points in this direction. Rising costs of raw materials may not present an insurmountable difficulty, but they are hardly conducive to more rapid growth.

Investment policies. The Soviet Union benefited in its drive toward industrialization by inheriting from Czarist Russia a respectable industrial base. In particular, the railway transportation network was extensively developed. Although the Russians have added to railway trackage, the system contains only one-third of U.S. railway mileage, despite the vast area of the country. More than 80 per cent of Soviet freight is moved by rail; only 50 per cent in the United States. One of the ways that so much capital was supplied for industry was through intensive usage, almost exploitation, of the railroad network. With the growth of total tonnage, the Russians have reached the limit of this particular method of economizing on capital. Considerable sums will have to be diverted to improve and extend the railway system. Moreover, if the Russians desire to use motor transport to any great extent, vast sums will have to be poured into the construction of a modern highway network.

An increasing proportion of Soviet capital will be going into replacement rather than net investment. Soviet construction has been notably deficient, particularly in housing, but also in industrial facilities. These can no longer be neglected. The upshot is that the *proportion* of investible funds available for industrial expansion will tend to decline. It may be further noted that the Soviet Union has benefited in the past by being able to take over the methods of production developed by advanced Western technology. This particular advantage is gradually disappearing, as Soviet industry catches up with the West.

The growth of amenities. Any sizable effort to raise the level of living of the Soviet people inevitably will tend to reduce the rate of industrial growth. Housing conditions are truly wretched, but new construction will be competing with resources that might otherwise go to industry. Khrushchev has promised a seven-hour day; this implies lower output. Provision of additional consumer goods in volume will tend to restrict the sums that would otherwise be available for industrial expansion.

External relations. Any increase of Soviet assistance, no matter how small, will represent some drain. Soviet credits and assistance have increased very modestly, but even the provision of a few hundred million dollars per year will represent a change. The Soviet Union presumably will have to be more brotherly now in its dealings with its satellites and with Red China. The fact that external relations with the bloc and with the under-developed nations may require an outflow of Soviet resources implies an enormous net change in the Soviet position. In the immediate postwar period, Soviet rehabilitation and growth was fostered by a sizable inflow of foreign resources. The Soviet occupation forces stripped bare both Eastern Europe and Manchuria under the guise of claiming war booty. In addition, Soviet hegemony permitted the exploitation of the satellite economies in the interests of the Soviet Union. How much was channeled to the Soviet Union by the joint companies established in Eastern Europe, for example, is hard to say, but it has been estimated that Soviet "reparations" in kind should be valued at more than $20 billion.[7] This particular source of external assistance seems unlikely to be reopened; instead, capital will probably flow in the opposite direction, and, as a result, Soviet foreign activities are likely to prove increasingly expensive, probably with some repercussions upon the domestic rate of growth.

These are the four factors that tend to indicate retardation of the Soviet growth rate; they must be weighed against the possible determination of the Soviet leadership to maintain the rate of growth at all costs. It is hard to prophesy just what the future will bring, but the evidence to date does suggest the likelihood of some retardation. The growth rate in the period 1950-1955 was lower than it had been in the period 1928-1937. In the years since 1955, it has declined still further. Soviet statistics indicate that it fell from 13.1 per cent to 11 per cent (the last being the figure cited by the director of the CIA). The most recent figures of the National Bureau study indicate a growth rate of 6 per cent between 1956 and 1957. In any case, many recent events—the demise of the Sixth Five-Year Plan, the reductions in the Soviet armed forces, increased emphasis upon agriculture, the pressures for assistance in Eastern Europe, and possibly the cancellation of the Yugoslav credits—point in the direction of economic difficulties which will make the task of maintaining the rate of industrial growth a formidable one.

Opinions differ as to whether this recent reduction represents a tendency toward retardation or a temporary aberration. As might be expected, the high-estimate and low-estimate schools diverge on the question of the degree to which retardation may be anticipated. The high-estimate school, while agreeing that some retardation is likely, sees no reason for assuming that it will be large. It is argued that the periods 1928-1937 and 1950-1955 are the typical ones under planning, and that we may therefore expect continued rapid growth. On the other hand, Nutter, who has surveyed the entire Soviet period and has argued that growth tendencies are similar to those discernible in the American economy in an earlier period, expects that the Soviet economy will exhibit roughly similar tendencies toward retardation. It should be noted that Nutter has followed *the Soviet practice* in judging the period 1913-1955 as a whole, rather than emphasizing particular plan periods. During this 42-year period, he has found an industrial growth rate of 4.6 per cent a year—a somewhat less rapid one than the American industrial growth at a comparable stage of development (1885-1927). In terms of time lags, the typical Soviet industry was further behind its American counterpart in 1955 than in 1913. The median lag was thirty-five years in 1955, while it was only twenty-eight years in 1913.[8] Recently, Soviet growth rates have exhibited the tendency toward retardation that might be anticipated on the basis of roughly comparable growth trends separated in time by three decades.

Nutter's critics in the high-estimate school have pointed out certain misleading features in the use of the 42-year period as a basis of comparison, even though this is the period on which the Russians stake their claims. It included two destructive wars, one violent civil war, two periods of serious social unrest, and intermittent periods of rearmament—hardly an appropriate period for comparison with the less troubled American scene. Moreover, the comparable American statistics stop in 1929, thus conveniently obscuring the sizable retardation of American growth that occurred during the depression of the thirties.

On logical grounds, the high-estimate school would seem to have the better of the argument. At a very minimum, allowance would have to be made for wartime devastation and the stagnant period of the twenties in making such a comparison. The ideal would be to have some statistics, both long-range and normal, on peacetime growth—under planning of the type that has existed since 1928. The high-estimate school argues, at least inferentially, that the 1928-1937 and postwar periods do, in fact, represent such normal growth trends. But the proposition that such brief periods are representative of the long run would appear highly debatable, and this is the reason for the longer period in the National Bureau survey. (Unfortunately for statisticians, there are never any periods that are entirely suitable for statistical comparison.) The 1928-1937 and postwar periods were short periods of intensive effort following longer periods of stagnation or wartime destruction. Experience suggests that economic progress comes in spurts, and typically such spurts have followed periods of stagnation. In the postwar period, the Soviet Union has not been alone in experiencing an economic spurt following in the wake of the war. Since the war, for example, France, West Germany, and Japan have all exhibited rates of industrial growth that compare quite favorably with that of the Soviet Union; and France, at least, has carried a sizable armaments burden, although not so heavy as that of the Soviet Union.

In view of the tendency for economic progress to come in spurts, we would be unwise to assume that the two shorter periods are any more representative of the long-run trend of the Soviet economy than is the 42-year period. The degree to which retardation may be expected must be based on evidence more broadly based than that provided by these historical periods. Undoubtedly, the weight of the factors enumerated does point to some tendency toward retardation of the rate of growth. But the resources available to the Soviet Union have also grown. The Soviet Union does not possess a market economy, and it does not need to wait for the growth of demand in order to spur industrial development. Therefore, there is no certainty that the Soviet Union will exhibit a degree of retardation comparable to that which has occurred in the United States. It may appear likely, but we cannot be certain. If the Soviet leaders possess Stalin's drive and if they can maintain the *élan* of the Soviet people (two highly debatable propositions), it is certainly not impossible, with their control over the rate of capital formation, that they could maintain steady and high rates of industrial growth over a long period.

3. The Long-Run Prospects

Up to this point, the following propositions have been put forth: (1) the Soviet industrial growth rate *at the present time* is substantially greater than the comparable American rate; (2) there has been some tendency to exaggerate the Soviet growth rate; (3) the weight of the factors points to some retardation of the rate of growth; and (4) if the Soviet leadership possesses the power, the will, and the determination, there is a possibility, however remote, that these factors may be overborne. What are the longer-run implications of these propositions for the comparative development of the Soviet and American economies?

There are several conclusions that may be drawn. The first and most important will prove unpalatable to the majority of Americans. It consists of this simple statement: *it is in the nature of the Soviet economy and society that the Soviet Union can, and probably will, catch up with American production in several of the basic industries.* In coal and iron-ore production (extractive industries), this is likely to occur in the next decade; but for most manufactured products, the process will take much longer. In steel, for example, which is so frequently taken as a symbol of industrial power, it is difficult to envisage the Russians matching us in terms of capacity before 1980 [9] at the earliest, and they have put greater emphasis upon steel than upon other industries. But the point is that, in time, the Russians can catch up in any particular industry that they desire to do so. The Soviet government controls both the direction of economic activity and the rate of capital accumulation. The Russians have, in the past, stressed basic industrial production, and continue to do so now. Even if Soviet industrial growth rates have been exaggerated, the over-all rate is substantially greater than in the United States. If they continue to stress the basic industries, they will catch up in time. In fact, it is not impossible, if the gap in industrial growth rates remains the same, that at some point, perhaps within the next century, the Russians will overtake us in terms of total industrial production. That event is too far in the future to concern us, but within the next several decades we must expect Soviet production in the basic industries to be roughly comparable to American production. Such an event seems inevitable in view of the wide differences in the *present* goals of the Soviet and American economies. If we wanted to prevent such an occurrence, quite likely the only way would have been to wage war when our relative power was at its maximum. This opportunity, if it can be called that, is now past. We must therefore be prepared to watch the gap narrow.

In view of this prospect, what should our attitude be? We should not be unduly alarmed. Of course, it might be observed, with American resources, we could easily stay ahead in the production of the basic industrial commodities. We might now embark on an expansion of our industrial capacity. But what would be the point? Would it serve some economic or strategic purpose—or would it be merely to stay ahead? In the nature of the American economy, it is assumed that industrial capacity must serve some purpose. The expansibility of American industry, when the need exists, is well-documented. For example, in the six-year period after the outbreak of the Korean War, American steel capacity was increased by 30 million tons, when it became clear that the demand existed. In absolute terms, this exceeded the expansion of Soviet steel capacity by some 7 million tons during the same period. Yet this prodigious expansion was accomplished without strain in order to meet the market. Undoubtedly, if we wished to stay ahead, we could spur the rate of industrial growth. But again it may be asked, what purpose would the additional capacity serve? Clearly, if there is no demand, it would not serve consumer well-being, and we would be better advised to make use of our resources in other ways. On economic grounds, we would be little short of lunatic if we created additional and superfluous capacity merely to stay ahead.

But the question arises as to whether industrial expansion might serve a strategic purpose. The strategic implications of economic capacity have already been considered. In the discussion of resource allocation, it was suggested that if we so desired, we could, by the proper mixture of incentives, spur the growth of capacity in any sector in which it was needed. Certainly, if it were deemed essential, the proper steps might be taken along these lines. But subsequently, it was argued that the strategic significance of general economic capacity has been very much exaggerated. Its importance lies in the fact that it may provide flexibility and rapidity and serve as a social emollient in meeting the demands of limited war. It might also provide reserve capacity for achieving recuperation from a nuclear war. Aside from these factors, however, the strategic importance of economic growth is chiefly psychological, in its impact on the underdeveloped areas.

Manifestly, a nation will at some point reach a plateau in terms of economic capacity, at which level all of the relatively modest demands of limited warfare may be met. It is true that expansion beyond this level may provide greater assurance of recuperation in the event of nuclear warfare, but the relationship of economic capacity and nuclear warfare is so nebulous that there are no conceivable bench marks for determining the suitability of the recuperative power provided by economic capacity in the post-attack period. Even in this contingency, the advantages of additional capacity may be doubted; to expand capacity simply for this purpose would be to pay for a costly and possibly useless form of insurance in the face of the unknown. Consequently, after a certain point has been reached, the *strategic* importance of additional industrial capacity rapidly declines. It might be said that this plateau represents a stage of industrial plenty, similar in some respects to a condition of nuclear plenty. After a position of industrial plenty has been attained, it makes as little strategic sense to add to industrial capacity as it does to add to the stockpile of megaton bombs when the stockpile has reached such proportions that all potential foes may be destroyed three times over.

After major powers have reached the plateau of industrial plenty, differences in relative economic capacity provide no strategic advantage, aside from the issues of the disposition of that capacity, and its relative vulnerability to attack. To be sure, it has been pointed out that *at the present time* the vast superiority of American over Soviet economic resources provides the West with a strategic advantage. But this is true only in the sense that the United States has reached a position of industrial plenty and the Soviet Union has not. This should not be taken to mean that the Soviet Union does not possess sufficient industrial resources to wage an effective war of the conventional type, if she should bend her efforts in that direction, but Soviet ambitions are numerous, and the Russians do not possess the resources to accomplish all their desires—rising living standards, further industrial expansion, a bold international policy, and maintenance of a high level of military preparedness. High Soviet aspirations, combined with a lower level of resources, have meant that the Russians have subjected their economy to continual strain. Because their system operates under forced draft, it may be less adaptable than is our own to sudden demands upon its resources. This implies that the West may subject the Russians to harassment as they attempt to attain their objectives. But it would be inadvisable to overstress this advantage, for a reduction by the Russians of their domestic goals would free an impressive array of industrial power for their strategic objectives. In several sectors of their economy, the Russians already possess sufficient capacity for all strategic needs. Under any circumstances, moreover, it would be unwise to exaggerate the importance of sheer industrial power. The Russians, like the Germans before them, have demonstrated a remarkable ability to make do with less.

Until the Russians reach that pleasant plateau at which all potential strategic demands are within the capacity of their industrial mobilization base, we in the West will possess some strategic advantage, and it is desirable that the advantage *disappear as slowly as possible*. However, the time period that will elapse before the advantage disappears will depend on the growth of Soviet capacity taken by itself rather than on its relationship to American capacity. Harassment is open to us, but speeding up our own rate of growth will not delay the Soviet achievement of a condition of industrial plenty. Since the strategic significance of additional capacity soon diminishes, and since no economic function is served by creating for production not desired by consumers, it would be foolish for the United States to embark deliberately on an industrialization drive at this date simply to stay ahead of the Russians in certain lines of industry. Industrial growth in the United States is desirable when it serves some purpose, but it is hardly an end in itself. We must expect the centrally controlled Soviet economy, if it continues to pour its resources year after year into industrial expansion regardless of the desires of consumers, to close the gap gradually in industrial production, and even to surpass us in certain categories of output.

We would be making a serious error if we were to accept the Stalinist yardstick of comparison. The fundamental ethos of the Soviet Union—based, as it is, on the desire to catch up with and surpass the advanced capitalist countries in terms of *per capita* industrial production—is a phenomenon that can only be described as "neurotic." The significance of purely quantitative norms has been terribly overestimated, yet we in the West have shown an unhealthy tendency to accept these norms as a basis for competition. The differences between the Soviet and American economies mean that the requirements of the two societies are not identical. In many ways, the Soviet Union is a "hardship economy" that must exert greater efforts to obtain the same results achieved with greater ease in the more congenial American setting. Take the case of coal production, in which Soviet output has almost reached the American level. The immensity of the Soviet land mass and the rigor of its climate are not blessings, except during periods of invasion. It has been estimated that one-third of Soviet coal production is consumed in transporting it to the point where it is needed. More coal is required to provide physical comfort for its citizens in winter. Should these facts be disregarded in comparing Soviet coal output with American output? Or should the facts that coal is an inferior fuel for many purposes, and that American railroads have been completely dieselized, while Soviet railroads are just starting the transition, be ignored in the comparison? Or should we neglect the declining quality of Soviet coal production, since lignite now constitutes some 30 per cent of production, as opposed to 4 per cent in 1928, with a corresponding decline in calorific content of 12 per cent?

Clearly, the significance as well as the physical quantity of production must be considered. The Soviet Union now produces 30 per cent more passenger railroad cars than does the United States; its production is at the American level of 1890, prior to the automotive revolution. Should we compete in what so many consumers regard as an inferior form of transportation? The Soviet Union is far ahead in both production and consumption of hard liquor on a *per capita* basis. Is *per capita* liquor consumption a gauge of the progress of society? In other words, conditions in the Soviet Union are such that the average citizen feels obliged to imbibe liquor in quantities greater than Americans have been in the habit of consuming since around 1870. Here is one quantitative record about which the Soviets have been disturbed, but it is illustrative of the folly of quantitative comparison of a wide range of goods.

It is an unhealthy sign that Americans have accepted production statistics of specific items as a serious form of competition. Clearly, the prosaic features of Soviet industrialization goals lend themselves more to jest[10] than misguided alarm and imitation (the sincerest form of flattery). Few features of Communized life are less appetizing than the spectacle of officials reciting dull statistics on the *per capita* production of granulated sugar. Surely Western civilization can provide goals of life more inspiring than this dreary spectacle.

If we are sensible, we will not be unduly disturbed as the Soviets reduce the gap with the West. What we cannot avoid— or, similarly what it would be folly to compete with—we might as well learn to accept and, if possible, to enjoy. There are several ironical aspects to Soviet development for us to consider. Not the least of these is the spectacle of a Marxist society inaugurating the age of plenty by exploitation of the workers, and with total indifference to the desires of consumers. In the long run, the level of material prosperity must rise, and it will be interesting to observe the softening effects on the Soviet character, as the stern Soviet virtues are dissolved in an orgy of luxury and sloth. It has frequently been said that "a revolution devours its children"; in the Russian case, however, the revolutionary process has continued for so long that, in the end, the children are likely to devour the revolution.

One additional aspect of the long-run implications of a rapid rate of industrial growth should be considered, and that is its psychological impact on the underdeveloped countries. Undoubtedly, if the underdeveloped lands continue to stress the growth of industrial capacity as opposed to the levels of living (and this seems to be a general characteristic), the appeal of the Soviet example and of totalitarian techniques increases. This is a misfortune for the West, but it hardly pays to compound the misfortune by stressing industrial growth in our propaganda, when the underlying importance of Soviet industrial growth is essentially propagandistic. It is ill-advised to stress quantitative norms in a statistical war that we are likely to lose. It is the level of living that we should stress rather than industrial growth. If the underdeveloped areas are impressed by purely quantitative norms and reject the grossly materialistic West for the higher aspiration of increased production targets, so much the worse for them. It cannot be prevented, in any event.

4. A SOVIET BUSINESS CYCLE?

One interesting long-range possibility that has not previously been considered, because it is sheerly speculative and is more of an economic curiosity than a factor bearing directly upon the issue of national security, is that of a Soviet business cycle. In all of the recent discussions concerning economic trends and prospects for the Soviet economy, surprisingly little attention has been paid to the possibility of sizable fluctuations. The experts continue to argue over the rate of Soviet economic growth, and in the nature of the problem, definitive conclusions have not been reached. The following facts, however, do stand out: the Russians are devoting a substantial proportion of their production to capital formation—more than 25 per cent of the total; investment is concentrated in industry, particularly the basic industries; in recent years, Soviet industrial production has been growing at a rate substantially in excess of present American rates of growth, and comparable to the rate of growth in the period of most rapid expansion of American industry, 1880-1929.

The latter date, 1929, should be at least suggestive. All the knowledge that economists have painfully acquired concerning business cycles suggests that a sizable conjuncture is in the making in the Soviet Union—how severe remains to be seen. In their writings, the great business-cycle theorists from Juglar to Schumpeter have emphasized the following factors as the *real* underlying causes of cyclical fluctuations: an intimate connection between growth and instability, the pulsating nature of innovational processes, imbalances between the capital-goods and the consumer-goods industries, and the principle of acceleration of demand. Current assessments of the Soviet emphasis on economic growth clearly suggest that in the Soviet case we may find all of the underlying elements of the "real" business cycle.[11] No society has ever placed more emphasis upon growth; in no society has the imbalance between the capital-goods industries and consumer-goods industries been more spectacular; and in no society has the attempt been greater to compress the innovational process into a short span of time. Finally, in no society have the potential acceleration effects been greater, because of the unique dependence of the demand for final goods upon the process of growth itself.

The significance of these factors may be indicated most quickly by delving into the operation of the accelerator principle. This principle refers to the phenomenon that the demand for investment goods depends upon the *rate of change* rather than *level* of the demand for final goods. A period of rapid growth requires an expansion of the capital-goods industries to a level in excess of the long-run demands upon those industries. To take a simple example, if the demand for shoes is growing, the capital-goods industry in question, the shoe-machinery industry, will be under extra pressure because it must supply *new* machinery for an *expanding* market, not merely replacement machinery for a stable market. When, however, there is a decrease in the rate of increase of demand for shoes, there will be a mild depression in the shoe-machinery industry. As the demand for shoes levels off, the shoe-machinery industry will have excess capacity, since it will only be called upon to replace shoe machinery that is wearing out or becoming obsolescent. It will no longer be called upon to expand the production base of the shoe industry, and consequently its rate of activity will slacken—even though there has been no decrease in the demand for the final product, shoes.

What is true in the example for the shoe-machinery industry seems applicable to Soviet industry as a whole. To a remarkable degree, the final use of the output of Soviet industry (what we would call "demand" in a market economy) is to provide the capital goods for the further expansion of industry. A high rate of investment is necessary to absorb the type of goods that Soviet industry produces. A sudden reduction in the rate of growth and, consequently, a reduction in capital-goods requirements would place many Soviet industries in a condition of excess capacity. On a vast scale, it would seem that at some future date the Russians will be forced to consider this issue.

The Russians have placed great stress upon the basic industries, but in order for the output of those industries to be used effectively, a high rate of investment activity must persist. Suppose, for example, that in the steel industry, the rate of expansion of the Fifth Five-Year Plan, 12 per cent a year, had been maintained;[12] then, by 1968 the Russians would have a capacity of roughly 150 million tons. In what ways could the Russians use this immense output of steel? At the present time, most steel production is used either for investment purposes or for the production of military hardware. The steel industry itself, as it expands, absorbs a substantial proportion of steel production. The greater the steel production and the production of other basic industries, the greater is the necessity of maintaining a high rate of growth simply to absorb that production.

The problem of absorption of the output of her industries will grow, as long as the present emphasis on industrial expansion is continued. Increasingly, the Russians will be faced with a dilemma: they may either maintain the rapid pace of expansion, thus using the supply of industrial materials, and put off the long-run problem; or they may reduce the rate of investment and face the possibility of reduced production and underemployment of men and equipment in the basic industries. To some extent, the problem may be tempered by the diversion of industrial materials to consumer-goods production. But the production of consumer durables, even at the American rate, does not absorb all of our steel output; a major portion of steel capacity must be used for investment purposes or not at all.

The Soviet Union must anticipate some fluctuations in the use of its industrial facilities. If she were to maintain the pace of industrial expansion that she desires, within a decade or two, the issue might be resolved with staggering force. The greater the present neglect of the possibility, the more violent will be the subsequent adjustment. The problem, in short, is that the growth of Soviet industrial capacity is outstripping a rather narrow consumption base. Consequently, unless the Russians soon begin the process of conversion of their industry, they will be faced at some point in the future with the dilemma of whether to use industrial capacity simply to expand capacity further or whether to accept the consequences of structural maladjustments in their economy by permitting unemployment and idle capacity.

Differences between centrally controlled and market economies must, of course, be taken into consideration. The Soviet economy is capable of making certain adjustments that may not be possible in market economies. Soviet industry does not produce for markets, and may continue to operate irrespective of the use made of output. Production could be discarded or wasted in one manner or another. There are indications that the Russians have, on occasion, already employed some such devices in order to deal with troubles essentially cyclical. The manifestations of cyclical forces may be different under the two economic systems, but they exist, nevertheless, in both systems. Disguising excess capacity is not the same as eliminating it—and the possibilities of effective disguise diminish as the volume of excess capacity grows. To be sure, the Russians may have to deal only with real cyclical factors, and not with the crumbling of the financial system, which played so large a role in the Western collapse of the thirties. For this reason, the 1929 analogy may not provide the correct inference, since the American depression would have been much milder had the real factors alone been operative. Nevertheless, the Soviet Union can no more abolish the effects of disproportion between the capital-goods and consumer-goods industries than it could abolish the rate of interest, which represents the productive efficiency of capital under any economic system. Clement Juglar, the early French analyst of business cycles, stated in his most famous apothegm that *the unique cause of a depression was the preceding prosperity.* "Prosperity," in the technical sense, means a period of rapid capital formation, through which the Soviet economy has been going. We have learned that instability is the price of rapid growth, and in the course of time the Russians are likely to gain this knowledge as well.

The choice confronting the Soviet Union is clear. It might permit growth to taper off by degrees, and thereby permit the gradual adjustment of industrial production. The fact that there has been in the past few years a sizable reduction in the Soviet growth rate may indicate that the Russians have encountered and recognized this type of difficulty, and are attempting to make intelligent adjustments. If this is so, it would tend to suggest that there has been a permanent retardation in the rate of industrial growth. However, it seems more likely that the recent difficulties have been simply fortuitous, and that *their ideological outlook prevents the Russians from perceiving the conversion problem.* In the Soviet setting, industrial growth has both an ideological and a propagandistic role, and the passion for industrialization probably continues unabated. The Russians may choose the other alternative and push on with the drive to catch up with the West in terms of *per capita* industrial production, particularly in the basic materials. In this case, the later adjustment problem will be correspondingly more massive. Under the Soviet system, to be sure, industry could be kept in production whether or not there was any use for the output. But it must be doubted that even the Soviet system could long tolerate the massive misuse or waste of productive effort. Ultimately, the adjustment problem would have to be met, and this would mean idle resources and reduced output—although not necessarily the type of unemployment found under free enterprise.

Soviet passage through such a time of troubles might evoke an attitude of malicious enjoyment in the West. No doubt, there would be an element of poetic justice in observing a Marxist economic system suffering from crises despite the absence of the *bourgeoisie,* and ultimately because of the lack of purchasing power on the part of the exploited workers. It would constitute an entrancing bit of historical irony, except for the possibility that, in true Leninist fashion, the Soviet Union might be tempted to find an outlet for its surplus capacity in the form of foreign (that is, imperialist) adventures.

To speculate in this fashion means, of course, that we must take a long-range view, and before such a period might be reached, a revolution could occur in the world power structure, in which the Soviet Union might become more closely associated with the West. But in the meantime, consideration of the possibility of fluctuations in the Soviet Union does serve a further purpose, reminding us that the operation of economic systems is more similar than persons on both sides of the Iron Curtain like to think. When nations are confronted with industrialization, their problems are likely to be similar—mass organization, bureaucracy, economic balance, and change versus security. The major differences between systems appear in their social and political ramifications, rather than in the economic structure. The equivalence of the economic pressures of industrialization may be observed in the recent tendency for the methods of economic organization in Soviet Russia and the West to draw closer together in certain respects. In the West, we have moved closer to national economic integration through greater centralized control, while the Russians have been making sporadic movements toward greater decentralization. Since so much parallelism exists, ultimately the success of an economic system depends not merely upon the system itself, but upon the attitudes, the will, and the determination of the men who operate it. In the Soviet case, we have seen that an economic system that is inefficient in the sense of satisfying the desires of consumers may be highly efficient in the development of industrial power, because of the fierce resoluteness of the men who run it. It would be an error to prejudge the efficiency of an economic system purely on the basis of *a priori* preferences.

8

THE UNDERDEVELOPED AREAS:
ECONOMIC PROSPECTS

In attacking the problem of the possibilities of economic progress in the underdeveloped areas, it may be wise at the outset to sketch the *general sort of problems* facing these areas. It must be emphasized, of course, that the areas represent a heterogeneous group, differing substantially in many respects and bound together only by their present relative poverty. In the second section, the specific cases of China and India will be considered: first, because Asia has come to be the main focus of the problem of development; secondly, because these two countries are the largest and are roughly representative of much of the rest of Asia; and thirdly, because there has been some attempt to narrow the complex policy issues involved into a microcosm of the comparative performances of India and China. In the third section, we will attempt to deliberate upon the general economic facts that cast light on the policy questions to be discussed subsequently.

It is a tricky problem to generalize about the underdeveloped areas, bound together as they are, not by the similarity of economic conditions, but by the psychological bond of mutual poverty. It would be unwise to treat the problem of all underdeveloped countries as inherently similar. Some are underdeveloped in the sense that they are underpopulated and the natural resources of the country have not been fully exploited. The solution to the problem in this case is simple—just develop.

Iraq and Brazil might fall into this category, but in a real sense, by this criterion, it is more fitting to call Australia or Canada underdeveloped than India or Egypt. Others—and these are by far the most important cases—are referred to as "underdeveloped" only by courtesy, since quite commonly their natural resources, particularly their agricultural resources, have been developed quite extensively. Such countries are called "underdeveloped" because of the extremely low *per capita* incomes, but the natural-resource base relative to the population may be skimpy, and the prospects for development much more ample in a land with higher incomes. Typically, such countries are characterized by a shortage of capital and the engagement of the bulk of the population in subsistence agriculture. Frequently, there is a burdensome excess of population, although this condition does not apply universally. Manifestly, the reasons for calling Iraq, India, Bolivia, Greenland, and the Sahara "underdeveloped" vary. Iraq possesses great natural resources and an adequate flow of capital, but is troubled by social and political instability. India possesses political stability, but lacks the capital resources for development and struggles with a staggering population problem. The last three are not only undeveloped but, to varying degrees, undevelopable. Only under rare circumstances can extensive industrial, commercial, or agricultural development take place in the high mountain regions of the world such as Bolivia or Tibet, though undoubtedly some amelioration of living conditions can be achieved. Greenland has no agricultural resources, and what natural resources it possesses are inaccessible. The Sahara cannot, under present technological conditions, serve as the focus for large-scale development.

Plainly, therefore, it is difficult to form a composite picture of the underdeveloped areas. In this study, the term will be used without precision to apply to all regions in which *per capita* income is low—$200 a year or less—but this embraces more than two-thirds of mankind.

1. THE GENERAL PROBLEMS

Despite the wide disparity of economic conditions and opportunities, it is, nevertheless, possible to discern certain characteristics that do apply quite broadly to the underdeveloped areas. Virtually all have expressed aspirations for higher standards of living, and for most of them this has connoted industrialization. Many have already adopted plans that look forward to steady economic advance. In most, the ferment for progress has disrupted social ties and stirred discontent. To these events, the dramatic phrase "the revolution of rising expectations" has been applied. But in addition to the widespread similarity of attitudes, virtually all face, to a greater or lesser degree, an array of problems which can be summarized under five headings: breaking the social "cake of custom," capital formation, the population conundrum, the agricultural bottleneck and the problem of a balanced economic structure, and the planning "fetish." Although the list is not exhaustive, the items go to the heart of the major issues affecting the economic prospects of the underdeveloped areas.

Breaking the social "cake of custom." In the bad old days of international frankness and callousness, the countries now known as "underdeveloped" were referred to as "backward." This harsh term, displaying, to be sure, all of the chauvinism and cultural insularity that typifies mankind, points to an important fact. Typically, the underdeveloped lands are held back not merely by their poverty, but by a social system that resists the transition to modern economic life. The latter requires the movement of factors of production, economic rationality, the acquisitive instinct, and so on, but in the underdeveloped regions the pattern of life is governed by tradition.[1] Typically, life is carried on in accordance with the established customs within the setting of the agricultural village. The economy is nonmonetary; economic calculation plays an insignificant role in the determination of behavior. The process of development implies the disturbance of these ancient patterns. Labor must be siphoned off to urban areas, partly in response to economic motivation. A monetary economy is introduced; cash crops may replace subsistence crops. The familiar lines of authority are strained, and rational calculation replaces tradition as the guide to behavior.

The decay of the traditional pattern of life creates a problem that is belied by words like "backward" and obscured by words like "underdeveloped." The breakdown of the indigenous culture will, in itself, give rise to a serious social problem of restlessness. With the evaporation of the older pattern of standards and expectations, the individual, cast adrift with no resources but his own, feels the tinglings of frustration and resentment and is receptive to any political movement that will bring about a golden age. It is on such feelings that Communism feeds. Inevitably, development, under the best of circumstances, would be a long and painful process. When the term "backwardness" was popular, it was assumed that there was little intrinsic value in the native culture, but so long as the latter did not interfere with world (that is, Western) commerce, there was no objection to its survival. In principle, the term "underdeveloped" carries with it no such low evaluation of the traditional culture, yet in practice it is implicit that the older standards are outmoded and must be swept away. Inevitably, a low estimate is placed on both the merits and the staying power of the traditional way of life.

In economists' discussions of development, observations like "any defects or impediments in the market processes should be eliminated as rapidly as possible" are tossed off rather casually. The market imperfections in question happen to be the customs according to which social life has been carried on for generations. They are not readily eliminated in order to make way for progress. Moreover, these social customs have supplied the tethers of society; with their elimination, rootlessness flourishes, with all its promise for extremist movements.

The older attitudes die hard. A basic problem in improving economic organization is the lack of trained personnel—engineers, technicians, administrators, accountants, and the like. Since the ancient ways held it unseemly for educated people to engage in manual tasks, there exists some tendency for superfluous numbers to appear in the so-called "genteel" or "reflective" professions. Relatively speaking, there is a superfluity of lawyers, philosophers, political scientists, and economists. They appear to be more interested in the preliminary task of programming or philosophizing about development, rather than in the actual laboring for the stated goals. Consequently, a scarcity of trained technical or specialized personnel is one of the major obstacles to economic development. It is not an unmixed blessing that the intelligentsia constitutes the governing group in the underdeveloped lands.

Capital formation. In order for investment activity to be carried on successfully in any country, it is necessary, first, to free resources through the act of saving (that is, refraining from the consumption of all production), and, secondly, to have access to capital goods. It is most important to recognize the low capacity for savings characteristic of the underdeveloped areas. The bulk of the population is near complete destitution, with incomes at perhaps $50 a year. The higher-income groups are too small and frequently lack the inclination to contribute usefully to savings—savings taking the form of land acquisition or the acquisition of mercantile stocks, rather than investment in productive industry. Since aggregate income is extremely small and the percentage that will be saved is slight, the aggregate figure for savings must be small.

The problem of capital supply is further complicated by limited demand in underdeveloped areas. An individual, even on a very small income, might be willing to make some small-scale investments, if he were able to discern any market for the goods he could produce. But the prevailing poverty of the inhabitants implies that the potential markets for the commodities that could be produced are quite restricted. Thus low incomes, which hinder the growth of substantial domestic markets, act on the demand side to limit further the supply of capital, which could not be large under the most favorable of circumstances.

The limited domestic capacity to save and to invest may, of course, be supplemented by the inflow of foreign capital. In the past, this has been true. Moreover, foreign trade has supplied the means by which domestic savings can grow, since the increase in incomes in the export sector of the economy that arise from international specialization has played a crucial role in spurring growth in the past. But there has been an immense change in the international climate, in regard to both capital flows and international trade. The rise of nationalism has reduced both the opportunity for and the attractiveness of international capital flows. The presence of foreign capital is resented. Onerous restrictions are placed upon the level of earnings and the amount of profit remission. In addition, there is the ever-present threat of expropriation. It is not surprising the flow of capital is not strong. Moreover, many developing lands resent dependence upon foreign trade, which may well be the most effective form of economic activity. Foreign trade lies outside the scope of planning; it is regarded as demeaning. Better to build up domestic industry, but this means forgoing the advantages that trade has supplied in the past and, in many cases, can continue to supply today.

It is necessary to have access to capital goods for development, but in most underdeveloped lands, domestic industry cannot supply the need. Reliance upon foreign supply is unavoidable, but this implies a need for foreign exchange which neither export earnings nor the inflow of capital can supply. The greater the desire for industrialization, the greater will be the demands upon foreign exchange; yet the fervor of nationalism that accompanies development is likely at the same time to be reducing the availability of exchange.

In the early years of development, the demand for capital development may be especially great, because of the lack of those basic facilities which are a prerequisite to industrial expansion—roads, harbors, railroads, schools, and so on, the so-called "social overhead." Characteristically, creating the social-overhead capital is extremely expensive and time-consuming, yet pays low immediate returns in relation to the magnitude of the investment. An immediate hurdle is placed in the path of development; simultaneously, the foreign capital that previously filled the need has become more chary.

Finally, it is frequently the case that the lack of capital is not, in itself, the limiting factor. It has previously been observed that there is a shortage of trained personnel, the labor force is insufficiently trained, and the social structure is somewhat inflexible. Therefore, *the capacity of the economy to absorb capital may be limited,* even when the capital is available. In the absence of this barrier, however, the available supply of capital is insufficient in most cases to achieve the desired rate of growth.

The population conundrum. The most dismal of the prophecies of the dismal science was the Malthusian, which postulated that incomes could not for long rise above the level of subsistence, for the consequent increase in population would encroach upon any expansion of resources. There were too many mouths to be fed at "nature's mighty feast." Despite the modification of the original Malthusian dogma over the years, the danger remains that the excessive growth of population will wipe out the gains of economic progress. In several regions of the world, examination of the demographic statistics points to the conclusion that any prospective economic revolution will shortly be succeeded and eliminated by a Malthusian counterrevolution. Egypt, with its rich but limited resource base and high birth rate, is perhaps the clearest and most startling example. The International Bank for Reconstruction and Development, in approving a request for partial financing of the Aswan Dam, observed that this vast project would not actually increase Egyptian living standards, but instead only held out the hope of braking its rate of decline.

The world population is now some 2.75 billion; it is anticipated to be nearly 6 billion at the end of the century. But the rate of increase has been accelerating over time, due not to rising birth rates but to sharply falling death rates. In Ceylon, which is a frequently cited example, the death rate has fallen from 28.9 per thousand in the period 1920-1924 to 11 per thousand today. In the same period, the birth rate has declined from 38.5 to 37.9 per thousand. The net growth rate has therefore risen from 9.6 to 26.9 per thousand. This implies that a nation which had been "enjoying" (I use the term loosely) a demographic equilibrium is now expanding at a rate that will double the population roughly every generation, and one that will cause some deterioration in a moderately favorable economic situation. Unfortunately, it is just those regions in which economic prospects have been least favorable that the rate of population increase has been most rapid—that is, the underdeveloped areas.

However, the rapid expansion of population in the underdeveloped areas has not been solely a recent phenomenon. To be sure, the recent burst has been associated with the introduction of modern sanitary and medical techniques which have reduced the death rate. The impact of colonialism itself was roughly similar on nations that had been enjoying a demographic balance. The colonial regimes increased economic opportunities and provided a degree of personal security previously unknown. The result was not higher living standards but an enormous expansion of population made possible by this technological revolution. When the Dutch came to Java, for example, the population was approximately 4 million; when they departed, it had risen to 55 million. There seems little doubt that population growth will continue to interpose a barrier to increased levels of living.

The problem of agriculture in a balanced economy. The fourth problem is not distinct, but is closely intertwined with the first three. This is the problem of the agricultural sector and the crucial role it plays in economic development. In the absence of massive outside assistance, a developing economy must achieve economic expansion in a balanced way. Without provoking a crisis, agricultural production must expand rapidly enough to sustain industrial growth, but the agricultural sector of the economy normally is the least susceptible to stimulation and to government manipulation.

As a consequence, in the attempt to achieve development, Communist and non-Communist nations alike came up against the ineluctable agricultural problems, although they diverge on the appropriate solution. The root of the problem lies in the fact that the husbandman is an uncompromising traditionalist. From the standpoint of government officials, he is not easily socializable—in fact, not even sociable. He retains a zest for private property, that "little worm," as Nikita Khrushchev has recently referred to it. The peasant remains singularly unaffected by the demand to devote his energies to the abstract "welfare of the community." He remains, by and large, the complete individualist—unmodernized and unreconstructed.

An underdeveloped economy is primarily agricultural. In order to achieve economic progress, it is necessary to extract from the agricultural population an increased food surplus, for two reasons: to be able to feed a growing industrial population, and to infringe upon over-all consumption in order to obtain the savings that provide the possibility of investment. At a minimum, the same amount of food must be obtained from a diminished number of hands.

Man is controlled in his economic habits by either persuasion or compulsion. Under ordinary conditions of economic growth, when farmers have produced a surplus (or possess the resources and can be persuaded to produce a surplus), they may be persuaded to part with the surplus through the availability of consumer goods, which provide amenities and lighten the burden of abor by reducing the necessity for the self-supplying of goods. Under these conditions, in other words, we find the efficiencies that characterize the division of labor.

In the traditional agricultural societies of the type in which we are now interested, the methods of voluntary exchange have not been the route by which the non-agricultural population obtains its food supply. Characteristically, we find a sharply skewed distribution of income, in which the agricultural surplus is extracted by landlord, loan shark, merchant sharecropper, and the like. Society is organized to enforce this legal extraction of agricultural surplus from the peasantry. It is understandable that the peasantry becomes resentful of the "parasitical elements" that seemingly rob them of their hard-earned produce. It is on this hatred of the legal compulsion to provide for the rest of society that Communism relies in its quest for power in the underdeveloped nations. The road to power follows from the promise to relieve the peasant of the exactions of the loan shark or landlord, who may be taking 50 per cent of the crop or more.

Suppose the Communists obtain power by promising land to the peasants. In so doing, the mechanism for extracting a consumable surplus is abolished, and the regime is left face to face with the necessity of finding a substitute, through taxation, in order to supply agricultural goods. In order to obtain the necessary supplies, the regime must resort to naked compulsion or else provide incentives in the form of consumer goods. Under democratic regimes, the results may be similar. A democratic state that has not expropriated the village *bourgeoisie* is similarly under pressure to adopt reform measures which will sharply restrict the incomes and the role of the landlord and loan shark. Such action, by tending to reduce the agricultural surplus, will also tend to reduce the margin of resources available for investment. How can this vicious circle be broken?

To observe the problem in perspective, we might draw upon the early experiences of the U.S.S.R. During the period of the NEP (new economic policy), Lenin's plan was to obtain agricultural supplies through voluntarism—that is, "to give the peasant nag its head." The policy was frustrated because inadequate incentives were provided. In the years up to 1928, Russia was chronically plagued by what became known as the "scissors crisis"—a growing disparity between agricultural and industrial prices. The shortages and high prices of consumer goods led to a slackening of effort on the part of the peasantry and to the hoarding of grain. After a decade of unsatisfactory progress, it was Stalin's view that the Soviet Union must industrialize or perish. The peasantry had to supply the agricultural surplus without compensation in the form of consumer goods. At the outset of the First Five-Year Plan in 1928, Stalin was faced with the choice of collectivization (a method of compelling the provision of grain) or the necessity of pulling in his industrial horns. He chose the method of compulsion, and proceeded with collectivization, regardless of cost, which mounted into millions of lives. This is, by the way, an extraordinary example of the impact of the individual on history, hardly conforming to the theoretical tenets of Marxism.

Thus the Russians broke out of the vicious circle and achieved the only successful example of forced industrialization to date. Rather than permitting the prerevolutionary surplus to be dissipated into easier living for the peasantry, the state intervened, and it was the industrialization program that became the beneficiary of the now-departed upper classes. We must remember that the resources available to a Stalin are not necessarily available to nations now attempting development. For better or worse, the idea of democracy is afoot throughout the world; the technique of mass slaughter is not easily reconciled with the expectations of the newly "liberated" peoples. In addition, the

Russians had achieved, prior to the revolution, a relatively high degree of development. They had unutilized resources and a people traditionally submissive to despotic rule, so long as that rule was effective. The Russians achieved their breakthrough via the combination of brute force and favorable factors, but even then it was touch and go. The opportunities open to the Soviet Union are not available to the same degree in other lands. To be sure, there may be greater external assistance, but there is also external enmity, the pressure of military expenses, and less favorable economic circumstances.

In selecting the method of procedure for coping with the agricultural problem, the underdeveloped nations face a dilemma. If they rely upon relatively free markets and incentives, they may dissipate their resources upon light industry with little expansive power, and may be forced to forgo the heavy industrialization that they desire. They must also reckon with the additional possibility that their underfed populations may not desire consumer goods, but may prefer more food—thereby reducing the agricultural surplus which is the basis of savings and capital. This route probably means a modest rate of economic growth—too modest to satisfy the expectations that have been created in the developing regions.

On the other hand, as an alternative to persuasion, a government sufficiently potent *and* undemocratic may well embrace the other possibility for controlling economic behavior—direct compulsion. This is the path being followed by China. From the standpoint of the results achieved, it may well be the superior road. But if it runs into Khrushchev's "little worm"—the peasant's zest for private property—it may generate the passive or open resistance that could frustrate the achievement of the plan. An in-between program, with the provision of some consumer goods, may be the right type of temporizing, but it also means the slowing down of the rate of growth.

Oddly enough, it is the desire to industrialize and to achieve national self-sufficiency that has brought the agricultural problem to the fore. In the past, industrial growth might come fortuitously through foreign trade. Through trade, a nation might rely upon other nations to supply food or capital. But with the growing emphasis on nationalism, which in so many subtle ways undermines the basis for trade, economic growth must be balanced, and agriculture cannot be permitted to lag even temporarily. This would not be the case if there were truly a world economy; under those circumstances, balance between the agricultural and industrial sectors of the individual economy would not be required.

The planning "fetish." At the outset, it should be recognized that, in its proper setting, planning can be useful for a developing state. Provided that industrial development, in itself, is accepted as a national goal, management of the economy may contribute something to this specific end. This is particularly true when managerial ability is in short supply and the supply must be stretched to accommodate many purposes. Of course, these conditions would not pertain in a free economy in which ends are determined by the interaction of millions of individual decision makers and a specific form of development is not accepted as a national goal. In the underdeveloped countries, proper planning may, however, serve to spur growth.

Having said this, it must be observed that the penchant for planning has gone too far. It has been hailed as a panacea rather than as a limited technical instrument. Following the Soviet model, the plans are usually extended over a five-year period, rather than four or six. Paradoxically, it has not infrequently been American advisers who have encouraged a rather inflated notion of what planning can accomplish. At its best, a plan cannot serve as a blueprint for society, because achievements and difficulties cannot be foreseen. A plan must be flexible—in Stalin's words "a plan is a living thing, which may be changed en route." In early Soviet days, planning had been considered an exercise in the prediction of likely developments, rather than the active pursuit of specific goals. But even after the change of emphasis under Stalin, the need for flexibility was fully recognized. Oddly enough, in the underdeveloped areas which lack the instruments of compulsion and control available in Stalin's Russia, there is less recognition of the need for flexibility. Targets are more than aspirations which may or may not be achieved; they are firm commandments which the state can only neglect at its own peril.

Three misconceptions about planning are common.[2] First, planning does not necessarily create anything new; instead, to a considerable degree, a plan merely corroborates what would have occurred anyway in the absence of the plan. Second, planning need not necessarily be wise; in fact, it can lead the development of the economy in a direction other than the one for which it is best suited. Third, planning does not create additional resources for the society. Through planning, the illusion has been created that there are resources to be drawn upon which do not exist in fact. Moreover, planning in itself can be an expensive process; instead of conserving administrative personnel in short supply, it is recklessly prodigal with them, and deprives the operating sectors of the economy of needed direction.

The greatest drawbacks to planning are that it may result in the creation of expectations that cannot be met, and it may create rigidities in a situation that is essentially fluid and in which flexibility provides the route to most rapid advance. The disease of "planitis" is particularly acute when resources are limited and society is controlled by the intelligentsia. Its symptom is paperwork. Although the United States has similar financial fetishes of its own,[3] since planning bulks larger in the underdeveloped areas, the unfortunate concomitants of its more extreme manifestations are naturally all the more important.

From this brief discussion of five general problems in achieving development, it should be clear that the barriers to economic expansion, if not unscalable, are imposing. It seems clear that increases in *per capita* income will not be large unless the population problem is brought under control, thereby allowing a better balance between population and resources. But when will this occur, if at all? The other difficulties suggest that, at best, progress will be slow and perhaps sporadic. The situation, unfortunately, is ripe for the breeding of romance rather than realism. In the underdeveloped lands, economists are not infrequently more missionaries of the impossible than they are

detached observers, pragmatically weighing the limits of resources. If the role of the economist, under such circumstances,
is the trivial though indispensable one of reminding us, on
occasion, that a people cannot consume and invest more than
they produce, then this role cannot be played by observers in
the underdeveloped lands without running the risk of losing
all influence. The wish is father to the thought, and foreign
advisers are not in a position to tell their "clients" the truth.
They must romanticize about free capital and the availability
of nonproductive labor and so on, implying painless growth.
Both economically and sociologically, growth is painful and
disruptive; but one cannot afford objectivity in an era of mes-
sianic fervor. The rude awakening comes only after the plans
have failed.

2.   CASE STUDIES: CHINA AND INDIA

It is appropriate now to examine in detail, in a set of case
studies, the programs and the difficulties posed for individual
nations. However, it is advisable to recall the wide variety of
conditions prevailing in the underdeveloped areas, and the
consequence of this variety—that no particular case study can be
typical. It is particularly important to emphasize this point in
view of the choices of China and India for case studies. China
is a law unto itself, and it is chosen for obvious reasons. China's
great expanse, its immense population, and the fact that it is
the only power in Asia attempting to industrialize along the
lines of the Soviet model—all point to the necessity of including
China in the survey. India, to be sure, is the largest non-Communist nation in Asia; it is one of the few with a well-articulated
program for development. Yet there are drawbacks to the inclusion of India in this survey. It may encourage the common
assumption that the contest in Asia is a two-sided one. From
what has been said about the variety of conditions in the underdeveloped areas, India ought not to be taken categorically as
representative of the countries even in Asia, still less of the
relatively underpopulated countries of Africa or South America.
It has frequently been stated that the crucial test for the

free world is whether a country like India can achieve a rate of economic progress comparable to that of a totalitarian state like China. Though this sort of statement does conform to the ruling ideas and passions of our era, it simplifies the intricate problems of American diplomacy by making the economic factor determinate; and by so doing, as we shall see, it makes the future of the West in Asia appear even bleaker than it otherwise might. Furthermore, it overdramatizes the conflict in Asia by implicitly understating the diversity of conditions, both economic and political, that prevail. In the absence of the use of military force, it is doubtful whether the rest of Asia will follow India's path; in fact, the reverse might be expected. Iraq's position, for example, is entirely different; its economic possibilities are impressive, but it is the political situation that is doubtful. Surely, Pakistan and, to a lesser degree, Burma are not likely to follow the trail blazed by their larger neighbor, toward whom they have hostile or ambivalent feelings. Nevertheless, despite the danger of fortifying the impression that India is the surrogate of the West in a two-sided struggle for Asia, it is desirable to include India because of its own importance in the survey. India, moreover, illustrates the obstacles to development even under circumstances that are politically most favorable.

Economic conditions in China and India exhibit many similarities, as well as several dissimilarities—and the dissimilarities are growing as a result of the divergent social organizations. Both nations are relatively overpopulated, highly agrarian countries characterized by extremely low incomes and low *per capita* industrial facilities. India has had the initial advantage of a trained civil service, somewhat greater industrial development, and a more efficient railroad network. China has a somewhat superior natural-resource base. Until about 1950, the economies of both countries had been deteriorating—as a result of the struggle with the Japanese and the civil war in the case of China, and as a result of World War II and the horrors of the partition in the case of India. Both nations had experienced declining standards of living since the thirties. For both at the end of their times of troubles, there existed a twofold problem:

the achievement of economic rehabilitation, and the spurring of additional economic progress.

Let us attack the problem chronologically, and turn first to China. In 1949, when the Communists obtained control of the mainland, the Chinese economy was operating at a low level. In that year, the estimated *per capita* income was a mere $27. According to the Communist figures, industrial production was only 56 per cent of the pre-1949 peak level, while agricultural production was some 25 per cent below the previous peak.

By 1952, an impressive recovery had been achieved by the regime. The precise nature of the recovery is difficult to judge because the statistical data are neither comprehensive, exact, nor consistent. According to government sources, production had been raised above the previous peak; despite the expansion in output, this particular claim is difficult to verify. On the basis of the given data, it is impossible to tell whether Manchuria was included in the prewar estimates; and since Manchuria was the most industrialized part of China, there would be a considerable difference. Moreover, sometimes the pre-1949 peak performance is falsified by changing the nature of the statistical comparison. Grain production (inclusive of soybeans), for example, was reported as 110 million metric tons in 1949; by 1952, it had risen to 163.9 million metric tons. Communist pronouncements maintained that this was a sizable increase over previous peak levels, but careful analysis of the statistics, including those for both Manchuria and certain minor crops not included in grain production in the prewar estimates, suggests that the total was only slightly more than the 1931-1937 average, if, indeed, there was any gain at all.[4] This is not to belittle the vast expansion of almost 50 per cent that did occur between 1949 and 1952, yet it does suggest that the comparison with the previous levels was not nearly so favorable as the regime would like to have us believe. By using low-base years and manipulating the included data, the regime has attempted to exaggerate its accomplishments. All in all, however, rehabilitation had been accomplished by 1952, and the stage was set for spurring economic growth.

The Chinese have chosen the route of centrally planned development. In the First Five-Year Plan (1952-1957), the undisguised emphasis was placed upon heavy industry. Of the funds for capital construction, 58.2 per cent were scheduled to be devoted to industry, with only 7.6 per cent designated for agriculture and allied resources. Table II presents some production statistics for certain key industries in 1952 and 1957, and, in addition, the stated goals of the First Five-Year Plan and the approximate goals of the Second Five-Year Plan ending in 1962. It will be noted that for the First Five-Year Plan, with the exception of oil production, all production targets for industries *that are not affiliated with agriculture* (such as steel, coal,

TABLE II

SELECTED PRODUCTION STATISTICS FOR MAJOR INDUSTRIAL AND AGRICULTURAL COMMODITIES, COMMUNIST CHINA—
1952, 1957 (target); 1957, 1962 (target)

Commodity	1952	1957 (target)[a]	1957	1962 (target)[b]
Steel (million tons)	1.35	4.12	5.24	12.0
Coal (million tons)	63.5	113.0	123.9	230.0
Electric power (million kwh)	7.3	15.9	19.0	44.0
Petroleum (million tons)	0.44	2.01	1.44	5-6
Cement (million tons)	2.9	6.0	6.7	12.5
Paper (million tons)	.37	.66	.91	1.5-1.6
Cotton cloth (million bolts)	111.6	163.7	156.2	235-260
Sugar (million tons)	.45	1.10	.84	2.4-2.5
Food grain (million tons)	154.4	181.6	185.0	240.0
Soya beans (million tons)	9.5	11.2	9.7	12.5
Cotton (million tons)	1.30	1.64	1.64	2.15

Source: *Economic Survey of Asia and the Far East 1957*, United Nations (Bangkok: 1958).

[a] These are the original target figures of the plan. Subsequently, the targets were revised to bring them in line with production developments.

[b] The 1962 targets, originally fixed on September 28, 1956, were revised on December 7, 1957—upward for coal, power, and steel, but downward for cement. In agriculture, the food-grain target was reduced from 250 to 240 million tons, and the raw-cotton target from 2.4 to 2.15 million tons. The later figures are included here. No attempt has been made to update them in view of the reported targets of the "great leap forward." The contrast between the 1962 target of 240 million tons for grain production and the reported output of 350 million tons in 1958 should be noted, however.

electric power, cement, and paper) appear to have been exceeded. On the other hand, those industries affiliated with agriculture (cotton cloth, sugar) failed to reach the targets. In this respect, the accomplishments have been similar to those of the Soviet Union. It will be observed that the gains have been impressive in relative, if not in absolute, terms. It may be that the low industrial base from which the development started has eased the problems of achieving large *relative* expansion at the outset. In any event, the planned 90 per cent expansion of industrial output during the first plan appears to have been achieved, roughly speaking. The official claim is that the goal was surpassed—industrial output expanding by 119 per cent, although this figure arouses the usual doubts concerning Communist composite indexes. It should be noted that in the last year of the plan, difficulties were encountered. It was reported that planned investment was cut back by 20 per cent and the budget ran unexpectedly into the red. These difficulties seem to have spread from the agricultural sector.

In agriculture, the results appear to have been less promising. The terminal plan target for grain production (including soybeans) was revised on several occasions. In 1957, it was hoped that grain production would reach 201 metric tons, somewhat above the original goal of 192.8 million metric tons, but somewhat below the revised goal of 202.2 million metric tons. The final figure reported, after a disappointing harvest, was 194.7 million metric tons. Over the five-year period, grain production rose by almost one-fifth—in absolute terms, an impressive expansion, and a rate of increase of approximately 3 per cent per year. But as Mao Tse-tung observed, the growth in grain production has been barely sufficient to keep pace with the needs of China's growing population. If the census figures may be believed, on a *per capita* basis, production appears to have remained *somewhat lower than in the period prior to the Sino-Japanese war.*

It was claimed that national income increased in the four-year period 1952-1956 by some 40 per cent—64 billion *yuan* to 90 billion *yuan*. (The official exchange rate is approximately 2.4 *yuan* to the dollar, but 3 *yuan* to the dollar probably gives a more accurate idea of its value.) This figure gives a misleading impression, however, of the rate of growth in China. First, starting from a low industrial base, any increase in industrial production for which the monetary value is high tends to increase the monetary value of national income at a rapid rate. Secondly, much of the growth occurred between 1952 and 1953, and to a lesser extent in the 1953-1954 period (the end of the Korean War strain). In the following years, the growth rate fell to a much lower level. Thirdly, the failure to report a figure for 1957 suggests that the regime considered the results unfavorable. Living standards, moreover, especially in food consumption, improved only very slightly in this period—a reflection of Chinese emphasis upon industrial expansion.

Clearly, by the end of the period of the first plan, the swift pace of the early years had been slowed. This was reflected in the poor agricultural picture and the slow growth of the industries dependent upon agricultural raw materials, which, it must be remembered, despite the stress on the heavy industries, constitute half of China's industry. Reports of food shortages, grain rationing, and bad harvests were sufficiently frequent to raise at least a question concerning the accuracy of Peiping's figures on grain production. In fact, it was suggested that the bad harvest of 1957 may have shaken the regime's control over the populace.

For reasons of its own, which undoubtedly included economic difficulties, the regime decided to delay the inauguration of the Second Five-Year Plan, which was presented to a Party congress in 1956. From the figures in Table II, it will be seen that the original version of the Second Five-Year Plan continued to stress heavy industry. Reports from China indicated that in the final revised version, much greater stress would be placed upon agriculture. Even before the delay of the second plan, Mr. Po-I-po, its director, had been laying much greater stress on the need for "flexibility" than hitherto.

It has now been recognized that agriculture represents the key to growth. The entire system is dependent to a marked degree upon agriculture—for food, for industrial raw materials, and as a source of foreign exchange to purchase capital goods, since extensive foreign assistance cannot enter into Chinese calculations. Maintaining a steady growth of industrial production would appear to be the easier half of the problem for the Chinese, but inevitably, whatever occurs in industry will reflect the achievements or the failure on the agricultural side. At the beginning of expansion, there are several "simple" ways to increase agricultural production through the use of insecticides, fertilizers, better seed, and so on. As soon as these possibilities are exhausted, however, the leeway for rapid improvement shrinks. Chinese planners, like the Russians before them, tended to simplify their problems by disregarding the major difficulties in agriculture. They fell into the habit of preparing their targets or projections by taking the yield on the most productive acreage and multiplying it by total acreage, thereby assuming that the yield on all acreage can be raised to the level of the best. But it is a simple fact that production will vary according to the quality of the land and labor, rainfall, climate, and the degree of mechanization. To achieve its agricultural goals, the regime had to invest much greater resources than had hitherto been assumed.

Recognition of the dependence of its industrial goals upon the performance in agriculture has been met only in part by a reduction of the targets for industry. Instead, the regime has increased the pressure on the countryside, and has diverted much of its energies and some of its investment program from heavy industry to agriculture and allied activities. Rightists and cadres of Party members alike have been sent to the countryside. Masses of peasants have been mobilized during slack seasons to contribute their time to the development of roads, dams, irrigation and flood-control projects, and the like. Despite setbacks and some unfavorable results of collectivization, the regime has pushed ahead. The methods it has employed have occasioned some surprise.

In September, 1958, the decision was announced that the society was to be organized into vast communes of producers, which would not only encourage greater production but enable the regime to increase its control over the populace. By the end of the year, the process was reported to have been completed, and the communes were said to be flourishing. The reaction of the peasantry can only be surmised, but it may be doubted whether, outside of a few "show" areas, the communes do more than exist on paper. The regime has reported, however, that its astonishing new target of 350 million metric tons of grain production in 1958 was surpassed, and it has projected a further 70 per cent increase for 1959. Such figures do suggest that the nature of Chinese statistics has been transformed, and that pure fabrication is now in the ascendant. The organization of the communes has been part of China's "great leap forward," in which it is supposed to become a great industrial power and overtake Great Britain in production in fifteen years. This is a relatively modest goal, for such an accomplishment, when population is taken into account, would mean that Chinese industrial production would only be one-fifteenth of the British level, on a *per capita* basis.

As part of this leap forward, China has concentrated on a more rapid expansion of steel production than that projected in the Second Five-Year Plan. A new target of 10.7 million tons for 1958 was reported to have been exceeded, and a similarly large increase was projected for 1959. In their spare time, Chinese adults and children were set to producing pig iron in backyard furnaces. These developments must be treated with healthy skepticism. To find parallels for the technological methods of production, one must retreat to antiquity. Even with the factor prices prevailing in China, they probably represent an enormous expense of effort with relatively little to show for it economically. The main purpose is probably propagandistic—to awaken enthusiasm among the population and to impress foreigners. At any rate, much of the crudely refined pig iron has proved to be unusable without further processing.

The new wildness of Chinese claims probably reflects underlying economic and political difficulties and a turning away from rational methods of dealing with these difficulties. An economic system operating under forced draft can accomplish only so much. It is clear that we have had less and less reliable information coming out of China. All we have is signs; one such sign is the almost complete cessation of exports at the end of 1958 and the beginning of 1959. Nevertheless, the regime does have

UNDERDEVELOPED AREAS: ECONOMIC PROSPECTS

sizable resources at its command which it may be able to mobilize to push forward with its goals. It would be folly, therefore, to predict the future.

Let us turn now to India. In some ways, the path India has followed is similar to that of China, yet the chronological sequence of steps has been reversed. Initially, the Indians concentrated on the agricultural sector with some success, and it was only after the decision was made to emulate the Chinese example and concentrate upon industry that difficulties were encountered. Recovery from the effects of war and partition was tardy in India; consequently, the First Five-Year Plan was intended to complete the recovery and at the same time create a foundation for future industrial expansion by concentrating on the agricultural sector of the economy. Thus, at the outset, the Indian program was sharply distinguished from the Chinese one, which had initially concentrated on industrial expansion. In Table III, some statistical data on various important sectors of the Indian economy are presented—for 1950-1951 and 1955-1956 (the period of the First Five-Year Plan), and the targets for 1960-1961 (the terminal date for the Socond Five-Year Plan). Examination of the figures will indicate that the purpose of the first plan was to set the stage for rapid industrial development by strengthening agriculture. More than one-fourth of India's total investment of $4.2 billion was devoted to agriculture and irrigation. In contrast, 7.6 per cent of China's $14 billion investment in its First Five-Year Plan was allocated to agriculture. Production of grain and cotton increased (though the relative rise was no greater than in China). In the industrial sphere, it is clear that the emphasis was upon supporting light industry (fertilizer, cement, cotton textiles, and paper), rather than upon heavy industry (steel, coal, and iron ore), although production of aluminum and electric power did grow impressively. In overall terms, the first plan must be regarded as successful. Over the period of the plan, Indian national income rose by 18 per cent from 9,110 *crores* of *rupees* to 10,800 *crores* (or, roughly, from $19 billion to $23 billion).[5] This represented a rate of increase of better than 3 per cent a year—considerably below the comparable Chinese figure, although the latter was undoubtedly inflated. In the period 1952-1956, the growth was particularly rapid, better than 2 per cent a year *per capita,* and this was reflected in rising living standards.

TABLE III

SELECTED PRODUCTION STATISTICS FOR MAJOR INDUSTRIAL AND AGRICULTURAL COMMODITIES, INDIA—1950-1951, 1955-1956, and 1960-1961 (target)

Commodity	1950-1951	1955-1956	1960-1961 (target)
Steel (million tons)	1.1	1.3	4.3
Coal (million tons)	32.3	38.0	60.0
Iron ore (million tons)	3.0	4.3	12.5
Aluminum (thousand tons)	3.7	7.5	25.0
Electric power (million kwh)	2.3	3.4	6.9
Cement (million tons)	2.7	4.3	13.0
Fertilizer (thousand tons)	101.0	500.0	2,170.0
Paper (thousand tons)	114.0	200.0	350.0
Cotton textiles (million yards)	4,618	6,850	8,500
Food grain (million tons)	54.0	65.0	75.0
Cotton (million bales)	2.9	4.2	5.5

Source: Government of India, Planning Commission, *Second Five-Year Plan,* 1956.

The Indians were much encouraged by the success of the plan and, in particular, by the fact that agricultural production had exceeded the targets of the plan. It was felt that the successful refurbishing of agriculture had laid a "certain foundation for future development," and that they could now embark on an industrialization program similar to that of the first Chinese plan. Certain facts about the first Indian plan ought, however, to be kept in mind. Bumper crops were, to a considerable degree, simply a consequence of unusually favorable monsoons. The plan itself was not, in the main, a governmental program for the spurring on of greater production; instead, it was a coordination of projects already afoot at the time the plan was promulgated. Some of the success may be attributed to the rehabilitation from the stagnant period following the partition. India did stage a marked recovery from the effects of war and partition, yet consumption levels remain somewhat lower than prewar.

The relative success of the first plan, plus the fact that the Chinese industrial growth had been even more spectacular (a comparison to which Indians, as well as others, are sensitive), induced the government to project for the second plan a much higher rate of growth—5 per cent a year. In the Second Five-Year Plan, emphasis was to be placed upon the long-deferred expansion of heavy industry. The impressive targets for steel, iron ore, coal, electric power, cement, and aluminum may be noted in Table III. With the exception of fertilizer, the growth of lighter industry was correspondingly de-emphasized. In contrast to the first plan, less than 20 per cent of the total was to go into agriculture and irrigation, with almost 60 per cent allotted to power, industry, mining, and transport and communications. More than half of total investment in industry was to go into steel capacity. Thus, the plan is, in a sense, the parallel of the Chinese First Five-Year Plan, with its even more drastic emphasis on heavy industrialization. It calls for an immense effort to double the level of investment to some $10 billion over the life of the plan[6]—with the rate of investment increasing from 7 per cent of GNP in the first year to 11 per cent of GNP in the terminal year.

The financing of the plan is of particular interest because, from the first, it has been recognized as a shaky structure. Of the contemplated $10 billion public expenditures, one-quarter (or $2.5 billion) was to be paid for by taxation, and another quarter by tapping internal savings through the sale of bonds. The third quarter was to be financed through the creation of additional money (currency inflation). It was hoped that external sources (that is, foreign loans and gifts) would contribute another $1.7 billion, and the final $800 million was simply referred to as the "gap" that would have to be covered from other internal sources not specified.

During the period of the plan, the foreign-exchange deficit was expected to be a little more than $2.3 billion. Foreign gifts, loans, and investment would, it was hoped, supply almost $1.9 billion. The balance of the foreign-exchange gap would be filled by the drawing down of India's foreign-exchange reserves by some $420 million over the five-year period.

Little comment is needed on the financial soundness of the plan. From the first, it was recognized as a gamble. It is risky to launch a program based upon the deliberate inflation of the currency, the using up of a quarter of the nation's foreign-exchange reserves, and the expectation of enormous foreign assistance. The Indians chose to take this gamble. It was felt that the rate of advance in living standards under the First Five-Year Plan had been *too slow to be satisfactory*—particularly in view of the tacit comparison with China—and it had to be speeded up. It was argued that to hope for less was to admit defeat. As a matter of fact, Indians began to take a little pride in deliberately ignoring the arithmetic of caution. Mr. T. T. Krishnamachari, the finance minister at the time, observed that the plan was not "an exercise in budgeting by an accountant." Eventually, doubt came to be treated as a sacrilege. When the World Bank mission to India mildly suggested in its survey that the plan was somewhat too ambitious, and urged caution with respect to deficit financing, the response was one of injured feelings.[7]

Economically, the results have been little short of catastrophic. Even with considerable outside assistance, it may be that some of the damage will be permanent. Within a year, the $420 million in foreign exchange that was to be used over the entire plan period had been exhausted. A change in the law governing legal requirements for foreign-exchange holdings provided an additional $210 million, but through the summer of 1957, the drain continued at $15 million a week. In November of 1957, the government took the decision to throw all of its remaining sterling balances of about $700 million into the gap. In 1957, foreign-exchange holdings of the Reserve Bank fell by almost $500 million, and the drain continued into 1958, though at a reduced rate.

India was thus plunged into a foreign-exchange crisis. Commercial credit became increasingly hard to obtain. As a result of the world boom, import prices rose, adding to the difficulties. Domestic inflationary pressures were also felt. The rapid rise of cereal prices led to demands for increased wages. The government's initial response to the rising costs of the program was to *increase the total expenditures* in order to save the plan. But in the budget of 1957, the finance minister recognized that too much was being attempted, and called for "some rephasing of the plan." He was insistent, however, that what was called the "core" of the plan—that is, investment in steel, coal, transportation and power—was inviolable. Even to achieve this goal, massive outside assistance was required, and, prior to his resignation, Mr. Krishnamachari was moderately successful in obtaining additional assistance from the United States and West Germany.

The assumptions upon which the plan was based have proved to be invalid. The estimates of the costs and of the foreign-exchange deficit were too low; the estimates of the Indian capacity for saving and of the ability to absorb currency inflation were too high. These developments might have been foreseen if there had been a more cautious appraisal in the planning period. In any event, the plan has disrupted the economy. There is the foreign-exchange crisis; there is inflation; there is the threat of a partial breakdown of the economy and the spread of unemployment. In the attempt to save the plan, the budget of 1957 put increased pressure on private firms—and even beforehand, the attitude toward private enterprise had been ambivalent, almost pathological. The determination of the government to carry through the core of the plan, whatever the cost, as expressed by Mr. Nehru,[8] has provoked criticism in India. "The plan was made for the people," observed one publication, "not the people for the plan." The difficulties have been compounded by unfavorable harvests. Yet there is one favorable result, and that is a growing note of realism—a recognition that aspirations based upon hope rather than resources tend to be disruptive rather than beneficial.

Broadly speaking, it would appear that both China and India have been heading in the same direction. China discovered the defects of simply forging ahead with industrialization, and has increasingly placed more emphasis upon primary production. The Indians, after some success in agriculture in their first plan, have bitten off a larger lump of industrial expansion than they can chew. It may be that the Indians also will decide that the expansion of heavy industry is too expensive in the early stages of economic development, and will turn back toward light industry and agriculture.

At the present time, it would appear that the long-run prospects for China are more promising than those for India. The rate of capital accumulation is between two and three times as great. With centralized direction, both the rate and the direction of capital investment are easier to control. Using her energetic population as a form of human capital, China has been able to mobilize masses of men for developmental projects. The slack periods in the eternal time pattern of a peasant population are now used "fruitfully." At the moment, therefore, China's prospects are more favorable, but much depends upon the question of whether the collectivized population will respond as demanded. The regime is driving hard, and there is a point beyond which human endurance cannot be stretched; an explosion is not impossible. Barring this contingency, however, there seems to be no reason to doubt the capacity of China to outstrip India. It is more difficult to succeed, in the case of India, since her economy is a halfway house, lacking the mechanism of compulsion. India has been unable, moreover, to energize her population to the same degree that China has.[9] She has aspired to accouterments of the welfare state, while lacking the resources of the Western powers. Consequently, India has been unable either to provide incentives for private savings and enterprise or to obtain the degree of capital accumulation possible in a totalitarian system. Although India's position is improved by outside assistance—for example, the agricultural problem is not so pressing as in China—she tends to develop balance-of-payments difficulties. Whether the halfway house can be maintained is a question. As time goes by, the attempt to expand heavy industry puts upward pressure on the prices of consumer goods, and the tendency is to go further and further in the direction of stringent controls. The alternative is to concentrate on agriculture and light industry.

3. Implications for Future Trends

Any survey of the possible guidelines for American policy in the underdeveloped areas must come to grips with certain harsh economic realities which set limits on the alternatives open to us. Unfortunately, recent American discussion of our policy goals has disregarded the economic realities and fostered wishful thinking. There has been a good deal of romance about the underdeveloped areas; and before we turn to a discussion of policy, we must attempt to dispel these economic illusions. We are all, to be sure, interested in what American assistance can accomplish, but our thinking on the subject has been confused in recent years. The three main sources of confusion concerning the possibilities in the underdeveloped world are what we shall call "the illusion of growth," "the population myth," and "the dream of American power." Let us treat them one by one.

The illusion of growth. The West should be under no illusions, because of plans and hopes and graphs, as to the possibilities for expansion. These are *backward* economies, frequently over-populated, characterized by a cultural inertia which may not easily be reconciled with economic progress. It is dangerous to break down cultural traditions too rapidly, since this leads to frustration and rootlessness; yet, if the cultural traditions are not broken down, economic progress is impeded. If all goes well, and if the populations prove tractable, these economies may have the resources to expand at the rate of 3-5 per cent a year, but these are big *ifs.* Even under the most optimistic assumptions, it seems unlikely that living standards can be raised much more than 1 per cent a year *on the average*—certainly not more than 2 per cent. The percentages may sound impressive, but we must remember the low base from which we start. Indian *per capita* incomes are now estimated at $56 a year, barely one-fortieth of the American level. It was hoped that by the end of the Second Five-Year Plan, it would rise to $69, and it was vaguely envisaged as doubling by the mid-seventies. The rise of living standards would, of course, be less rapid. Thus, even under favorable conditions, not likely to be fulfilled, the absolute level of growth will be quite modest. An income level of $100 *per annum* is not likely to quell dissatisfaction, particularly as the gap with the outside world increases.

The absolute levels of investment are extremely low—in India, which is a pace-setter, about $2 billion a year, spread out among 380 million persons. One can hardly expect large absolute gains. India, to be sure, could *absorb* more capital, but the capacity of many of the underdeveloped lands for capital absorption remains extremely low. It is no overstatement to say that "the curse of the poor is their poverty." Finally, it must be remembered that in some respects the conditions for growth in India and China since 1950 have been unusually favorable; it is therefore possible that the recent performance has been more rapid than we can anticipate in the future.

The population myth. We in the West are becoming obsessed with the question of population. Population is now being viewed as the main, long-run index of power. In the underdeveloped lands, the population is enormous in relation to that of the West. What if all these peoples were equipped with modern implements and were universally hostile? Then we extrapolate trends—the population growth rate and an assumed economic growth rate—and we become alarmed. These are the coming great powers. Possibly, this is true, but the time element must be considered. To be sure, the balance of power is gradually shifting to those regions of the non-Western world which have been neglected for so long. It will be a long time, however, before the power is sufficient to challenge the West directly, and there is no reason why the West should be unable to maintain sufficient power to protect her own interests. A trend does not continue indefinitely.

Moreover, we should be aware of the drawbacks of large populations. When not well equipped with resources, they may be more of a liability than an asset. The importance of mere numbers is exaggerated, and it is partly for this reason, as we have seen, that we tend to overstate the possibilities of development. It is certainly not clear that the West itself has escaped from the Malthusian specter. It is clear, however, that the present rapid rate of population growth in the underdeveloped areas subjects the resource base to continuing pressure. The problem has been stimulated by improved health and sanitation, and it promises to become worse before it becomes better. Population pressure is not solely a matter of mouths to fill: high birth and death rates also imply a population structure within which a considerable portion is nonproductive. Typically, in an underdeveloped country, half of the population will be under twenty-five years of age; sometimes, half will be under twenty. Frequently, death will occur before an individual enters his productive period, so that from the national point of view, there is nothing to show for the investment of resources.

Sometimes, in the attempt to dismiss the problem of population pressure, it is pointed out that population densities in China and India are less than they are in Europe *at the present time.* Although this is true, the implications are misleading. The present population of Europe has come into existence *subsequent to* and *as a consequence of* the expansion of economic opportunities through industrialization. In Asia, industrialization must chase population, rather than the other way around. Moreover, European resources are unusually favorable in relation to the size of its land mass. Overpopulation in Europe exists in the sense that it is dependent upon foreign sources of supply to maintain its present standard of living. The meaning of overpopulation in Asia is entirely different, and the problem cannot be eliminated by pointing to European conditions, which are by no means parallel.

For a brief period, recognition of the population problem came from an unexpected source. In 1957, Communist China—which previously had regarded its enormous population as an asset and had, in orthodox Marxist fashion, denounced Malthusian ideas—launched a vigorous birth-limitation campaign. Despite its industrial difficulties, the government promised to expand the production of contraceptives fivefold and to cut their prices in half. Success in curbing population growth would have eliminated one relative advantage that India possessed. Yet, despite its propaganda machine, its war on family-oriented motives, and the difficulties of life under the new order, the regime was unable to achieve its purpose. It did not, however, admit defeat; it simply and abruptly terminated the birth-limitation campaign in the spring of 1958 and returned to the older position of regarding its immense population as an asset. The regime looks forward to controlling more than a billion Chinese well before the end of the century. Nevertheless, because of Chinese ambivalence and Indian concern over the problem, the Soviet Union has felt obliged to cease its attacks upon discussion of population pressure, formerly dismissed as simply a *bourgeois*-imperialist plot against the colonial peoples.[10]

The dream of American power. Many of us suffer from an illusion of American omnipotence. Curiously enough, many of those who hold that population is the long-run index of power are able at the same time to exhibit a touching faith in American omnipotence. There is a left-wing as well as a right-wing variation of the disease.[11] We exaggerate what can be done, and what we can do. If low standards should be raised, why, let us raise them. If there is poverty in the world, it is America's fault, or at least her responsibility. We can achieve anything, if only our attitudes and our policies are correct.

Any realistic assessment of our ability to extend aid will quickly deflate the estimates of what we can accomplish. When we consider that $65 billion of domestic investment is now raising American output by 2-3 per cent a year for a population of 170 million, we must recognize that assistance of $2 billion or $3 billion a year is going to have a relatively modest impact on a population of more than one billion in the underdeveloped world. Our support in the developmental process can never be more than marginal. A massive assistance program, in which we undertook to supply all the capital that could be absorbed, would undoubtedly accomplish more, but even in this case the short-term results would be limited. Moreover, it is politically unrealistic to assume that the American taxpayer would, or even should, provide this degree of assistance. For the underdeveloped world as a whole, American assistance cannot have more than a modest impact. We must recognize that we are only playing around with the tail of the dog, rather than with the dog itself. To be sure, if we were to concentrate our assistance on selected countries with relatively small populations, we could accomplish a good deal more. But this takes us into the political problem of selection—and it is a long way from the belief in American omnipotence. Even if international affluence could solve our security problems, which is debatable, we should recognize that it is an objective beyond our capabilities. We should not deceive ourselves; whether or not we extend aid in massive doses, most of the world will continue to be poverty-stricken for the foreseeable future. Moreover, economic progress in the West and in the Soviet Union implies that the gap between the living standards of the advanced and the underdeveloped worlds will continue to grow.

Enough has been said to indicate the problematical nature of the issue of economic development and the limits on our own power to affect it. Aside from the general statement that economic prospects are brighter in the advanced regions than they are in the underdeveloped regions, there are far too many imponderables to say with any assurance just what the future will bring. Although we have indulged in a great guessing game, it is impossible, in fact, to predict the economic future of the underdeveloped areas. We should neither frighten ourselves nor comfort ourselves on the basis of imaginary projections, nor should we base our present policies on the effects of the hypothetical expansion of income in Asia, which is a half-century away at the least. We need to guard ourselves against spurious policy dilemmas posed by such observations as: "Much of the future course of world history will be decided by the economic competition between India and China." We can predict with some certainty the resolution of that particular contest, and it is within the capacity of the West to make its adjustments, whatever the outcome.

It is true, however—and it is a fact that ought never to be forgotten—that although what we would regard as acceptable standards of living are many years in the future in coming to Asia, *the instruments of power may be constructed on very low levels of living.* Although economic possibilities are limited, the strategic possibilities are not without significance. Although we cannot eliminate poverty, we ought not neglect the potential for hostility. Foreign adventures may be a partial substitute, in fact, for higher living standards. Despite her recent difficulties and industrial cutbacks, China is continuing with her expansion of armament industries. Since the industrial base that can support a military posture adequate for certain types of international conflicts is much more modest than the one that would be required to support high standards of living, we ought to be alert to the possibility that economic development may occur in the sense of supplying the factor of power, without its occurring in the sense of raising *per capita* incomes above the poverty level. When we discuss economic development, we ought to know clearly what we have in mind. It may be that a modest growth of industry—sufficient to affect the balance of power, but insufficient to raise living standards substantially—represents the most realistic assessment of the possibilities in much of the underdeveloped world.

The discussion in this chapter of the economic possibilities in the underdeveloped areas is of enormous import in appraising the foreign policy of the United States. An understanding of the economic factors involved is essential in disentangling fact from fiction in an evaluation of just what economic assistance can accomplish. For this reason, it is desirable to summarize briefly the main conclusions we have been able to develop:

1. Because of the cultural, demographic, economic, and political conditions generally prevailing in the underdeveloped world, economic prospects—while not unfavorable when related to the whole history of the human race—are quite poor in terms of the present aspirations of the populations.

2. In the underdeveloped world, the rate of growth in *per capita* incomes is likely to be extremely modest, and even more modest in terms of levels of living. How low the rate will be depends in no inconsiderable measure on the rate of population growth.

3. Economic growth in the underdeveloped world starts from an astoundingly low base. The gap between Western (and Soviet) standards of living and those in the underdeveloped areas *will continue to increase.*

4. The capital requirements alone that are necessary to reduce the gap between the advanced and the underdeveloped worlds are immense in view of the relative populations involved. The capital is not likely to be forthcoming. Large-scale flows of private foreign capital are unlikely. As a source of capital, foreign investment is inadequate and is currently subjected to political harassment. In order to make even a dent in the requirements, governmental aid would need to be so massive as to be politically unthinkable.

5. However, nations differ in numerous ways. In some of the underdeveloped countries, particularly those not subjected to population pressure, the prospects are far more promising.

6. Totalitarian regimes possess three great advantages over those which reject totalitarian methods: they are better able to control the rate of capital accumulation; they can more easily direct the flow of investment into those industries which foster rapid industrial growth; and they can more easily (or more ruthlessly) dissolve the "cake of custom."

7. China, for these and other reasons, probably has a sizable advantage over India, if—and this is the crucial question—she can avoid costly or explosive disaffection among the peasantry.

8. The standard of living in underdeveloped areas is not likely to be substantially affected by aid programs, unless that aid is concentrated upon relatively few beneficiaries.

We in the West might just as well face these facts now, because extravagant statements in recent years have tended to mislead the public as to what could be accomplished. If such statements are accepted at face value, they are likely to lead at a later date to great and politically dangerous disappointments.

9

THE UNDERDEVELOPED AREAS:
POLITICAL CONSIDERATIONS

To take issue with the widespread supposition that the principal aim of our foreign-aid program should be to spur general economic development in the underdeveloped lands is to move against the currents of fashion. Increasingly, the military aspects of the program have been criticized by those in public life as narrow and misdirected; but correspondingly, the hopes for the developmental aspects of the program have grown. As a consequence of the concern over the future relations of the West with the newly emerging lands of Asia and Africa, a program of fostering economic development has been seized upon as the best answer, if not the only answer, to the problem of curbing the expansion of Sino-Soviet power into the affected regions. This growing enthusiasm has been reflected in the vigorous support given to the foreign-aid program, and particularly to the developmental portions of that program. The public has been subjected to a stream of statements in behalf of foreign aid from an impressive group of notables. Opinion of the informed variety seems virtually unanimous in support of the program.[1] A bipartisan committee organized by the President is now attempting to "sell" a long-term aid program to the American public. Recently, the House Foreign Affairs Committee reported that curtailment of the foreign-aid program "would immediately mean that we would lose the cold war." One United States

Senator has argued that the destiny of the world will be determined by what occurs in the underdeveloped nations of Asia. Another Senator has commented that the 2 billion people in the underdeveloped regions are, collectively, the greatest resource in the world. Both are members of the Foreign Relations Committee. The Vice President has stated that we can never be secure "as long as misery and poverty exist in any substantial manner in any part of the world." Secretary of State Dulles, who possessed a knack for converting political issues into theological ones, observed that the foreign-aid program "is an expression of the moral law under which we live." Even more vigorous support can be found in the Democratic camp. Examples could be multiplied, all supporting the conclusion that the overwhelming majority of the nation's leaders are presently committed to the belief that economic development of the underdeveloped nations is likely to provide security for the United States. One brief quotation from the President's 1958 State of the Union Message concisely summarizes all the hopes that are held for the present program: "The countries receiving this aid become bulwarks against Communist encroachment . . . Nations that are conscious of a steady improvement in their industry, education, health, and standard of living are not apt to fall prey to the blandishments of Communist imperialists." [2]

Granted that many of the more dramatic statements have been issued with proselytizing intent—the Foreign Affairs Committee wishes to bring pressure to bear on the Appropriations Committee, and so on—still, there has been an astonishing degree of uncritical acceptance of the claims made in behalf of the assistance program. The issues have been phrased in terms of black and white, and economic development has been treated as a panacea. On questions of this sort, however, political unanimity may not be a sign of health. Some of the claims put forward in behalf of economic development are mutually inconsistent. It is necessary, therefore, for us to attempt to disentangle the fact and the fiction, and to indicate what foreign aid can accomplish and what it cannot.

At the outset, it should be recognized that the assistance program is fundamentally a political issue. One's conclusions must depend upon one's assessment of the non-economic factors involved, and, therefore, there is relatively little that the economist, as such, can contribute to the discussion. The principal insight of economic analysis that bears upon the problem is the recognition of the insatiability of human wants, which are limited only by the availability of resources. It would be impossible to quench the aspirations of the underdeveloped nations by the contribution of any finite amount of resources from the West. Poverty is a relative matter; with each increase in the standard of living, new desires and new dissatisfactions emerge.

But it may be inquired, is there not such a thing as absolute poverty? Cannot the misery of half-starved, shelterless wretches be eliminated? The harsh answer is probably not, certainly not in the foreseeable future. The expansion of income that would be required to raise living standards for the huge and burgeoning populations of the underdeveloped world to what we would regard as a tolerable level simply staggers the imagination. In view of the limited resources of the underdeveloped nations, the institutional barriers to advancement, and the population pressures, assistance from the West of even more massive proportions than has yet been contemplated would hardly permit *per capita* incomes to rise by more than 1 or 1.5 per cent a year. These are the fondest expectations, but starting from so low a base, it would mean that at the end of a century, the degree of poverty would still be appalling.

We must reckon with the fact that even if poverty lies at the root of our difficulties in dealing with the new nations of Asia and Africa, it is not likely to be eliminated. It is doubtful, however, whether we can ascribe our difficulties to poverty *per se*, or to the workings of what is called "belly Communism." Recent history is replete with cases of poor peoples who have been impervious to Communism, and of prosperous people who succumbed. Apparently, the appeal of Communism was greater in Czechoslovakia than in Turkey. Ireland has had less Communism than has France. The well-paid factory worker is more susceptible than the impoverished peasant, and if the latter follows Communism's banner, it is less because of his poverty than his resentment of the affluence of his landlord or the local loan shark. Apparently, the poverty explanation of Communism is far too simple to be of any value. In fact, it may be argued that Communism is incompatible with absolute poverty. Communism depends upon some notion of progress, upon the conviction that some improvement in living conditions is a *possibility*.

It seems invalid to assume that the door to Communism would be closed by improvement in living standards. On the contrary, it is the impact of commerce and industry upon what has been a closed society that creates a fertile field for Communism. Individuals are uprooted, ancient patterns are disrupted, and the idea of progress is unleashed, accompanied by rather unsophisticated notions of the ease with which progress may be achieved. Thus the stage is set for "the revolution of rising expectations," about which so much has been said in the literature on development and the American aid program.

It should have occasioned no surprise that when the possibility of improvement had been discerned, man's desires would outrun his means. The idea that "a man's reach should exceed his grasp, or what's a heaven for?" is imbedded in Western thought and the thought of other cultures. What is surprising about this age is the belief that the rising expectations might ever be satisfied, and that heaven could be achieved here on earth. In the nature of things, these rising expectations can never be satisfied, but the fact that mankind has been encouraged to allow its hopes to outrun its capacity is a political condition with which we in the West must now reckon.

We should recognize, however, that we Americans bear a particular responsibility for these rising expectations. Fortunately situated as we have been, on a virgin continent isolated from the penalties of war, we have fallen prey to the idea that evil men and outmoded institutions present the only barriers to rapid economic progress. We have gone around the world spreading the "gospel of plenty," raising the level of expectations, cajoling skeptics into the need for higher aspirations. We have been unable to fight a war without developing grandiose objectives. In World War I, we fought "to make the world safe for democracy." In World War II, in the message of the "four freedoms," we added to the traditional democratic objectives of freedom of speech and religion the unobtainable objectives of freedom from want and freedom from fear—in part, a simple extension to all mankind of the political attitudes engendered domestically by the depression of the thirties.[3] Inevitably, in the postwar world, the hopes raised by these evanescent slogans have been deflated. Yet the effects of the slogans have lived on—and have been sustained by the words we utter. The failure to realize the rising expectations is bound to be blamed upon America and the West. Somehow, the United States is responsible when the promise of easy progress goes unfulfilled.

The question raised by Western relations with the newly emerging countries can never be primarily economic. The economic element is chiefly a limiting one: it suggests that the rising expectations about which we hear so much cannot be fulfilled. Though economists have not been loath to offer programs, the principal elements are political and psychological. The future of the underdeveloped areas will be determined by the direction in which the peoples of those areas *conceive* their interests to lie. Only in marginal cases can it be hoped that the element of economic aid will alter the balance. The attitudes toward the West will be determined, in the final analysis, largely by factors other than economic, unless we are so blind that we deliberately take actions that directly undermine the economies of the underdeveloped nations. It is therefore quixotic to believe that countries receiving aid will become bulwarks against Communism. If they do become bulwarks, it will not be the aid but some other cause that controls the attitudes of the population. Economic relations may simply be the vehicle through which underlying sympathies or antipathies are expressed.

Since the broader social attitudes and the conception of self-interest is likely to dominate the relations between the West and the emerging nations, it is, perhaps, only the better part of wisdom to recognize that in many of these countries the attitude toward the West varies only between ambivalence and hatred. This antipathy is a product of past and present grievances, real or imaginary; to what extent it can be alleviated by sympathetic treatment is problematical. It is a mistake to assume, however, that unless we are successful in making them see our virtues, these powers will slip into the Soviet camp. The analogy of the bipolar world can hardly be applied mechanically in Asia and Africa. The countries of these two continents are jealous of their newly found liberties. Failure to dissolve the hostility to the West does not necessarily mean that Soviet power will be extended or that the rest of the world will gradually form an anti-Western coalition.

What we cannot change we must endure. Failure to recognize our limited capacity for affecting the dominant ideologies in the underdeveloped lands has led the West into a rather frantic frame of mind: we must not let them get away; we must do something. For this reason, we are inundated by dramatic advice which, if we accept it, we are promised will lead us to a golden age of international harmony; but if we reject it, we are inevitably on the road to ruin. Such attitudes would seem to combine in themselves both wishful thinking and romantic pessimism.

1. THE ADVANTAGES AND DISADVANTAGES OF AID

In all economic activities, among which we must include the aid program, advantages are mixed with compensating disadvantages. Particularly for the contributing power, the case for aid is hardly straightforward, as has been assumed in the recent discussions of the issue, even if it is agreed to disregard the sacrifice of resources that is involved. In any given circumstance, the contributing power must reckon with unfavorable by-products of the aid program created in the minds of the recipients. It is, therefore, incumbent upon us before we construct a long-term assistance program to weigh carefully the pros and cons, in order to make most effective use of the invested resources.

The main significance of the extension of aid is, of course, that the recipient nation is provided with additional resources with which to achieve its broad social goals. Since the assistance is in the form of foreign exchange, of which the underdeveloped nations are chronically short, it may have additional leverage; but the impact of the aid is roughly dependent upon the ratio between the resources supplied by aid and those available domestically. Consequently, the larger the recipient, the less will be the relative impact of a given amount of aid. The increment of resources may permit higher consumption levels, greater investment activity, or a more formidable military posture.

The contributing power may benefit in any one of several ways. It may obtain a weighty instrument in the propaganda war. It may obtain a more effective military ally. Its international position may be strengthened by the greater degree of social stability in the recipient country that is made possible by the aid. It may benefit internationally, since the recipient country is likely to be reluctant to take positions that will endanger future assistance. Finally, it may benefit from the gratitude of those in the recipient countries whose living standards have been raised or whose political life has been made easier by the assistance. Even in this last case, it should be recognized that the beneficiaries may not be aware of the cause of the relative improvement of their position. Moreover, the distributional impact of the benefits must be considered. If the benefits are limited to a particular segment of the population, or seem to be limited to a particular segment, support of that group may be forthcoming, yet the rest of the population may resent the relative deterioration of their position. In a politically unstable society, this may imply that the non-benefiting "outs" will eventually take over and express their pent-up resentment toward the contributing power.

Over-all, however, the advantages to the contributing powers may be substantial, but there are also compensating disadvantages. As in all human affairs, the reactions are bound to be mixed. Although none of the compensating disadvantages is likely to be as important as the initial advantage, they are more numerous, and may make up in quantity what they lack in weight. When taken in conjunction with the taxpayer's sacrifice, they may point to the conclusion that foreign aid is ill-advised, despite its obvious benefits to the recipient nations. One obvious drawback, which is simply the reverse of the primary advantage, arises from the possibility that political alignment of the recipient power may be reversed, and whatever resources have been supplied now contribute to easing the problems of one's rivals on the international scene. But there are other disadvantages, and we shall analyze them under three main headings: the psychology of the beneficiary, mutual jealousy, and the penalties of involvement.

The psychology of the beneficiary. Depending upon the initial attitudes, the reaction of the beneficiary may well be exactly the opposite of that which was expected. That disillusioned but perceptive observer of the ways of men, Sir Robert Walpole, once defined "gratitude" as the "expectation of favors about to be conferred." But Sir Robert may have been unduly sanguine in this respect. When assistance is *regularly* conferred, it may be incorporated into the pattern of expectations of the recipient and regarded as a right. When assistance is regarded as a right, the recipients are likely to turn to brooding about the niggardliness of the aid, and come to the conclusion that they are *entitled* to more.

In the particular circumstances of aid to the underdeveloped nations, these underlying reactions are complicated by the belief, which is impossible to eradicate, that the wealth of the West and the poverty of the underdeveloped world are mutually attributable to colonial exploitation. This is, to be sure, a myth based on the merest suggestion of fact, but it is a powerful myth. Economically at least, colonial relationships were mutually advantageous, evidenced by the fact that in most cases the former colonies are maintaining and expanding upon the pattern of economic activity first established under colonialism. It is arguable that the colonial powers obtained the lion's share of the benefits under the colonial system, but this is a far cry from the vulgar myth of "exploitation," which holds that colonial powers stripped away the assets of their colonies.

In light of the myth, any support from the West may be viewed simply as justified restitution of what rightfully belongs to the underdeveloped countries. American aid is considered vicarious atonement for what the other Western powers have done. In fact, American aid may be viewed as confirmation of Western guilt. Under these circumstances, no amount of Western aid will be viewed as anything more than a partial payment on the vast sums that have been stolen. Unfortunately, the strange expressions of guilt uttered by some Americans—that we should be so prosperous in a poverty-stricken world—have tended to support the belief that we feel our guilt. And the last thought that we should desire to strengthen in a political or psychological sense is the notion that the West is guilty.

Nobody likes the position of seeming to be dependent upon alms; the attempt is therefore made to justify this position. Resentment toward the contributing power is exacerbated. The search is made for motives, even lower than the usual motives of self-interest, that influence the giver. To the extremists, the aid program is seen as a more sophisticated type of exploitation or a way of utilizing surplus capacity and avoiding unemployment. Resentment against the contributing power may be particularly keen if the beneficiaries of the aid can be presented to the mass of the people as the lackeys of the West.

Mutual jealousy. As soon as assistance is accepted as commonplace, it is unavoidable that envy develop among the recipients and potential recipients regarding the shares allocated among the underdeveloped nations. Unfortunately, there are no real standards for the allocation of aid; it must be done on the basis of expediency. Under these circumstances, it is inevitable that few, if any, of the recipients will be satisfied with their allotted shares. The Pakistani will resent the large share of aid going to India. The Indians will attribute their economic difficulties to defense preparations necessitated by the arms aid to Pakistan, for which their own share can in no way compensate. Firm allies of the West will resent aid to neutrals, and wonder if their loyalty is well advised. The South American republics that have firmly supported Western policies will resent being neglected because they are taken for granted. The Arab countries are not likely to appreciate assistance, as long as aid to the Arab bloc, narrowly defined, is but 1 per cent of the aid to Israel on a *per capita* basis. And so on.[4] Those with smaller shares, in general, will look at the principal beneficiaries and feel that they have been short-changed. This may not be compensated for by the increased appreciation of those receiving larger shares, since they may view the aid in terms of their own internal problems and feel that it is insufficient. Inevitably, the lack of precise standards will introduce difficulties into the aid program.

The penalties of involvement. It is too infrequently realized that the contributing power may have to pay a price in terms of lost respect in an assistance program, if the program includes involvement in the internal affairs of the recipients. The penalties arise from two sources, personnel relations and the responsibility for success. To a greater or lesser degree, an assistance program requires administrators, experts, program officers, clerical personnel, and so on. Few are the foreigners who can fit easily into an alien environment. Among them, Americans are rare. Americans easily offend local sensibilities with their colonies and their high standard of living, which may stand out like a sore thumb in an impoverished community. They are resented, and rightly so.

One of our scarcest resources is that of intelligent and tactful personnel. In planning the foreign-aid program, we should not simply assume that the manpower is there to be utilized. We must be cautious in shipping troops of experts or so-called experts to other lands—where they may promote envy, contempt, or ridicule through their strange ways. Even the Europeans, who are as used to our ways as is possible, were provoked to a mixture of resentment and amusement by the horde of authorities that accompanied ECA. For many of the officers fresh out of college, it constituted a post-collegiate "grand tour" with unemployment compensation—a brief but pleasant interlude before settling down to the serious problems of life. In the interim, they might solve a few of the production and social problems that the local inhabitants had been unwilling to come to grips with. In the underdeveloped areas, feelings are more easily ruffled by the casual effrontery of Americans and the display of the comforts with which we Americans find it so hard to dispense.

Perhaps a more fundamental problem is the acquisition of responsibility for the results of the development program. If we are involved in the planning, or if we require that the plans for development be submitted to us for approval, then it appears that the United States has guaranteed that the project or projects will be successful. When projects fail, and failures are not rare because of overplanning, it appears that the United States has been deficient in meeting the responsibilities that it has accepted. The Soviet Union, in granting assistance, has generally followed the practice of accepting whatever plans are put forward; in this way, the responsibility is placed on the recipient alone. In view of the cultural conflicts and the advisability of avoiding responsibility for the failure of projects, it may well be that the aid program would be more successful, in the propaganda sense, if the money were to be granted directly without the subsequent control of its use.

It is arguable that the soundest prescription for getting along with other nations is to have as little to do with them as possible.[5] Latin Americans, for example, seem to be continually irritated by the *nordamericanos,* with whom they have such close contacts. But there is one area of the world where the United States is admired and Americans are universally popular: that is the great belt of Eastern Europe stretching from Turkey to Finland, where knowledge of the Russians has been so intimate. Our ways, which seem so lovable to us, are no more endearing to other peoples than are their ways to Americans. It is illusory to believe that increasing the contacts between peoples will make them like each other; the reverse is more likely to be true. The price of involvement is high, and it may affect the net results of the aid program.

2. THE ALTERNATIVES

When both the advantages and the disadvantages are weighed, it appears to be uncertain whether or not it was initially wise to embark upon a program of economic assistance. This is particularly true when we take into consideration the sacrifices imposed upon the taxpayer, and the likelihood that the taxpayer will resist expenditures of a size sufficient to make an effective contribution to the recipient nations. In a sense, a program of limited aid brings the disadvantages of aid immediately into operation, but it requires an extensive program to make the advantages effective. But the decisions that have been made cannot be made over again. We are interested in what our policy should be today, not what it should have been at some time in the past. We must recognize that a great disadvantage of an aid program is the resentment that would be provoked if it were abruptly terminated. Aid that is taken for granted and treated as a right will cause more dissension if it ceases than if no aid had been given in the first place.

Many and varied are the proposals which have been brought forward concerning the proper direction of the aid program; the majority envisage an expansion of aid to the underdeveloped areas. Some have based the case for aid largely upon humanitarian motives; others have gone on to say that the dispensing of aid is both a duty and a privilege; and for some, perhaps too heavily imbued with Marxist notions concerning the danger of substantial unemployment in the United States, aid is considered to be more than a privilege, it is a necessity. These suggestions are perhaps, at best, too politically unrealistic to require much comment; the economic benefits of aid are too limited, the humanitarian motive too frail to serve as the basis of a long-term program. The majority of the proposals, however, whatever their conclusions, are based to a greater or lesser degree upon what the proponents consider to be the long-term security interests of the United States. In this section, we will analyze three types of proposals that have been made, and which are broadly representative of the elements included in the larger universe of proposals.[6] These proposals may be classified as: the free-enterprise approach, the Millikan-Rostow approach, and the eclectic approach. The first two represent the poles of American opinion; the third is, in a sense, a modified version of the Millikan-Rostow approach.

The free-enterprise approach.[7] The simple prescription for economic aid here is to abolish it. This may require a generous terminal grant to the recipient nations in order to allay the resentment expected to result from a precipitate curtailment of the program. It should be pointed out that the free-enterprise approach poses no objection to military assistance, provided it contributes to the effective military position of the West and helps to further our political objectives. But economic aid, it is argued, rather than furthering our security, actually undermines it. Consequently, it is this aspect of our foreign economic policy which is criticized, although up to the present time the amounts contributed have been relatively small.

The basic assumption of the free-enterprise approach is that "it is clearly in our national interest that they (the underdeveloped countries) satisfy their aspirations for economic development as fully as possible in a democratic framework." The West cannot survive as a free island in a totalitarian world. It is held that true democracy can only survive in an economy characterized by free action and free markets; socialism only partakes of freedom to the degree that the private sector of the economy survives. On this ideological base, it may be understood why our present program of assistance, requiring centralized and coordinated plans of development and relying upon intergovernmental grants and loans, is considered to be detrimental to our long-run position. A program of direct assistance expands the government sector of the recipient economy rather than the private sector. Requiring a coordinated plan of development is not only less efficient than fostering the growth of the free market, but it creates attitudes that encourage the growth of totalitarianism; and thereby, it endangers our security. Only the Communist nations can fully qualify for aid under our standard of coordinated plans; the United States and other Western nations, despite rapid economic growth, could never have qualified for assistance, since economic development in the West occurred despite the absence of such a coordinated program. Our present assistance program, it is therefore held, will retard development and speed up the process of Communization.

On the positive side, this school holds that more can be accomplished in fostering both development and democracy by eliminating obstacles to private international trade—that is, removing all tariffs over a period of five to ten years, and encouraging the flow of private capital. Our purpose should be to "release the energy of millions . . . chained by ignorance, custom, tradition." If this can be achieved, and it is assumed that it can be, then the pace of development will be quickened.

It may well be that, intuitively, the free-enterprise school has arrived at the best prescription for foreign assistance, but its ideological foundations must be severely questioned. It is not at all certain that the furtherance of democracy is a purposeful strategic objective of the United States. It is not demonstrable that the spread of democracy necessarily improves our strategic position; the converse might be argued equally well. Nor need we assume that we will be unable to get along with societies with planned economies—whether they be socialist, semi-socialist, totalitarian (narrowly defined), or even Communist. Nor is it certain that the West could not survive in an otherwise totalitarian world. Since we cannot control the destinies of other states, their internal arrangements ought to be a matter of indifference to us, at least in terms of policy formation. Our policies ought to be based, not on the internal social organization of other states, but rather upon their foreign policies and the attitudes they take on the international issues that are of concern to us.

To be sure, there is an element of paradox present when a nation so wedded to the tenets of free enterprise as is the United States requires other countries to develop a centralized program to make use of the proffered aid. But this is a paradox rather than an inconsistency. It is probably inevitable that when intergovernmental aid is given for economic purposes, some such demand should be made. We ought not assume that such assistance automatically will weaken private enterprise, or that in the absence of such aid, private enterprise will receive more favorable treatment at the hands of the government. Moreover, it ought to be recognized that in view of the political and social conditions prevailing in some societies, there is no real choice but to plan. The alternative in some cases is stagnation. It may be well to talk of unchaining individual initiative and eliminating ignorance and customs that interpose a barrier to progress; but traditions are not easy to change, disruption creates unrest and rootlessness, and, in the final analysis, the social and psychological foundations for private initiative may well be absent. Nor ought we to assume that it is a simple thing to remove entirely the barriers to private trade or capital flow— or that in this divided world of armed camps, we ought to try. Democracy itself may well be a fragile growth suited for certain environments, but not for others. If we wish to encourage the growth of democracy or private enterprise, it may be done most effectively by unconscious example, rather than by allowing it to become a direct policy consideration. We should maintain an attitude of respectful indifference toward the social arrangements of other states; in the long run, such a policy will be most conducive to our security. Consequently, "making the world safe for free enterprise" does not appear to be a tenable political objective.

The Millikan-Rostow approach. By far, the proposal that has received the most attention up to the present time—in a doctrinal if not in an appropriations sense—is that emanating from the Center of International Studies at M.I.T.[8] It has earned for itself a number of enthusiastic proponents on the Committee on Foreign Relations of the Senate,[9] and has from time to time influenced the thinking of the Administration. The Millikan-Rostow approach shares with the free-enterprise position the view that the West, and particularly the United States, could not survive as an island of freedom if the underdeveloped nations were to turn against democracy—though its definition of "democracy" is sharply different. In contrast to the free-enterprise approach, however, the M.I.T. proposal strongly opposes substantial military assistance to the underdeveloped areas, since it channels resources away from what the underdeveloped nations are, *or should be,* interested in—economic development. In substance, it is proposed that the United States should sponsor, under international auspices, a new long-term capital fund which would make available to underdeveloped countries as much capital as they can use productively. Since the economic organization of most of the underdeveloped areas is so rudimentary, it is assumed that their present ability to absorb capital is limited; thus the program need not prove expensive. At the outset, it is anticipated that the underdeveloped countries would absorb between $2 billion and $3 billion annually. The United States should make available $10 billion to $12 billion, and the other industrial countries some $2 billion to $3 billion over a five-year period. The program is envisaged as continuing for a decade or more.

The underdeveloped countries are, according to the argument, divided into those in the "precondition" stage and those in the "transition" stage. In the former stage, the preconditions for economic progress—men and institutions that can effectively utilize resources, including capital—are absent, and must be developed. In this stage. it is argued, small amounts of technical assistance are all that is required. In the transition stage, the nation possesses the organization and institutions to absorb substantial sums of capital profitably, yet it is so poor that it is unable to generate sufficient savings to maintain an acceptable rate of growth. It is at this time that substantial flows of capital from outside become necessary. As the transition period draws to an end, much of the increase in income is plowed back into savings; thus the nation develops the savings capacity with which it can maintain growth without the flow of outside capital. The flow of assistance in the transition period helps to enable the underdeveloped country on its "take-off" into "self-sustained growth." The latter is a third stage of development, which the advanced countries have all reached, in which a substantial proportion of national income—some 10-20 per cent—can be saved, economic development continues unimpeded, and apparently the danger that the nation may turn to Communism out of hopelessness and frustrated aspirations largely disappears.

Most of the underdeveloped nations are considered to be in the precondition stage. A prominent exception is India, which is now entering the transition stage, along with a few other nations. It therefore can absorb more capital than it can supply from domestic savings, and at the present time may be considered the principal claimant for outside assistance.[10] The authors are careful to point out what economic assistance cannot be expected to accomplish. Growth will not be rapid; even under the most favorable conditions, it will not exceed 2-3 per cent annually in terms of *per capita* incomes. Aid cannot be expected to bring about reliance upon private enterprise. It will not bring us friendship—nor would we want such "fair-weather friends." It will not, nor should it, strengthen foreign military capabilities. It will not stop the spread of Communism by eliminating hunger. It will, however, allay the unrest created by disruption of traditional patterns, by providing a dream that will sustain the underdeveloped countries through the hard years ahead. And we are reminded not to underestimate the importance of spiritual elements, since the West already is condemned for its materialistic emphasis upon the mere physical gratifications involved, which are apparently only a small part of the developmental process.

Three comments should be made concerning the Millikan-Rostow proposal. First, the authors are insistent that no "strings" be attached to the aid, and have developed an international structure for administering it that minimizes the possibility. But strategic implications are inherent in aid programs, just as they are in trade. The strings are either explicit or tacit; they may be ignored, but they exist, nevertheless. If a nation were to go Communist, presumably the aid would be cut off. No matter how loosely held, there is always a string on a long-term aid package, as the Yugoslavs have recently rediscovered. All that can reasonably be asked is that we refuse to make use of the strings—at least for petty purposes.

Secondly, despite the small size of the initial annual contributions, it may be expected that the costs would rapidly rise as the absorptive capacity of the underdeveloped countries improved. Since the indicated standard is all the capital that a nation can use productively, the amounts would rise to astronomical figures, eventually surpassing the fondest hopes expressed in the United Nations literature, unless some rationing process were instituted. Since the capital is freely offered, it would be expecting too much of the underdeveloped lands not to help themselves to as much as possible. In fact, through public policies, they might prolong the so-called "transition" stage, that interesting period of non-self-sustaining growth, and continue to absorb foreign capital. Were the contributing powers to suggest that the potential savings exceeded the actual savings, and the potential was not being realized, would that not be crass intervention in the internal affairs of the recipient nation? But what more could be expected of the materialistic West?

Thirdly, despite the over-all tone of optimism, the authors fully recognize in guarded phrases and qualifications how bleak the possibilities are, which we have analyzed in the preceding chapter. If incomes were to rise by 2.5 per cent annually, it would take until the turn of the century for Indian income in *per capita* terms to reach $100—hardly a firm barrier to despair and resentment. The authors are inclined to rely upon the spiritual factors in a development program. At one point they observe: "It should be plain to us that if all that we have to offer to offset the disturbing effects of the breakdown of traditional cultures and the development of widely expanded expectations is the actual physical increment of new product created in two or three years by development, the picture is bleak indeed." [11] Even to the most hopeful of American observers, the facts, when they wish to consider them, are sufficiently bleak to support the pessimistic conclusions of the previous chapter. At base, this program is a calculated risk at long odds, and gives little cause for optimism. In the final analysis, it is a long-term program that can hardly cope with our problems, which are inherently short-run.

The eclectic approach. The third proposal may be treated more briefly, since, in essence, it is a modified version of the second. It exhibits a broad sort of eclecticism, and is lacking in the doctrinal elements that characterize the first two approaches. [12] The fundamental basis, it is held, for the extension of American aid can only be its contribution to American security; economic motives are lacking in force, and humanitarian impulses lacking in political realism. The policy issues are recognized as many-sided and not simply the promotion of economic development. For this reason, sharp exception is taken to the belief that the assistance program should eschew military objectives. The military risks in Asia, at least, are substantial, and sole emphasis on economic development is likely to prove self-defeating.

Nevertheless, it is also believed that exclusive attention to military aid is too narrow a foundation for our assistance policy. Most of the nations in the underdeveloped world have aspirations for economic growth, but will be unable to achieve even the most modest rates of growth without substantial outside assistance. We should provide assistance for development, in the hope that this will maintain political stability in the areas concerned. For better or worse, the old order is breaking down, and the emerging nations are passing through a period of change. It is a wise course for us to attempt to channel this change, to influence it to some degree—although, in the final analysis, we must recognize the stringent limits to our power. We would be silly to expect friendliness from these nations, or to desire them to adopt social systems similar to our own. The essential element is that if these nations can maintain political stability, we can live with them; we might not be able to do so with the alternative. The alternative is Communism—and Communist China and the Soviet Union, it is feared, may have immense attraction for nations as they start to develop.

This proposal differs sharply from the Millikan-Rostow one in that the aid would not be given without any strings. In fact, the political considerations may well be the heart of the matter. When a region is politically unsettled, or if a nation is indulging in blatantly anti-Western activities, economic assistance would be contingent upon, and a means of achieving, a political settlement. We should not be deterred from giving if a nation is neutral, but it is fully recognized that at some point the assistance would be terminated if political developments were displeasing to us.

It will be recognized that under this proposal, the aid extended would be substantially less than under the Millikan-Rostow approach, and a higher proportion of the total would tend to go to military allies and to friendly countries generally. It may well be that the eclectic approach has overestimated the degree to which limited Western aid may further either development or Western security, but by recognizing the paramount importance of the security aspect and the inevitability of political considerations, it provides a superior framework for policy. One weakness of the eclectic approach is that it has failed to lay down firm guidelines for specific tactical decisions in the granting of assistance.

3. A SUGGESTED POLICY FRAMEWORK

It is a logical misfortune, but a practical necessity, that the amount and the allocation of foreign assistance must inevitably be based upon compromise between conflicting pressures, in which expediency as opposed to rules of policy will have some role to play. A policy framework, however, can be formulated within which the majority of specific issues may be judged as they arise. The first rule is a positive one: whenever we give aid, we must recognize and make use of its strategic implications, just as we should in the case of trade. Insofar as they are related to foreign-policy objectives, trade and aid should be viewed as equivalent and coordinate weapons to the same general end—to influence the international environment favorably to our own interests. This does not, of course, imply that whatever advances our interests must do so at the expense of others. The chief advantages of trade and of aid—the commercial weapons of strategy—are that they permit the conferring of mutual benefits, so that the interests of both nations may be served and coordinated by economic ties.

A corollary of the first rule is recognition of the fact that of the two weapons, the role of aid must generally be subordinate. Though assistance programs and trade are two methods of supplying foreign exchange, the former has drawbacks that the latter does not share. Assistance that implies dependency creates resentment between benefactor and beneficiary to a degree not characteristic of trade, which is less emotion-laden, since it is part of the ordinary commercial routine. Trade relationships may be viewed as permanent, whereas aid must be viewed as a temporary phenomenon. In any quantitative appraisal, trade must loom much larger than aid. Probably until the day that hope succumbs to disillusionment, the American people will be willing to supply some funds for economic assistance; but in the nature of things, these sums will not be large, and it may well be in the interest of the recipient nations that the desire to assist not be abused so that it is soon exhausted.[18] The taxpayers will demand that their interests be taken into account in the evaluation process.

Consequently, it may be argued that our policies have been moving in the wrong direction in recent years. We have encouraged expectations of aid which will not be forthcoming in the long run, and at the same time have been laggard in encouraging trade, on which the main burden in the end must lie.

The Eisenhower Administration entered office using the slogan, "trade, not aid." It has resisted the pressure to return to high tariff policies, yet it has belied its lofty professions of adherence to liberalized trade by using restrictive devices other than the tariff to limit imports. In particular, by imposing quotas upon oil imports and by forcing the Japanese to limit the exportation of textiles, china, and other items to this country "voluntarily," the Administration has made it appear that "aid, not trade" might well be a more appropriate epitaph to its foreign economic policies. In recent years, the Administration has endorsed the aid program with ever-increasing vigor. But aid is inevitably a weak substitute for trade; it does not provide the permanency of trade ties, especially in view of its weak domestic political support. There can be little doubt that in the long run, it would be advisable to rely increasingly upon the trade weapon.

It is important to recognize how restricted are the short-run economic possibilities in the underdeveloped areas, and how limited is the capacity of aid or of trade to alter those conditions. In this regard, we must disabuse ourselves of a number of economic illusions. Frequently, the more enthusiastic proponents of the aid program assert that its goal is to reduce the gap between our living standards and those in the underdeveloped areas, thereby reducing envy and resentment of the West. Dr. Lewis Webster Jones, president of Rutgers University, for example, in a recent report to the Senate on our assistance program in South Asia, observed that "the gap between their poverty and our affluence is as obvious to them as it is to us; and the necessity for narrowing the gap is as important to us as it is to them." [14] But the gap refuses to be narrowed; half a century from now, it is likely to be greater than it is today. Even if the levels of living in underdeveloped areas were to double in the next generation—a most optimistic and unlikely aspiration—the absolute gap would increase because of the expansion to be expected in the advanced economies. When this unpalatable fact is mentioned to the enthusiasts, they are likely to argue that perhaps the gap in living standards is not the important issue—that is, rather, to spur industrial growth, or at least to make the attempt. This may be true, but it points to a certain degree of confusion over just what our objective in extending aid should be. Clarification of the purposes of the assistance program is essential, and we need to take care that there is some relationship between our objectives and the actual possibilities in the underdeveloped areas.

The amount of aid we can extend is limited; the task of development is herculean. Inevitably, the problem of selection arises, and in the selection process two factors stand out. First, because of the limited capacity of the aid to speed development, the propaganda and foreign-policy aspects of the program should be considered more important than the developmental aspects *per se*. Secondly, the greater the dispersion of the aid, the less will be its impact upon the economies of the recipients; the more concentrated, the more effective it will be. Even if we were to recognize fully the difficulties that stand in the way of development, the United States would probably continue the foreign-aid program because of its implications for our international position—specifically, its propagandistic aspects. But if the strategic aspects rather than the developmental aspects become paramount, we should recognize the implications.

This leads to a second proposal as a rule of policy which broaches the issue of neutralism: aid should be used in strengthening the international position of the West. Throughout the cold war, the United States and other Western powers have sponsored regional military alliances to counter the threat of Communist expansion. Much criticism questioning the wisdom of such a policy has appeared, some of it penetrating; but as long as we rely upon such military arrangements, any aid program must support rather than weaken this instrument of foreign policy. Having given strong support to the broad policy objectives of the West, our military allies should never be treated in a fashion that conveys the impression that non-alignment, and even active opposition to Western policies, may frequently bring a nation greater rewards in terms of foreign aid. To cultivate such an impression is to provide an incentive for wholesale desertion from the Western camp.

It follows that whatever assistance we extend to the underdeveloped nations should be graduated in accordance with the support given Western policies and the degree of resistance to the policies of the Sino-Soviet bloc. That this is a harsh rule from the point of view of the Indians or the Cambodians cannot be denied, but they must accept the penalties as well as the benefits of their general foreign-policy orientation. The argument that some of our military allies would make ineffective use of additional aid is misleading. The wasting of aid, in itself, is not relevant to the more fundamental question of whether an allied power deserves more at the hands of the West than a state with a different orientation. Furthermore, it is doubtful whether the West should insist on its allies setting higher economic objectives. To encourage rising expectations and dissatisfaction with the prevailing degree of progress (or lack of progress) may simply further unsettle an already unsettled world.

As a power, the United States has been inclined to ignore its strong points in the attempt to shore up its position at its weakest—hardly a wise tactic if it leads to a weakening of the strong points. The maintenance of the political cohesion of the West, especially in our relations with Europe, should remain the primary consideration of American policy. Despite the existence of some antipathy toward the United States, the nations of Latin America have consistently given support to American policy, and they should never be given cause to believe that our treatment of them has been less satisfactory than that accorded less "reliable" countries. In Asia, our behavior has appeared on occasion to be something less than politic. It should not have been difficult to anticipate the reaction of the Baghdad Pact countries when, shortly after extending a $225 million loan to India, the United States promised to distribute $10 million among the pact members, as occurred in January, 1958. Such action suggests that alliance with the West does not pay. Unless the allocation of aid is closely correlated with our foreign-policy objectives, the program will not represent even a calculated risk but simply a miscalculation. Such an allocative procedure is supported by developmental considerations. Since aid is limited, it should be concentrated in a manner that will achieve maximum long-run results. This would imply that Latin America should take precedence over Asia as an object of our attention. To rephrase the second rule: never should the aid program place a premium upon opposition to Western policies, or neglect Western strong points.

There is an additional prescription that, in the long run, we would be well advised to follow. Financial irresponsibility ought not to be *underwritten,* with aid graduated either in accordance with the degree of recklessness of the recipient in handling its domestic affairs or in proportion to its ruthlessness in acquiring assistance. In other words, the amount of aid should be roughly predictable in advance, or else it may come to be regarded as a sort of expansible crutch useful for offsetting crippling domestic policies. If aid is determined by the size of the foreign-exchange deficit or by the pace of inflation, a premium is placed upon the acceleration of the very spending that is the initial cause of the economic difficulties. Although a lenient attitude may be taken with respect to waste in the aid program, certainly the program should not be organized in a way that provides an inducement for excessive expenditures.

On the basis of such considerations, the advisability of attempting to salvage India's current Five-Year Plan, for example, is open to question, particularly with respect to its long-run implications. The plan was overly ambitious, and it was so admitted from the first, but officials refused to reckon with the cold statistical facts, since they held out insufficient hope for progress. The magnitude of the "planned" *rupee* and foreign-exchange gaps was staggering, and, in practice, the original estimates proved to be too low. Expanded assistance now would mean that we place a premium upon overambitious (unrealistic) planning. Some observers have suggested that a most valuable result of this experience has been a trend toward greater realism among Indian planners. How wise is it to attack this new sense of realism by assistance that carries with it the implication that no matter how reckless a scheme, the United States stands ready to bail out the party concerned? Not infrequently, this issue is similarly posed by Latin American nations with chronic inflation and exchange problems. In the final analysis, it would seem advisable, despite the temptations, not to grant aid on the basis of simple expediency, since it encourages what might otherwise be temporary emergencies to become chronic.

Another seemingly obvious rule might be mentioned because recent experience suggests that it is likely to be neglected. *The aid program ought not to be based simply on neurotic reactions to Sino-Soviet activities.* This brings up the painful subject of the current campaign to convince the electorate of the malignancy of the "vast Sino-Soviet economic offensive against the nations of the free world." The campaign has been organized quite frankly to sell the aid program; there appears to be a real danger that our policy makers will be deceived by their own propaganda, and that our policies will be designed to counter an imaginary threat conjured up for the American people.

The State Department figures on the Sino-Soviet economic offensive[15] indicate that since 1953, the bloc has extended some $1.9 billion in "aid," a figure that includes almost $400 million for arms and $285 million in now-defunct Yugoslav credits. Thus the net total of aid *pledged* to date is just over $1.2 billion. The bulk of it consists of credits, some of which are not yet operative. Only 10-15 per cent of the total has actually been used. Since the Soviet bloc trades bilaterally, the extension of credit should be compared to assistance rendered not only through the United States aid program but through all other Western sources—private investment, extension of credit by private firms, and credit from such institutions as the Export-Import Bank, the World Bank, the International Monetary Fund, and also, if the Western alliance is meaningful, by other Western nations as well. The State Department has chosen to compare bloc extensions of credit with the U.S. aid program, narrowly defined. Moreover, it has chosen to compare the American program with bloc activities on the basis of "commitments" during a particular time period, although American commitments are honored in the same year, while Soviet commitments include credits that are operative for as long as a decade.

Finally, the State Department has used these noncomparable

figures to contrast the activities of the U.S. and of the Soviet bloc in several of the underdeveloped countries in which the bloc has concentrated its efforts—such as Afghanistan, Egypt, India, and Indonesia. Since the American effort in these countries (carefully defined) is smaller than the bloc effort (generously defined), we are led to the inescapable conclusion that the United States must compete by enlarging its aid program. Any fair comparison, even in the selected countries, would suggest contrary conclusions. To take one example, in Indonesia, when American aid, credit from all sources, and trade are totalled, the Soviet program is dwarfed, without the inclusion of figures for the Western alliance as a whole. By such ingenious devices, however, the State Department has demonstrated the vast import of the Soviet economic offensive; though the figures are not falsified, the impression that is cultivated is deliberately misleading.

If the power behind this economic offensive is to be appraised fully, foreign trade should also be included. The Soviet Union has, since its inception, displayed strong autarkic tendencies, which will not be lightly surrendered. The same is true for other members of the bloc. This fact helps to explain why the Department prefers to talk in terms of bloc "capabilities" rather than in terms of the limited volume of trade.[16] The Soviet Union's external trade amounts to some $4 billion annually; but of this amount, about three-fourths represents intrabloc trade. Thus Soviet trade with the outside world is less than 10 per cent of the American level alone. The Soviet Union ranks sixth or seventh in world trade—following the United States, Great Britain, West Germany, Canada, France, and the Benelux nations (if they are considered jointly). If intrabloc trade is discounted—and for purposes of judging the economic offensive against the free world, it must be—the Soviet Union ranks between twelfth and fifteenth, following such nations as Switzerland, Sweden, and Brazil. Even with the inclusion of Eastern Europe and Communist China, the Soviet bloc contributes only 2.9 per cent of free-world trade. At least in the trade field, the Russians' claims that they have dwarfed the major European powers and are now the second economic power of the world ought to be rudely and scoffingly dismissed, rather than given serious treatment.

In no other field is the comparative power of the West *vis-à-vis* the Soviet bloc likely to be more impressive than in the international economic field. The present disproportion is little short of astonishing. We should welcome a sober and balanced appraisal of the opportunities open to the underdeveloped countries in dealing with the West rather than with the Soviet bloc; we ought not rig the evidence in favor of the latter. It is not in the interest of the Soviet bloc to give large-scale aid, or to promote development in the underdeveloped world,[17] for the very reason that aid proponents have emphasized—that extensive aid might, to some extent, allay the impulse to experiment with totalitarian techniques. The bloc program is designed to create dissension, to discredit the West, and to advance Soviet propaganda. With the unexpected assistance of the State Department, it may be succeeding. On the Soviet side, the main purpose of assistance is propaganda; on our side, it should not be ignored. The current American campaign represents a strange sort of propaganda, however; one in which one's opponents' efforts are touted and one's own performance belittled. Those who present information to the public on the government's behalf ought to recognize that the government's handouts are rarely read at home; when read, they may be discounted by Americans as the usual political hyperbole. In contrast, government documents are more highly regarded abroad; they may be both read and believed. Propaganda designed to impel the American people into some course of action is likely both to miss the mark at home and to hit the wrong target abroad.

A survey of the over-all picture is useful in bringing the problem of the Soviet economic offensive into perspective, but we must be aware that limited as the economic power of the Soviet bloc is, if that power is concentrated upon a few countries, they might succumb to the "bloodless revolution" of economic persuasion. As yet, the danger is remote—even in the case of Afghanistan about which so much concern was expressed several years ago[18]—but it is a possibility. We should be aware, of course, of the difference between *a vast economic offensive* and *the sharpshooting technique* actually available to the Soviet bloc. We ought to recognize that aside from keeping open the channels of trade to the West, with all that implies, there is relatively little we can do in this contingency. We must rely upon the judgment of the statesmen of the underdeveloped countries in avoiding the type of overdependence that is surely more alarming to them than to us. That this judgment will be forthcoming in the majority of cases, we cannot doubt, since the leaders of the newly independent countries will be wary of any real threat to their independence.

Surely, we ought not compete with the Russians in terms of economic assistance in whatever country they may be attempting to penetrate. This would open the gates to a game of blackmail that all underdeveloped countries could profitably play.[19] A nation would then be well advised to seek economic ties with the Soviet bloc, not because of the intrinsic value of the ties, but because it might be expected to provoke the intervention of a gift-laden Uncle Sam. Partly because of our neurotic antipathy to any trade ties with the bloc, this development is partially in progress in several countries. Nations having relatively little to exchange with the Russians have been encouraged to believe that Soviet credit and trade is the answer to all their difficulties.

If anything, we should encourage these nations to see for themselves how little there is in the Soviet connection. In practice, the Russians have been harsh traders; for the underdeveloped nations, a little experience may be worth far more than all the preachments from the West. If the underdeveloped nations have envisaged the Soviet Union, in George Kennan's phrase, as "the horn of plenty," what could be more advantageous for us than for them to see how empty the horn is. Heretofore, the Soviet Union has benefited internationally by being able to display its wares without being called upon for deliveries. The massed demand for credit and for trade agreements from all the underdeveloped countries can only embarrass the Soviet Union and disappoint the claimants. Since the end of the war, we have been criticized for basing our policies on negative reactions to Soviet moves. Here is one case in which

Soviet actions are fundamentally designed to cope with Western advantages. Instead of appreciating the flattery of imitation and taking some grim satisfaction in our advantages, we have become angry, resentful, and desperate.

The West possesses a decisive edge over the Soviet bloc in the realm of peaceful economic competition. In the long run, the conduct of our foreign economic policies should be based upon relatively simple rules. Trade and aid should be regarded as coordinate instruments. Aid should neither place a premium upon opposition to our foreign policies nor underwrite financial irresponsibility. We should not be lured into contesting any Soviet economic penetrations by unwarranted largesse. Trade should be our main instrument of economic competition, and the aid program inevitably would remain small. The bulk of total aid should continue to be used to maintain Western positions of strength, and also to deal with certain exceptional situations, such as the preservation of Yugoslav independence. It is impossible to develop any criterion for economic assistance that will not create dissatisfaction, since the needs of almost all recipients are insatiable and the only sound criterion is "more." For this reason, and because of the limited economic possibilities, we will have to disabuse ourselves of romantic illusions concerning how much aid can accomplish beyond the propaganda field. The claims of realism may appear cheap and tawdry to those who would have us dedicate ourselves anew to the ideals of Woodrow Wilson, but in the end there is no alternative, and the costs of undiluted idealism generally run high.

4. THE LONG-RUN PROSPECTS

In recent years, it has become increasingly difficult to interpret political events within the strict confines of the concept of the bipolar world. The nuclear stalemate has provided an opportunity for the nations that were formerly secondary players on the international stage once again to take actions independently of the wishes of the superpowers. Unable to get at each other directly, the chief participants in the power struggle now attempt to improve their relative positions by influencing events in other quarters of the globe. It is this vicarious nature of the power struggle that has brought the underdeveloped nations to the center of the stage, and those who have laid stress on development have seen this process more clearly than have those who still view the international scene in terms of the military alignments of the Korean War. But there are two additional aspects of the changing power structure that those who have viewed the international scene in terms of development have tended to neglect: first, the continuing evolution of the underdeveloped world away from its Western orientation; and secondly, the ability of the West to survive such a schism. The course of events in the underdeveloped regions is likely to prove most unsatisfactory from the standpoint of the West, regardless of the amount of assistance proferred. For this reason, it is likely to prove more satisfactory for the Soviet bloc; yet, in the longer run, the outlook is for an orientation independent of, and perhaps hostile to, the two great power blocs of today. The very fact that the power struggle has now shifted toward the underdeveloped world also implies that any setback suffered by either side will be of a marginal nature, not crippling to its interests, and therefore unlikely to provoke general war. No single event or chain of events is likely to affect Western interests so adversely that we would be unable to recover. So long as the West possesses the arms and the will to use them, it will be able to preserve its own independence.

Many persons have exaggerated the degree of dependence of the West upon Asia, and this partially explains why we have been unwilling to recognize and accept the progressive alienation of a large portion of the underdeveloped world. Lenin has been quoted in the West to the effect that "the road to Paris lies through Peiping and Calcutta." If it was really made, this statement must be viewed as a product of the curious revolutionary logic embodied in Lenin's theory of imperialism. The West need not collapse simply because what were once its colonial appendages succumbed. The road to Paris lies through Bonn and Sedan; if the West remains strong, there is no other path. Consequently, we must maintain sufficient power to defend our vital interests, and the outcome of the struggle in Asia may be viewed with a certain detachment.

The long-run evolution of the newly emergent areas is likely, because of ideological alienation, to be toward increasing friction with the West. Even at the present time, the characteristics shared by the emerging lands are a pent-up hostility against and suspicion of the West, and an admiration for the Soviet Union based upon three factors—a desire to annoy the West; a lack of familiarity with the Russians, in contrast to familiarity with Westerners; and the leftist orientation of the enlightened public, which is inclined to view Soviet methods as supplying the pattern for the development of their own countries.[20] For the moment, the impulse arising from these factors has been tempered by the older generation of leaders, who were trained in the West, and to whom Western associations are still meaningful; but the younger generation, by and large, exhibits scant regard for such connections.

The star of Communism has not yet reached its zenith in the underdeveloped lands—a fact with which we must reckon as we look into the future. In some of the former colonial nations, there is an inevitability about Communism that arises from the development problems and the dominant political attitudes just discussed. A substantial body of opinion is hostile to the West and views the techniques of Communism as the only answer to its economic needs. As the bleak prospects for economic development are considered, and as disappointments appear, what is more natural than to compare the grim realities with the promises of Communism? Communism, as George Kennan has observed, is already viewed by the prostrate as a "magic short cut to the emoluments of industrial and economic advance." Is it not inevitable that nations determined to develop rapidly will experiment with the techniques of authoritarianism? And who is more able to administer those techniques than the Communists?

The issue is complicated by the dominant position of the intelligentsia in most of the newly emergent societies, and the intelligentsia may be described as Schumpeterian[21]—that is, those to whom criticism of the *status quo* comes more comfortably than appreciation. Intellectuals are no more interested in freedom than are other groups—freedom for themselves, to be sure (from priest, or prince, or businessman), but not necessarily freedom for others. Inclined, as they are, to discern the cause of failure in the deficiencies of social organization rather than in the nature of things, they can be the most merciless of ruling classes as they attempt to remold men to their own liking. The road to power is attained by attacks on interest groups, internal and external, and the attacks will succeed as long as society fails to achieve its aspirations. In many of the underdeveloped countries, development is the god, and it will not be long before freedom is sacrificed on its altar. After all, the ultimate in rationality is Communism, in which the whole mass of people are viewed as one vast productive machine, with the state as manager.

The outlook is for evolution in an authoritarian, anti-Western direction. But the situation will remain fluid. As the influence of the West is withdrawn, the chief unifying element among the underdeveloped nations will disappear, and the centrifugal tendencies will appear. Some nations are likely to go Communist; their neighbors, perhaps for that very reason, are unlikely to go, at least voluntarily. The possibility that military power eventually will be used to compel adherence to Communism can hardly be dismissed—particularly Chinese power in Southeast Asia. Those who would exclusively stress economic and political factors are playing into the Communists' hands as fully as those who view the contest in nominal military terms. Unless the Asian countries have the will and the ability to protect themselves, they are unlikely to survive.

It would be a mistake to regard whatever Communist brotherhood that is established on the Eurasian land mass as monolithic. Unless all of human history is to be disregarded, there will be fissures and strains, interests and counter-interests upon which the West can play. Communists have shown themselves to be no more resistant than other ideologies to the attractions of a marriage of convenience. The vision of a firm array of Communist powers directed against the West would appear unrealistic. In fact, it is not unlikely that the over-all position of the West will be stronger in dealing with a ragged array of Communist states than in its present attempt to maintain a decaying social order. Perhaps the most reassuring of events that we may contemplate at length will be the vast cataclysm that occurs when the Russians discover that in the case of China, they have been nursing a Frankenstein monster to their Marxist bosoms. Among the major powers, Moscow joins Tokyo and New Delhi in having most to fear from an increase in Chinese powers, and it is not unlikely that much midnight oil is being burned in the Kremlin considering that possibility.

Therefore, we ought not view with trepidation the unfolding of events. We cannot control the evolution of the underdeveloped areas, and frantic efforts to do so are misplaced. On the other hand, we need not fear the creation of a solid phalanx directed against the West. It will do us little good to attempt to appease or propitiate; that is always understood as a sign of weakness, which brings on the very events it was designed to forestall. There is a disquieting similarity between the views of those who feel that we can control developments in the newly emergent nations simply by demonstrating what good fellows we really are, and the attitudes expressed during World War II on how to dispel Soviet hostility. Of all assets, goodwill that is not based upon mutual interests is the most evanescent. In the final analysis, our foreign policies will be most firmly supported if we seek the *respect* of the outside world, and not its love.

will not be surpr
each other, since
that we ought to
could be that the
people conscious
they serve a use
the reiteration o
crease the skep
mentos on ques
tions, if they ha
to running in t

Let us exami
attention. We ha
the recent wars
nation is rough
gross productio
properly refined
one among *seve*
potential has b
nomic capacity
this manner ha
Since the gene
power, it is ar
ened by reduc
economic poter
nation that red
economy will a

The facts p
United States
provides no p
which are like
the importanc
relation to th
we have retu
Revolution—cc
will, it can p
industrial bas
characteristica

10

EPILOGUE: COMMON SENSE IN THE CONTEMPORARY POWER STRUGGLE

National security is the problem of our age. In order to survive, the West will be obliged to combine intelligent analysis of strategic problems with effective action. It cannot allow its policies to be governed by the appealing but deceptive catch phrases that currently dominate political discussion of the security issue. In indicating the limits to our power and the benefits likely to accrue from alternative courses of action, political economy has its role to play. The economic element is, to be sure, only one of the several inhibiting factors that must be taken into consideration in formulating the policies designed to best achieve national security. Economics, sometimes called "the science of choice," is particularly useful in indicating how a nation may employ its resources in order to achieve its national objectives. The main lesson to be derived from economic analysis is contained in the principles of resource allocation, which are of broad applicability. In this study, we have examined the implications of these principles under various headings: (1) the allocation of total output to satisfy the desires of consumers, the need for investment funds, and the requirements of national security; (2) allocational techniques during periods of mobilization; (3) allocation of resources between the public and private sectors and within the government sector, as reflected in the size and composition of the national budget; and (4) international aspects of resource

255

by allocating a much higher proportion of their total resources for military purposes than we have in the West. Thus we can draw only scant comfort from the superiority of our resources for military purposes; it certainly provides no basis for complacency.

In practice, the economic-potential argument, designed to bring comfort to a troubled people, has served as the basis of two different sorts of alleged troubles. In the first place, alarm has been expressed that by excessive taxation and expenditures, we are destroying the nation's first line of defense, the economy. Traditionalists, who intuitively accept the dogma of economic potential, have become accustomed to a system in which the government's role is quite limited and have not been emotionally prepared to accept the sizable expansion of the government's activities that has resulted from the threat to national security. Consequently, they have argued that high rates of taxation and massive government expenditures are unnatural and intolerable under free enterprise, and that unless our rates of expenditure are sharply reduced, we will bring on the type of collapse that will leave us defenseless before our foe. Excessive expenditures thus become the chief menace to our national security, in the view of the traditionalists. Professional economists have been nearly unanimous in insisting that the nation's taxable capacity is not nearly so restricted as the traditionalists believe. It is simply a case in which political objectives have been reflected in the fashioning of alleged economic laws.

The second way in which the economic-potential argument has been twisted from a source of comfort to a source of alarm is in the evolution of our thoughts concerning the Soviet economy. For a long period of time, Americans have listened to and believed the refrain that we are protected by our economic capacity. It is therefore not surprising that we have insisted on interpreting what is a very palpable threat to our security in economic terms. Since we believe that our security cannot be threatened unless our relative economic superiority is challenged, and since the Russians pose a distinct threat to the West, we have been driven by our own misplaced logic to exaggerate Soviet economic achievements. Soviet industrial growth has been treated as some kind of ogre. Instead of recognizing that a

short run. We cannot, therefore, base ou
that the standard of living for the mass
underdeveloped areas will rise more rapidl
feasible. Neither the policy of staying ah
industrial power, nor the policy of bringi
nations to a par with the West is tenable
are emotional stop-gap policies convenie
the necessity of thinking out our long-rur
needs.

The deficiencies of the American persɪ
its proper long-range objectives have b
illustrated by the current discussion of bɛ
own aid program and what is referred to
bloc economic offensive" against the unc
the West. In our assistance program, ᵥ
economic progress will stem the tide of
reality the disruption caused by econom
centives held out by economic progress
influences encouraging the spread of tɔ
the Soviet stamp, if not of Communism
the belly motive for Communism is th
indulge in wishful thinking.

We have failed to recognize the weakɪ
nomic assistance, when in the nature of
there are no definite standards that can l
circumstances, the extension of assistan
apple of discord, since all potential rec
consider themselves to be the fairest of ɛ
lavished upon other states which they
A program of economic assistance is n
security of the West unless it clearly driv
nations the advantages of firm connecti
assistance program that seems to plac
straddling or on a pro-Soviet orientation
appear to be self-defeating. We have
damages of economic assistance, and h
of encouraging weakness by shoring
looking our strengths. Except in emerge

strategic menace may be based upon a rather modest economic structure, we have persisted in assuming that the underpinnings of a strategic threat must be economic, and have consequently concluded that Soviet economic growth must be fabulous. We have seen, in our examination of the Soviet economy, that the rate of economic growth is quite modest. Industrial growth, upon which the Russians have concentrated, is somewhat more rapid than our own, and they are catching up in certain types of basic production, but it will be a long time before they will be able to challenge over-all American economic superiority. Nevertheless, some public figures have concluded that the best way to arouse the American people to the dangers confronting us is to stress the divergency in the rates of industrial growth. This is a dangerous procedure—first, because it tends to confirm the underlying presupposition that economic capacity is the final arbiter of power; and secondly, because it leads to the policy conclusion, stated quite explicitly by some, that all we have to do to protect ourselves is to match the Soviet pace of economic growth.

It is unwise to overstate the importance of economic growth, *per se*. At some date in the future, the Russians will reach—in the strategic sense, at least—a position of industrial plenty. We may hinder that development by applying pressures of one sort or another, but in the absence of total war, it will come to pass. The ratio of our productive capacity to theirs at that point will have very little strategic significance. We could "stay ahead," but it would be pointless to create additional capacity that has no other purpose than to permit us to stay ahead.

The importance of economic growth has been exaggerated in yet another way. Many Americans have given credence to the notion that the West must necessarily collapse unless it has appeal to the newly liberated areas. It is argued that if economic growth in the underdeveloped areas is substantial, the West will have that appeal. But in the course of the argument, both the importance and the possibilities of economic growth have been exaggerated. On the one hand, in the underdeveloped areas, economic growth is viewed largely in terms of industrial growth, and if this is the case, the techniques of totalitarianism may be

expected to possess considera
possibilities for rapid econon
the underdeveloped countries
could be assured, which it c
between the underdeveloped
ing to increase rather than
garded as tolerable cannot
circumstances, in much less
economic development as the
underdeveloped nations, we
to a short-run problem.

In the discussion of eco
have been argued simultan
menaced by the Soviet bloc l
is too small and our advant
time, it is stated that we a
nations because our relativ
is a source of resentment. Q
relative economic power bc
time, which would seem to
the contemporary discussio
pace of the development ir
developed countries would
we were to use available V
build up the economies of
obviously the diminution of
to slow down the pace of V

In formulating our polici
First, we cannot base our s
taining the condition of in
acterized the United State
of growth, 7 per cent of tl
possess roughly 40 per cen
capacity, if the rest of the v
facilities. The Russians ai
share through the process
the economic preponderar
going to be diminished rap

tance should be provided to firm friends of the West, and others should be permitted to work out their destinies with lesser support. In other words, assistance should be geared to building up the strength of the Western coalition both militarily and economically, and not to encouraging general economic development—a project that can best be defended on humanitarian rather than security grounds. Once we are embarked upon an assistance program, it is difficult to disentangle ourselves. For this reason, we should be prepared to set the qualifications for assistance and stick to them.

The massive Soviet-bloc economic offensive is, in fact, an extremely limited economic phenomenon, the fundamental purpose of which is propagandistic. It has been exaggerated out of all proportion in the effort to whip up popular support for the aid program and the trade-agreements act. The Soviet Union is fundamentally an autarkic power. Aside from intrabloc trade, its external commerce is so limited that it is exceeded by such small Western nations as Switzerland and Sweden. The recent extension of credits by the bloc has been quite limited, not sufficient to make even a dent in the overriding preponderance of the West in international commerce. The Russians have given no evidence to indicate that they are willing to abandon their autarkic objectives and become dependent upon foreign sources of supply. Consequently, the total volume of trade that is open to the outside world is quite restricted. We should be certain that nations outside the bloc see for themselves how limited are the opportunities for trading with the Soviet bloc, not for just one or two small nations but for the large number of nations before whom the Russians have displayed lures. Instead of making the most of the immense advantages of the West as markets and as sources of supply, we have been frightened and treat any trade agreement between the Soviet bloc and an outside state as contaminating its character and setting it irreparably on the road to ruin.

The Soviet credit program is essentially propagandistic. It has no such grandiose ambition as to raise living standards and increase stability in areas where instability serves Soviet interests. Essentially, it has been adopted to disguise the enormous economic importance of the West to these areas. Instead of drawing the appropriate comparisons, in the effort to impress Congress and the public, we have furthered the only purpose of the Soviet effort—propaganda. We have exaggerated their accomplishments, made light of our own achievements. It is certainly a peculiar kind of propaganda that touts one's opponents and deprecates oneself. The only saving feature is that the reality differs to so great an extent from the picture drawn by our propaganda, that very few either at home or abroad take it seriously.

In the discussions of the Soviet threat to the West, we have also touted the Soviet rate of economic growth. Not only is the rate of industrial growth exaggerated, but it is taken as the sole criterion of economic efficiency. We have been lured into meaningless comparisons about the relative output of specific commodities. The slow rate of over-all economic growth in the Soviet Union has been ignored, along with the snail-like progress of living standards. But these are the very features of Soviet life that we should invite the underdeveloped areas to consider; instead, we concentrate upon a picture of Soviet industrial accomplishments that is somewhat larger than life. In this matter, our statements are taken more seriously because the lure of industrial development, even in the absence of rising living standards, is great in the underdeveloped areas. We should hardly encourage that tendency.

In dealing with the underdeveloped countries, we ought to dispense with the desperate feeling that if they are not on our side, they will be allied with the Soviet bloc. In these regions, the perspective of a bipolar world is least appropriate; we need to envisage the basic fluidity. Some nations in Asia may go Communist, but for that very reason neighboring states may be immune. On the one hand, the Soviet bloc has an immense advantage in that the appeal of the rapid industrial development through totalitarian techniques is widespread. But these nations are not likely to sacrifice their own independence of action in order to satisfy the Russians, who will decreasingly be masters of their own bloc. The West's greatest countervailing advantage is that supplied by trade, due to the complementarity of the economies of the underdeveloped countries and the West. We may use our advantages in trade to the fullest, without being misled into believing that trade provides any guarantee that nations will not turn against the West. At the present time, it is the strategic interest of the United States to eschew autarkic policies; we ought not, however, be deceived into believing that it is impossible for the United States to dispense with external sources of supply.

Expressions of opinion in the United States tend to run to extremes. Paradoxically, the grandiloquence of public statements may be due to the relative fixity of public opinion in a democracy.[1] Attitudes are slow to adjust, even in the face of necessity. Although, in the final analysis, specific national policies cannot be maintained for long if they affront public opinion, this public opinion is characterized by inertia. Consequently, it is tempting to try to speed up the adjustment of public opinion to new conditions and new policies through the use of political hyperbole. But the exaggerations that appear in public discussions are based upon something more than deliberate policy. In contrast to the stability of the views of the public at large, so-called "informed opinion," in itself, exhibits a high degree of volatility. Ideas may change with startling rapidity, though credos and conditions are altered only gradually. Consequently, opinions based on ideas and on the changing intellectual fashions are likely to be far more variable than are those of the general public, which are based upon existing conditions and inculcated precepts. Since ideas acquire a life of their own, the tendency toward self-deception among propagandists is great. Public debates may simply involve controversy over ideas that are largely divorced from a realistic appraisal of existing conditions.

In the war of words that has arisen from our disputes over policy, it has become increasingly difficult to disentangle the real problems facing the West from the transitory or spurious problems. Each group of proponents of some policy has designed its own economic test as to how well the United States is faring in the cold war. There is the economic-potential test, the taxable-capacity test, the Soviet-growth test, the China-versus-India test, and the foreign-trade test. Each of these tests carries within

itself the germ of an economic policy which, according to its
proponents, will provide security for the United States. In this
study, skepticism has been expressed concerning the value of
any such economic tests, and it has been argued that it is
dangerous to draw long-run policy conclusions on the basis of
such piecemeal analysis. The problems of national security are
subtle, and they defy analysis in narrow, quantitative terms.

The author of this study is aware that because he has dis-
paraged the importance of most of these popular indicators,
he will be accused of complacency. To some, it will seem incredible that so little strategic significance should be attributed
to Soviet economic expansion or to the Soviet trade and credit
offensive (at the present level). Others will argue that the
writer is mistaken in appraising the importance of economic
capacity, or that he would court destruction of our economic
system by asserting that a tax burden even greater than the
present is tolerable. But surely we cannot achieve security by
fighting what is unavoidable, and neglecting our real defenses.

It is the writer's belief that the complacent ones are those who
have presented these shibboleths as proper guides to the nation's
security. They have failed to realize fully the implications of the
enormous shift that has taken place in the international power
structure. Their arguments imply that there are easy solutions
to the problems of national security, and that these solutions
are economic in nature. All we need to do, it appears, is to
match the Soviet Union in industrial expansion, or adopt an
aid program to the underdeveloped areas that will bring home
to the inhabitants how effective and ethical are our methods of
social organization and how noble are our motives. In other
words, the tide now running against the West can easily be
turned by economic means, without substantial sacrifice.

Such hopes are illusory. It is typical of the American attitude,
cultivated as it has been in isolation and based upon the premises
of liberalism, to believe that any problem has a solution, and
that the basis of the solution is usually economic. In the 170-
year history of the American republic, experience would seem
to suggest that stability is the normal course for human relationships. Conflicts could be suppressed through law and order—

which in themselves were a reflection of the underlying stability of the American scene. Americans have not been laggard in attempting to apply the principles of law and order on the international scene. But the rest of the world has had experience with the permanent nature of conflict, and is by no means as enamored of the *status quo* as is the great satisfied and self-sufficient power of the New World.

There are no trick economic solutions to the problems that assail us. Mere economic growth will not protect us from the hostility of Communism in its virulent stage. Mere granting of economic assistance is no more likely to dispel the hatred of the West in the underdeveloped areas[2] than did our wartime attempts to convince the Russians that their suspicions of the outside world were unfounded, and that the world was fundamentally a harmonious and stable place. We will be no more liked or respected if we seem to dispense aid as a gesture of propitiation. The fact that the extension of aid is no solution to our security problem does not mean that there does not exist a terribly complex problem of the relations of the West and the underdeveloped areas; it simply means that no "solution" is possible, and Americans have always assumed that problems are solvable.

Surely these are not grounds for complacency. The West lives in an increasingly hostile world. The decay of our position in Asia over the past decade is woefully plain, and we would be unwise to believe that we, who are the symbol of the West, can ever separate ourselves from the other Western powers in the eyes of non-Westerners. The issuance of appeals, or advice, or assistance is not going to provide the West with security; only a combination of strength and of respect for that strength can do that. We are unlikely to convince outsiders that we are nature's noblemen, but we may convince them that it is our intention to protect our interests, our security, and our independence. If we are steadfast, if we do not allow our attention to be absorbed by spurious problems and easy solutions, we will be able to survive.

Rather than attempting to remake the world in our own image, and to solve economic problems that are not solvable in the

short run, we should pay more attention to the domestic implications of our existence in a hostile world. As yet, we have not
thought through the meaning for our type of society and our
type of economy of the existence of heavy and permanent expenditures for national security. The demands of national security
have raised a question about the preservation of our traditional
liberties, and this applies to more than the difficult task of
preserving civil liberties under conditions that call for political
cohesion.

Our type of society, with its emphasis upon personal freedom
of action, can hardly survive unless there is a considerable
dispersion of economic power. Since economic decisions must
be decentralized, ultimately it may be seen that free markets
are an important aspect of freedom. But the growth of the role of
the government carries with it the latent threat that the minimum of dispersion of economic power may disappear. The government's role as a big buyer, engrossing 20 per cent or more
of business activity and employment, may mean that the government's attitude will dominate all decision making. Unless this
power implicit in the government's position is handled with
great discretion and judgment, it may prove to be an element
imposing inflexibility and conformity upon the economic system.
Flexibility and economic variety would seem to be an integral
part of our type of free society. Considerable thought will have
to be given to ways of minimizing the impact of the government's extensive purchasing activities upon the whole of economic life.

An allied problem is that of the big budget. The rigidity of
the traditionalist attitude concerning the degree to which government expenditures and taxation are "tolerable" represents a
threat to our security. Surely, we must have adequate expenditures for national security, and surely adequate expenditures
are within the power of the world's most prosperous economy.
We have had far too much talk in recent years that too much
spending will lead us into insolvency or a hair-curling depression, or that Lenin's prescription for the destruction of capitalism
was debauchment of the currency. We cannot impose artificial
limits on military expenditures. The foreign policy and the

military posture of this nation are integral parts of the defense of our free institutions. Under no circumstances will they survive unless defense expenditures are adequate or more than adequate.

The abuse of the "intolerable budget" argument for purposes of domestic haggling over the tax load must disappear. The proper level of expenditures should be determined, and then the sources of funds found, rather than permitting expenditures to be determined by premonitions of taxpayer resistance. On the issue of the big budget and the tax load, we cannot afford "politics as usual," with the pleasant political assumption that a tax that strikes at the general standard of living is politically unacceptable. Part of the reason for the artificial limit imposed upon total spending in recent years is the artificial political limit imposed on the types of taxes that we have been willing to levy. We can no longer treat the problem of national security as a temporary disturbance; it will be with us continually. The gravest contemporary problem posed for our society is that of reconciling the free-market economy with the necessity of maintaining powerful forces in being for protection and as a diplomatic tool in the cold war. In the next quarter-century, this problem and its solution will be the touchstone of the success that we will have in maintaining a free society and a free economy.

Before we have settled our domestic problems, we ought to be modest in proposing solutions to the difficulties that other societies encounter. Our international goal should be the limited one of achieving security for both ourselves and allied Western nations, if possible. We cannot assume that the underlying disharmonies and rivalries that have always existed will now automatically disappear, simply because we have been thrust into the center of the world stage. Careful attention to domestic problems and a resolute determination to protect our international position in a hostile world, no matter how heavy the costs, will be the most fruitful and, in the long run, the most humane policy that we can follow.

NOTES

CHAPTER 1

1. Lionel Robbins, *An Essay on the Nature and Significance of Economic Science*, 2nd ed. (New York: The Macmillan Co., 1935), p. 16.

2. Ralph Waldo Emerson, in his essay, "On Compensation," developed a law of compensation which appears to be vividly applicable in economic problems. "The same dualism," he said, "underlies the nature and condition of man. . . . For anything you have missed, you have gained something else; and for anything you gain, you lose something. If riches increase, they are increased that use them. If the gatherer gathers too much, nature takes out of the man what she puts into his chest; swells the estate but kills the owner. Nature hates monopolies and exceptions. . . . Life invests itself with inevitable conditions, which the unwise seek to dodge."

3. I have avoided the use of the term "law of diminishing returns," with which many are familiar, first because I wish to include commodities as well as factors of production (resources)—that is, I wish to incorporate what is sometimes referred to as the "law of diminishing marginal utility." Secondly, the original use of the term "diminishing returns" applied to agriculture and referred to an expected decline in the average output as population increased, because of a shortage of good land. This use is more restrictive than is proper in the light of modern technology. All we can say today is that the returns from a particular factor of production will tend to decline as more of that factor is used *relative to the use of other factors of production*.

4. In his relations with each of the major political parties, the economist falls quite naturally into both of his roles, in turn. One party must be constrained; the other prodded. The spokesmen for one party announce that we can all enjoy higher real incomes; that public expenditures for

foreign aid, defense, welfare, and other civil benefits should be increased; that credit can be loosened; and finally, that the rate of investment and growth can be speeded up to match the Soviets. The spokesmen for the opposing party, on the other hand, give the impression that the society has little freedom in the allocation of resources; that any expansion of the government's activities is "unnatural"; that we cannot bear the present level of government expenditures or the present tax burden, and unless we get them down, we are heading for a "hair-curling depression." One would suppose that the economist would maintain a position of critical detachment. Yet few people like the role of disinterested observer; the economist, who is as swayed by emotion as the next man, discovers an affinity for one or the other of the two parties—based in no small measure on an emotional predilection for the role of either nay-sayer or yea-sayer.

CHAPTER 2

1. It should be stated in using the term "market value" in this example that all expenditures of the government on goods and services are weighed *at cost*, since market prices may not exist or may not be applicable..

2. In 1958, the Yugoslav credit providing for a power plant, two fertilizer factories, modernization of three mines, a hydroelectric plant, and an aluminum works was "delayed" for five years. It now appears that there will be neither a drain on the Soviet economy nor assistance to Yugoslavia. The rapprochement was of brief duration.

CHAPTER 3

1. Letter to Secretary of Defense Wilson, *Department of Defense Appropriations for 1956, Hearings before the Subcommittee of the Committee on Appropriations, United States Senate* (Washington: Government Printing Office, 1955), p. 4. The distinguished military historian Professor E. M. Earle has expressed the same conviction somewhat more cautiously but with the same implication: "It is true that production may be the decisive factor in an armed struggle now and probably will be the decisive factor in any armed struggle in the future." ("Characteristics of a Valid Strategy," lecture delivered at the United States Naval War College, March 12, 1951, reprinted in *Elements of Strategy*, pp. 4-5; reproduced by permission of Mrs. Edward Mead Earle.)

2. The most comprehensive treatment of the concept may be found in Klaus Knorr's excellent study, *The War Potential of Nations* (Princeton: Princeton University Press, 1956), Ch. 9-13. Knorr's approach is highly sophisticated, treating the economic factor merely as one of the several variables influencing national power. In treating economic potential, he works not only with the national-product figures but with the size and composition of the population, the structure of industry, and the role of

foreign trade. His treatment is much broader than the conventional view of the economic potential for war.

3. Benjamin H. Williams, *Reconversion and Partial Mobilization* (Washington: Industrial College of the Armed Forces, 1954), pp. 67-68.

4. There has been some tendency to exaggerate the Soviet manpower advantage relative to our own. We have fostered the public notion that we *cannot* match the Russians man for man. At best, this represents a half-truth based upon political considerations. The Soviet population is, to be sure, some 15 per cent greater than our own. This hardly represents a crushing superiority in numbers. It should be remembered that in World War II, when the Russians' advantage in population was 25 to 30 per cent, we mobilized more men than they did. Moreover, World War II resulted in the decimation of the birth cohorts that are just coming of military age in the Soviet Union, while expanding the same birth cohorts in the U.S.

5. W. K. Hancock and M. M. Gowing, *British War Economy* (London: His Majesty's Stationer's Office, 1949), p. 72.

6. See Thomas K. Finletter, *Power and Policy* (New York: Harcourt, Brace & Co., 1954), pp. 254-257. It is Finletter's contention that reliance upon economic capacity is anachronistic in this era:

> No longer will the United States . . . be able to build up its military forces and rely on its industrial potential after the war has begun. The nostalgic idea that our industrial power is our greatest military asset could ruin our military planning. There may not be any long war to give our industrial potential the time to bring its weight to bear. Our industrial potential may be smashed at the outset, and the war be over before we can recover.
>
> We must build our military force on the exact opposite of this industrial potential notion. We must have force-in-being ready to fight at peak power the day a war will open.

The deficiency of Finletter's work is that it does not seem to provide any place for limited warfare. On the contrary, he asserts that the "Korean war was artificial," illustrating the "drag of the past" by encouraging us to think that "strategy and tactics pretty much along the lines we followed in World War II" would suffice.

For the opposite side of the case, arguing for the continuing importance of economic capacity in both nuclear and limited war, see Klaus Knorr, "The Concept of Economic Potential for War," lecture delivered at the Industrial College of the Armed Forces on March 19, 1957, revised and published under the same title in *World Politics*, October, 1957, pp. 49-62.

7. Some writers have treated a high rate of growth as the panacea through which we can increase military expenditures or foreign aid without a decline in living standards. The weakness in this approach is that increased output redounds to the public in the form of higher incomes, which

are felt to be deserved. To take away more than the nominal fraction in taxation, which would be essential to obtain the resources under free enterprise, would meet resistance. It would not be too much harder to overcome the resistance to falling living standards.

8. R. E. Osgood, *Limited War* (Chicago: University of Chicago Press, 1957), pp. 19-20.

9. See William W. Kaufmann (editor), *Military Policy and National Security* (Princeton: Princeton University Press, 1956), p. 182; also pp. 122, 249-252.

CHAPTER 4

1. The farm bloc in Congress acquiesced in price controls only after it had obtained very large concessions on the level of prices at which controls could be instituted, as well as considerable restriction on the power of OPA.

2. Sir Dennis Robertson, *Economic Commentaries* (London: Staples Press Limited, 1957), pp. 147-154. "If we economists mind our own business, and do that business well, we can, I believe, contribute mightily to the economizing, that is to the full but thrifty utilization, of that scarce resource Love—which *we* know, just as well as anybody else, to be the most precious thing in the world."

3. In fairness to the Board, it should be observed that its assignment was an impossible one. The Preamble to Title IV of the Defense Production Act modestly proclaims the task assigned to the stabilization authorities as follows:

> It is the intent of Congress to provide authority necessary to achieve the following purposes in order to promote the national defense: To prevent inflation and preserve the value of the national currency; to assure that defense appropriations are not dissipated by excessive costs and prices; to stabilize the cost of living for workers and other consumers and the costs of production for farmers and businessmen; to eliminate and prevent profiteering, hoarding, manipulation, speculation, and other disruptive practices resulting from abnormal market conditions or scarcities; to protect consumers, wage earners, investors, and persons with relatively fixed or limited incomes from undue impairment of their living standards; to prevent economic disturbances, labor disputes, interferences with effective mobilization of national resources, and impairment of national unity and morale; to assist in maintaining a reasonable balance between purchasing power and the supply of consumer goods and services; to protect the national economy against future loss of needed purchasing power by the present dissipation of individual savings; and to prevent a future collapse of values.

It is indeed a laudable, but inconsistent, statement of aims. The conflict is phrased more succinctly in Title V: "It is the intent of Congress, in order to

provide for effective price and wage stabilization . . . and to maintain un-
interrupted production, that there be effective procedures for the settlement
of labor disputes affecting the national defense."

4. A further example is the emasculation of selective credit controls on
real estate credit. Under pressure from the construction industry, Congress
amended the Act in 1952 and prohibited the Board of Governors of the
Federal Reserve System (to whom the President had delegated his authority) from imposing down-payment requirements in excess of 5 per
cent when construction fell below 1.2 million units.

5. The actions of all parties in the dispute would appear reprehensible.
The industry demanded an unnecessary price increase; the union—perhaps
with most justification, in view of the lenient settlements elsewhere—pushed
its claims further than was warranted; and the Administration destroyed its
own position by becoming a protagonist in a dispute in which it was supposed to serve as a neutral. Politics, being the art of the possible, naturally
consists of compromise, but compromise does not mean the exclusive support of one participant in a dispute. The Administration contrived to make
controls ineffective as well as irksome.

6. Although inflation might be mandatory, the pace of the inflation
could be slowed by forcing groups to go through the *time-consuming, bureaucratic process* of appealing to the WSB or OPS to obtain the increases
in wages or prices.

CHAPTER 5

1. Quoted by Jesse Burkhead, *Government Budgeting* (New York: John
Wiley & Sons, Inc., 1956), p. 6.

2. It should be apparent that in the phrase "efficiency and economy,"
the word "economy" is being used in a sense different from that in which
it has been employed heretofore. Here, it means simply reduction of expenditures or budget reduction. This is, of course, a far cry from the broader
meaning of economy, as used in Chapter 1—that is, making the best over-
all use of resources. The reader should understand the dual use of the term,
and the fact that the conventional use of the term carries with it the
gratuitous and inaccurate implication that the best use of resources is
always achieved by giving less to the government.

Since this identification of economy in the true sense of budget reduction
has usually been made in the name of conservatism, it is perhaps appropriate to recall the balanced judgement of the father of modern conservatism
on the subject:

> Mere parsimony is not economy. Expense and great expense may be
> an essential part in true economy. Economy is a distributive virtue
> and consists not in saving but in selection. Parsimony requires no
> providence, no sagacity, no powers of combination, no comparison,

no judgment. Mere instinct may produce this false economy in perfection. The other economy has larger views. It demands a discriminating judgment and a firm, sagacious mind. (Edmund Burke, *Works*, V, p. 229.)

3. For a recent restatement of the marginal-utility approach to the level and distribution of government expenditures, see Arthur Smithies, "Federal Budgeting and Fiscal Policy, in *A Survey of Contemporary Economics*, edited by Howard S. Ellis for the American Economic Association (Homewood: Richard D. Irwin, Inc., 1952), pp. 192-193. For an earlier and more extensive treatment of the problem, see Hugh Dalton, *Public Finance*, 9th ed. (London: George Routledge & Sons, Ltd., 1936), pp. 18-20. For a critique of the applicability of marginalist analysis to budgetary decisions, see Burkhead, *op. cit.*, pp. 41-57.

4. For example, it is difficult to weigh, in terms of utility, the value of an additional aircraft carrier, as opposed to eight additional Polaris submarines (probably the relevant alternative). It depends upon the nation's objectives and its strategic doctrine—and upon its estimates of the likelihood of limited war as opposed to a nuclear one, and consequently, the value to be placed on deterrence or on tactical armed strength. Moreover, an aircraft carrier is a highly indivisible item which cannot be varied by small amounts at the margin. The impossibility of precise measurement of utility is clear, yet at the same time, in reaching a decision, a mental process that incorporates the notions of marginalism ought to be employed.

5. Lucius Wilmerding, *The Spending Power* (New Haven: Yale University Press, 1943), p. 143.

6. Senator James C. Couzens once remarked on the floor of Congress, "I think it is all folly to spend any time on appropriations bills, when whatever we cut out must be taken care of later in a deficiency bill." (*Congressional Record*, 69th Congress, 1st Session, p. 5419; quoted by Harold W. Guest, *Public Expenditure* [New York: G. P. Putnam's Sons, 1927], p. 133.)

7. In early 1958, Senator Dennis Chavez, chairman of the Defense Appropriations Subcommittee of the Senate, threatened to remove this bottleneck by writing a proviso into the appropriations bill forbidding the Bureau to withhold funds voted by the Congress.

8. Senator Harry F. Byrd has phrased the traditional position with great force:

Our free-enterprise system is the greatest deterrent in the world today to Russian aggression. It is our first line of defense. Our military forces are merely the tools through which the strength of this system is applied in war. Our competitive-enterprise system can only exist under solvent government. . . .

It is no exaggeration to say that there is literally nothing on earth more important than the preservation of the fiscal integrity of the Federal Government of the United States of America. (*Congressional Record,* vol. 103, Part 2, 85th Congress, 1st Session, p. 1947.)

9. Rep. George Mahon, rising to the defense of the Congressional sense of responsibility, has observed quite aptly: "Everybody in that period after World War II was going along hopefully with a much reduced budget. It was not Congress, but the Secretary of Defense and the Administration who were holding down the military program." (*Department of Defense Appropriations for 1957, Hearings before the Subcommittee of the Committee on Appropriations, House of Representatives* [Washington: Government Printing Office, 1956], p. 113.)

10. Arthur Smithies, *The Budgetary Process in the United States* (New York: McGraw-Hill Book Company, 1955), pp. 121-122.

11. *Department of Defense Appropriations for 1958, Hearings before the Subcommittee of the Committee on Appropriations, United States Senate* (Washington: Government Printing Office, 1957), p. 6.

12. Nothing that has been said should be taken to suggest that economical government is not a desirable objective in itself. A disquieting feature of the Washington scene, however, has been the tendency not only for the Director of the Bureau of the Budget, but also the Secretary of the Treasury, the Secretary of Defense, and even the President to imply that our chief policy objective should be to reduce government expenditures. For the record, at least, everyone has been concerned about economy and no one about policy fulfillment.

13. Compare the treatment in Smithies, *op. cit.,* pp. 287-296. Like Professor Smithies, I have been reluctant to involve myself in this complicated issue. Ignorant as I am of the technical questions involved, I have seen no other way to get across the *economic principles* involved in these decisions than to expose my ignorance rashly.

14. Though the Hoover Commission used the two terms interchangeably, economists have tended to concentrate on the term "performance budget" in recent discussions. It would seem, however, that "program budget" is the more appropriate term, since it implies consideration of policy alternatives, whereas "performance budget" would seem to connote evaluation of the past to see how much of a given program was actually achieved. "Performance budget" carries a connotation of efficiency as well, and it may well be that this term is the proper one to be used to integrate the two basic budgetary concepts—whenever the necessary changes in organization, procedures, and doctrine are achieved.

CHAPTER 6

1. I have taken the terminology from Albert O. Hirschman. See his excellent treatment of the theoretical aspects of the problem in the study,

National Power and the Structure of Foreign Trade (Berkeley: University of California Press, 1945), pp. 13-34.

2. Certainly, the British position can be explained largely on these grounds. The French and the Israelis had other objectives as well. But even in the case of the Israelis, the desire to open the Gulf of Aquaba to commerce played no insignificant role in the decision to attack.

3. John Maynard Keynes, "National Self-Sufficiency," in the *Yale Review,* Summer, 1933; see especially pp. 756-758.

4. Raymond Vernon, "Foreign Trade and National Defense," in *Foreign Affairs,* October, 1955, pp. 77-78.

5. *Trade Agreements Extension Act of 1953,* Hearings before the Committee on Ways and Means, House of Representatives (Washington: Government Printing Office, 1953), p. 406; quoted by Behrman and Schmidt, *International Economics* (New York: Rinehart & Company, Inc., 1957), p. 53.

6. In the Trade Agreements Extension Act of 1958, the national-security clause was strengthened along protectionist lines, further blurring the distinction between the vested-interest and the defense arguments for protection. The law now holds that "excessive" imports may impair national security not only directly but indirectly; since a strong economy is essential to national security, any imports that are "excessive" impair national security by threatening the economy. It should be noted also that the Office of Defense Mobilization has now been merged with Civil Defense to form the Office of Defense and Civilian Mobilization (ODCM).

7. It has been argued that the re-election bid of Senator Leverett Saltonstall played no insignificant role in the Administration's decision. The Waltham Watch Company was the one most directly affected by the decision. Under similar circumstances in 1950, President Truman had acceded to an increase in the tariffs on hats at the time of Senator William Benton's re-election campaign. The hat industry has a concentration in and around Danbury, Conn.

8. The chronology might be continued as follows: in May, 1958, the Vice President received his "very warm" reception in Venezuela. At his news conference on May 14, the President expressed his surprise at the resentments shown in Venezuela in the following words: "In Venezuela, on the economic side, you have had these rumors that the United States was ready to—was trying to impose quotas upon a country, quotas on the oil-producing countries; and, of course, there is no truth in the last one at all." (See the transcript in *The New York Times,* May 15, 1958, p. 14.)

9. *The Outlook for Energy Sources,* vol. III in *Resources for Freedom, A Report to the President by the President's Materials Policy Commission* (Washington: Government Printing Office, 1952), pp. 7-8, 10-14.

10. In testifying on behalf of the extension of the Trade Agreements Act, former Treasury Secretary Humphrey came to opposite conclusions. Admitting that there was a risk involved in relying on Middle Eastern

sources, he urged that sources in neighboring states be considered analogous to domestic production. See *Trade Agreements Extension,* Hearings before the Committee on Finance, United States Senate, Part 1 (Washington: Government Printing Office, 1955), p. 105.

11. George F. Kennan, *Realities of American Foreign Policy* (Princeton: Princeton University Press, 1954), p. 31.

12. This aspect of the matter has tended to be obfuscated by recent State Department propaganda in behalf of the aid program. The attempt has been made to portray Russian assistance to underdeveloped states as massive. The figure of $1.9 billion used by the State Department is probably correct, but it includes roughly $400 million worth of arms and $285 million of Yugoslav credits now lapsed. Most of the balance represents *credits* that will be drawn on in the *next decade.* It has been hard to obtain deliveries of goods based on credits, since the Soviets trade bilaterally. The State Department effort has been misguided, in my opinion. (The subject will be examined further in Chapter 9.)

13. Though the subject has not been discussed in this chapter, it should not be assumed that it will be desirable for the United States to continue to follow her traditional nondiscriminatory trading policy under all possible sets of circumstances. If the outside world grows increasingly hostile to the West, it may at some future date be regarded as desirable to use our massive buying power to obtain additional leverage in trade with which to reward our international friends and bring pressure to bear upon our international enemies. In such an event, the United States might find it advisable to make use of the whole arsenal of weapons provided by bilateral trading—in other words, to resort to illiberal (Schachtian) devices. In the last resort, maximum pressure would be obtainable through a government trading monopoly. It should be recognized, of course, that the United States would then be sacrificing potential economic gains for strategic advantages.

CHAPTER 7

1. Despite the clear evidence that the new plan is intended to cover up the failure of Soviet ambitions and a reduction of her goals, American observers have been disturbed by the projections. Khrushchev's boast, in announcing the plan, that "with the fulfillment of this plan, a decisive step shall have been made toward establishing the material and technical base for Communism and accomplishing the main economic task of the U.S.S.R. —overtaking and surpassing in a historically short period of time the most highly developed capitalist countries in *per capita* production" has once again excited a flurry of alarm that the Russians are catching up. With respect to the *imminence* of this danger that the Soviets will overtake and surpass the West, a sense of historical perspective is required. Consider the following statements, for example:

Stalin, 1931: "We are fifty to a hundred years behind the advanced countries. We must make good this distance in ten years. Either we do it or they will crush us." ("Tasks of the Business Managers," Feb. 4, 1931; reprinted in *Leninism,* Moscow, 1933.)

Stalin, 1939: "We have outstripped the principal capitalist countries as regards technique of production and rate of industrial development. We must outstrip them economically as well [that is, in volume of industrial production per head of population] . . . [We must do this] in the next ten or fifteen years." (*The Land of Socialism Today and Tomorrow,* Moscow, 1939.)

Khrushchev, 1958: "In the next fifteen years the U.S.S.R. will take first place in the world not only in total volume of production but also in per capita production, and the material and technical foundation for Communism will be laid in our country; this will also signify a great victory for the Soviet Union in its peaceful economic competition with the most highly developed capitalist countries." ("Khrushchev's Theses on the Seven-Year Plan," *loc. cit.,* p. 7.)

2. Gregory Grossman, "Soviet Economy and Soviet World Power," in *International Stability and Progress,* Eleventh American Assembly at Arden House (New York: Columbia University Press, 1957), pp. 44-45. Grossman was formerly associated with the Russian Research Center at Harvard University, which, along with the RAND Corporation, may be regarded as the center of the high-estimate school. A similar grim view of the issue by an English observer may be found in Alec Nove's "The Pace of Soviet Economic Development," in *Lloyd's Bank Review,* April, 1956.

3. Nutter has summarized his estimate in "Industrial Growth in the Soviet Union," in *The American Economic Review,* May, 1958, pp. 398-411.

4. This deficiency would also apply to computed growth rates for the United States, but probably to a lesser degree, because the emphasis upon and pace of development in these newer industries is greater in the Soviet Union.

5. Estimate in *Soviet Economic Growth, op. cit.,* p. 133. Though not intended to do so, this estimate would tend to corroborate the position of the low-estimate school. If, during the plan period, Soviet industry has grown by 10 per cent a year or more, and if we make allowances for the war period, industry should have increased at least twelve-fold, while agricultural production was rising by some 50 per cent. Yet the estimate states that from 1928 to 1955, the share of agriculture, forestry, and fisheries in the net product fell only from 42 to 28 per cent, while industry, mining, and construction rose only from 28 to 40 per cent. This would tend to suggest that the rate of industrial growth has been much less rapid than the high-estimate school has inferred.

Another way of putting the problem is this: according to the gloomy view, both agricultural and industrial production are roughly half the

American level. But in the United States, agriculture contributes only 5 per cent of national income, whereas in the Soviet Union it is alleged to contribute 28 per cent. This implies inconsistency in the position of the high-estimate school.

6. Allen W. Dulles, speech before the United States Chamber of Commerce, April 28, 1958, reported in *The New York Times,* April 29, 1958, p. 8. Mr. Dulles went on to point out that American industrial production, as a result of the recession, had declined by a similar amount in the same period. Whether this implies that there should be no fluctuations of output in a market economy is difficult to determine.

7. During the same period, it should be noted, the United States supplied some $60 billion in assistance, plus some additional billions in capital investment to the outside world. The different directions of the flow of capital in the case of the two superpowers ought not to be disregarded in considering the relative rates of growth of the two economies. A sizable reduction in foreign assistance by the United States would have permitted a more rapid rate of economic growth.

8. G. W. Nutter, "Some Observations on Soviet Economic Growth," in *The American Economic Review,* May, 1957, pp. 618-630.

9. Soviet steel production in 1957 was 56 million tons (51 million metric tons); according to the defunct Sixth Five-Year Plan, it was slated to increase to approximately 75 million tons by 1960 (68.3 million metric tons), but 65 million tons seems to be the probable output for that year. This will be less than half of our present capacity of 140 million tons. It should be remembered that capacity rather than output is the appropriate basis of comparison. Since American production fluctuates in accordance with demand, in a brief interval of time, Soviet production might surpass our own. Mr. Dulles, the director of the CIA, in his speech mentioned earlier, pointed out that in the first three months of 1958, Soviet steel production was 75 per cent of American production. This was due to the low operating rate of the American steel industry, and was meaningless as a comparison of industrial strength.

10. A recent article in *The Economist* (December 28, 1957), entitled "We Caught Up with Russia," presents a satirical forecast of the world of 1967, in which the West has accepted Soviet production standards, and Russia has accepted Western goals with respect to the standard of living. More of this sort of treatment of the issue is needed, and fewer desperate pronouncements.

11. The "real" causes of a business cycle refer to those that would operate even in the absence of a monetary framework. They should be distinguished from the "monetary" causes, to which some would argue that the Soviet economy, because of its centrally controlled nature, is immune.

12. The rate of expansion in steel fell to 4 per cent in 1958.

CHAPTER 8

1. It may be argued that Western life is no less governed by tradition than is life in the underdeveloped areas. But Western traditions have been created in a climate that fosters economic growth. Western goals and traits—ambition, progress, physical comforts, individualism, rationality, and so on—all are conducive to development. The factors that govern life in a traditional agrarian society are not. It is true that the West emerged from a similar agricultural setting, but it was a process requiring centuries—and it led to continual social unrest.

2. By pointing out the weaknesses of planning, I do not wish to associate myself with those who argue that the primary error of the underdeveloped areas has been to resort to inefficient planning, rather than to rely upon the market mechanism. The market mechanism is all right in its place, but it is dependent upon a framework of institutions and social attitudes that may be absent in underdeveloped areas. With our traditions of economic individualism, we have been able to obtain the results we desire through the workings of the market. Producers are guided by the market to make their contribution to national output, and they envisage their roles and functions through the mechanism of the market. Other nations, which lack our traditions of economic individualism, may find that the plan, no matter how grandiose in Western eyes, supplies the best method of coordinating economic efforts to the desired end. The plan provides the impetus to a change of social attitudes, and a framework within which individuals and groups may see the fruits of their actions in advancing the social goals. We may regard our methods as more efficient, as more decentralized, as more conducive to personal liberty; we have no right to insist that others so regard them.

In Chapter 9, I shall allude again to this issue in discussing the free-enterprise position on foreign aid. At this point, all I am pointing out is that planning, although not inherently defective, is no panacea. It can be terribly expensive in terms of limited entrepreneurial talent, and it is not unlikely to lead an economy along just that path of economic development that it should avoid.

3. The American subspecies of planitis is "budgetitis," the notion that through the mere appropriation of money, we can obtain workable solutions to vexing problems. More money for education, it would seem, can make up for shoddy standards, deficient doctrine, student apathy, parental indifference, and the low status and morale of teachers. On the international level, appropriations for foreign assistance will dissolve international rivalries, racial tensions, excessive population, low resources, and distress over unfair treatment.

4. See Yuan-li Wu, *An Economic Survey of Communist China* (New York: Bookman Associates, Inc., 1956), pp. 156-161.

5. A *rupee* is worth approximately 21 cents. A *crore* of *rupees* is 10 million *rupees*.

6. The original plan called for an outlay of Rs. 4,800 *crores*—subsequently raised, because of price increases, to Rs. 5,300 *crores*.

7. At its charitable best, the reaction seemed to suggest that the outside world could not understand India: *You Westerners, with your cold bankers' hearts, cannot possibly understand the aspirations of the Asian peoples or the spirit of India.* Resentment against the World Bank itself was somewhat assuaged by a loan for the development of India's railways.

8. See, for example, his remarks, as quoted in *The New York Times,* October 22, 1957, after the drought and crop losses in 1957: "The country will push through . . . India will go on if all the world is against her. There the matter ends. We will have to starve if necessary. But we will go on."

9. This may be due, in part, to climatic or cultural factors, which it is most undiplomatic to discuss.

10. The Soviet Union itself seems to have solved the problem of population pressure—in part, by the ingenious device of separating the men from the women. The local disproportion between the sexes in the Soviet Union is impressive. The men are herded together in the industrial towns, while the women remain behind to till the land. It might also be observed that the procreative instinct does not rank high in the list of virtues for dedicated Communists. On the question of family, the Soviet upper classes have fully absorbed the middle-class attitudes.

11. The right-wing version of American omnipotence has naturally received fuller treatment. Did China go Communist? It had nothing to do with the 600 million Chinese, but reflected the deficiencies of American policy (or worse). But the liberal attitude is comparable, and both reflect American experience which has not known failure; we can eliminate poverty, we can save the Indians, etc. Both the left and the right seem to have developed their own varieties of Asia-firsters.

CHAPTER 9

1. It is hard to corroborate this statement statistically. Any brief survey, however, of the expressed attitudes of leading public figures suggests that doubts are rarely stated concerning the desirability of American assistance for general economic development in the underdeveloped lands. The majority of public commentators of the press and radio lend support to the program. The Republican Administration has made it a cardinal point in its foreign policy, and if the Democrats are critical, they chide the Administration for attempting too little rather than too much. In addition to the President, the Secretary of State, and the Undersecretary of State for Economic Affairs, Douglas Dillon—who have led the Administration's fight for the program—the most outspoken support for a more extensive

program has come from Senators Cooper, Fulbright, Humphrey, and Kennedy; Averell Harriman, Chester Bowles, Paul Hoffman, Walter Reuther, Mrs. Roosevelt, and Adlai Stevenson. They have received wide support in the academic and journalistic communities. Governor Stevenson, the titular head of the Democratic Party, has been particularly fertile in developing programs of assistance. In 1958, for example, he suggested that the United States propose to the Soviet Union that we jointly finance development of the Nile River Basin. This scheme was designed to lure Colonel Nasser into the Western camp. The outstanding skeptic has been George Kennan, whose views have not been accorded the same sympathetic treatment in this field as they have received in others.

2. Reported in *The New York Times,* January 10, 1958, p. 8.

3. There is no need to go further into the naïveté of our wartime attitudes and the lack of realism in our political objectives. One has only to consider the policy of unconditional surrender, the primacy of purely military over political objectives, the touching faith in the reliability of the Russians, and the strange suspicion of our British allies.

4. This is the breakdown of *economic* aid given between the end of World War II and 1957 to the areas mentioned:

American republics	$ 1.2 billion
Pakistan	$ 278 million
India	$ 479 million
Arab states	$ 102 million
Israel	$ 407 million

(Source: *A Collection of Excerpts and a Bibliography, Relative to United States Foreign Aid,* prepared at the request of the Committee on Foreign Relations by the Foreign Affairs Division, Legislative Reference Service of the Library of Congress [Washington: Government Printing Office, 1957], p. 3.)

5. Mr. Dooley's comments on the American pacification of the Philippines after 1900 are germane in considering the advantages of minimizing contacts: "I was talkin' with a Spanish gintleman th' other day who had been away from the Philippines f'r a long time an' he said he wudden't know th' counthry. Even th' faces if th' people on th' sthreets had changed. They seemed glad to see him."

6. Some of the literature on development, particularly that emanating from the United Nations and its specialized agencies, has suggested much more dramatic and far-reaching proposals than those considered here. Essentially, the U.N. aspirations look forward to the establishment of a "welfare world"—that is, an international order along the lines of the several welfare states, but devoid of their nationalistic selfishness. The *locus classicus* of this approach is Gunnar Myrdal's *An International Economy, Problems and Prospects* (New York: Harper & Brothers, 1956), but an earlier version of the same general approach may be found in

Measures for the Economic Development of Under-Developed Countries: A Report by a Group of Experts Appointed by the Secretary-General of the United Nations (United Nations, 1951). The latter study recommended the provision of $10 billion to $14 billion of capital annually to the underdeveloped countries, chiefly through governmental grants and loans. Since, ultimately, the American taxpayer is requested to pay the lion's share of such assistance programs, it may be stated that no proposal that does not appeal to the American public is likely to be politically viable. For this reason, our discussion is confined to American expressions of opinion.

7. The free-enterprise approach has been most vigorously presented by Milton Friedman in his article "Foreign Economic Aid: Means and Objectives" (in *Yale Review*, Summer, 1958, pp. 500-516). For a more general treatment of the stimulation of market processes as the most satisfactory approach to progress in the underdeveloped areas, see P. T. Bauer and B. S. Yamey, *The Economics of Under-developed Countries* (New York: Cambridge University Press, 1957).

8. The proposal is most fully spelled out in Max F. Millikan & Walt W. Rostow, *A Proposal: Key to an Effective Foreign Policy* (New York: Harper & Brothers, 1957), but its implications are further developed in *The Objectives of United States Economic Assistance Programs,* a study prepared at the request of the Special Committee to Study the Foreign Aid Program by The Center for International Studies, Massachusetts Institute of Technology, no. 1. (Washington: Government Printing Office, 1957). I am critical of the views of the Center, but it should be understood that the criticism is not intended to question either the conscientiousness or the ability of the men associated with it. It should be noted, however, that whenever a center is launched with the support of the philanthropical foundations, the general conclusions are built into the institution. A center founded to find solutions to international problems will find solutions. Those who seek to work and are accepted for work at such an institution are bound to share in the ethical and economic presuppositions of the institution, so that there is a built-in bias in the selection of personnel. The foundations are likely to continue to give support so long as solutions are found—the more dramatic the better. Such an organization is hardly likely to reach the conclusion that the world looks pretty hopeless. Moreover, it must be admitted, when studies are prepared for the government, they are best received when they express what the policy makers would like to hear.

9. This fact, plus the nature of the M.I.T. proposal (as will be seen later), helps to explain why a Senate resolution in 1958 singled out India, among all the underdeveloped nations—allied, friendly, and neutrally hostile—as particularly worthy of support in its developmental program.

10. The Philippines and Burma are also mentioned; the latter, despite its difficulties, is probably included to augment the number of nations in

the transition stage. Since the Philippines already receives considerable assistance, the casual reader may get the impression that the intricate theological apparatus of growth stages has been formulated principally to achieve a grant to India of a larger share of foreign assistance than would be deemed advisable on other grounds. This helps to illuminate the Senate's specific concern over India in 1958.

11. *Op. cit.*, p. 23.

12. This point of view has been most clearly expressed in Edward S. Mason, *Promoting Economic Development: The United States and Southern Asia* (Claremont, California: 1955), especially in Chapter 1; and more recently in "Competitive Coexistence and Economic Development in Asia," in *International Stability and Progress, op. cit.*, pp. 59–97. Mason's views are broadly representative of a number of writers who look with favor upon economic assistance but cannot share the more grandiose objectives of the M.I.T. proposal. Some other writers, however, would place more stress than has Mason on the humanitarian impulse.

13. Once again, Sir Dennis Robertson's words seem particularly worthy of attention: "I think it needs saying that some of the claims for unlimited largesse made by the so-called under-developed countries, or by their self-appointed spokesmen in other lands, go far beyond what human nature can be expected to respond to, and can only end in disillusion . . . the more clearly those countries can make up their minds that the bulk of the job of development must be done by themselves, that it must be planned on lines and within limits dictated by climatic conditions and natural aptitudes, and that foreign funds and skills invited to co-operate must normally be hired and not demanded as of right, fairly treated and not bullied, the better are the prospects for a real, if slow and unspectacular, improvement in their living standards." (*Op. cit.*, pp. 153-154.)

14. Lewis Webster Jones, *South Asia*, report on United States foreign-assistance programs prepared at the request of the Special Committee to Study the Foreign Aid Program, United States Senate, Survey No. 8 (Washington: Government Printing Office, 1957), p. 3.

15. The current campaign to alert the nation to the Soviet economic threat was launched by the State Department early in January, 1958, with the issuance of a report on the economic activities of the bloc in the under-developed world. It represented a reversal of the Department's previous position, which had held the bloc's economic activities to be too small to be concerned about. A more complete study, *The Sino-Soviet Economic Offensive in the Less Developed Countries* (Washington: Government Printing Office, 1958), was released by the Department in June, 1958. Although both the earlier and the later study were factual, they were accompanied by a degree of fanfare that gave an alarming impression unsupported by the figures released.

16. *Ibid.*, pp. 14-20. Bloc capabilities are examined in terms of gross

national product and industrial production, as if the intention of the bloc
leaders was to use that output to mount an offensive against the West
in economic terms, whereas the historical evidence points to the opposite
conclusion—that the bloc will limit its connections with the outside world.
In the study, Soviet industrial growth is estimated at 9-10 per cent
annually, the growth of national product at "possibly as much as 7 per
cent." Since agriculture is growing very slowly, this set of figures would
imply that growth in the tertiary industries is in the neighborhood of
15 per cent annually, whereas their growth in the Soviet Union has
actually been woefully slow. Whether exaggerated or accurate, however,
discussion of bloc capabilities is beside the point in this particular case.

17. There is reason to suspect that Soviet generosity to India is viewed
with mixed emotions in China. To the degree that there is implicit competition between China and India, such Soviet assistance is aiding the
latter. In general, Soviet assistance to the underdeveloped regions is
designed to be sufficiently impressive to be used as propaganda, but not
sufficiently important to aid the regime in maintaining stability.

18. See, for example, Hamilton Fish Armstrong, "North of the Khyber,"
in *Foreign Affairs*, vol. 34, no. 4, July, 1956, pp. 603-619.

19. I pass on without comment the following report by an observer in
Cambodia, printed in *The Economist* of November 11, 1957:

> Cambodia is a visible disproof of Chou En-lai's dictum that a country's
> independence is measured by its ability to dispense with foreign aid.
> This nation of under five million people takes aid from all ideological
> quarters and uses its neutrality (the word "neutralism" is taboo in
> neutralist countries) to offset against one another the pressures which
> come from either side. A year ago observers here were engrossed, and
> distressed, to watch Cambodia almost publicly insulting the United
> States from whom it was receiving about $50 million worth of aid a
> year. The American giant under the implied blackmail: "We might
> go Communist if you stop the aid," continued to pay up and look
> as dignified as it could.

20. There is one other question that we might as well face frankly,
though it is a delicate one to raise. That is the issue of the color line.
Throughout much of the Eastern Hemisphere, at least, racial tensions are
on the rise. The newly freed countries are strongly opposed to racial discrimination and colonialism. But for them, racial discrimination may be
defined simply as abuse of non-European by European (possibly also by
Japanese); colonialism is the same trait writ large on the political level.
The quest for racial amity consists largely in putting the white man in his
place, which is something more than the redress of genuine grievances.
That Europe might be colonized, as was Hungary, or that the newly
emergent nations might abuse their power, as did Indonesia, is perceived

distantly, if at all. This problem is likely to increase rather than diminish, particularly in view of the brooding situation in Africa. For obvious reasons, it is unlikely to be a long-run Soviet asset, however.

21. Named after the late Joseph A. Schumpeter, whose unflattering and perhaps exaggerated picture of the intellectual appeared in *Capitalism, Socialism, and Democracy*, 3d ed. (New York: Harper & Brothers, 1950), ch. 13. To Schumpeter, the intellectual was the agent of destruction of existing society, since his livelihood depended upon the stirring of discontent with existing social arrangements through his poisonous criticism. The intellectual—and this is true in Asia—is a product of the rationalism of liberal society and is likely to destroy freedom.

I do not know whether the noun "intellectual" is of Marxist origin, but it has been popularized by Marxism, and it illustrates the Marxist abuse of rationality. Initially, "intellectual" was an adjective referring to a quality of mind; as a noun, however, it represents a disembodied trait—not fully human in proportions.

This should not be taken as a criticism of intelligence, which may be distinguished from "intellectualism." Intelligent men are always needed in society. In their beliefs, however, they *start with human nature* and build up to a social structure, making charitable allowances for the weaknesses of human nature. The intellectual, on the other hand—in the tradition of Rousseau, Lenin, or the modern totalitarian liberal—starts with an ideal social structure and works down to a concept of what the human being should be like in order to fit into it. If the human being fails to conform, he is "no man" and ought to be liquidated. Thus the intellectual lacks the sense of sin, which must be the basis of intelligence in dealing with social questions.

CHAPTER 10

1. As De Tocqueville observed (and no modern work purporting to examine the efficiency of American social institutions should fail to include a quotation from *Democracy in America*), "When once an opinion has spread over the country and struck root there, it would seem that no power on earth is strong enough to eradicate it."

2. On this question, I can do no better than to quote from Irving Kristol's penetrating review of Chester Bowles's *American Politics in a Revolutionary World*:

> It was the 19th century that witnessed . . . liberal revolutions. . . .
> The revolutions of the 20th century are of quite a different order; and if we fail to see this, we are easily confounded by the self-evident. Take, for instance, the anti-Americanism that is rampant in the new nations of Asia and Africa. Why do the Indians and the Indonesians and the Moroccans dislike us, despite our past friendliness toward their movements of independence? There has been an extraordinary

amount of ingenious soul-searching devoted to this question whose answer stares us candidly in the face. They dislike us because we are what we are, and they are what they are. They dislike us for belonging to the white race which has humiliated them; they dislike our power, which is greater than theirs; they dislike our wealth, which they do not think we merit; they dislike our individualism, which runs counter to their notions of a right social order; they dislike our hedonistic mass culture, which offends their moral sensibilities; they dislike our democratic system of government because of its instability and lack of permanent authority—they dislike us for our vices, and they dislike us for what we would regard as our virtues. There is nothing dark or mysterious about their feelings so long as one does not make the assumption that our values are theirs.

. . . Outside Europe . . . there are few parts of the world that have any faith, or even any interest, in the missions of Jefferson, Lincoln, and Roosevelt. For too long now we have been hypnotized by the mirage of a world conflict between the principles of freedom and those of totalitarianism in which our role is the gratifying one of preacher and savior. (*Commentary*, August, 1956, pp. 180-181.)

INDEX

Adams, Brooks, 58–59
agriculture, 35, 88, 89, 195–199, 272
aid comparisons, 246–247, 248–250, 262–263, 277, 279, 284
allocation of resources, 18, 19–21, 22–23, 24, 25, 31–33, 38–39, 40–45, 45–46, 49–50, 53, 93–95, 104, 108–109, 130–131, 170, 255–256
alternative cost, 18, 19, 24, 38
American attitudes, 4–5, 9, 52, 113–116, 258–259, 265–266
American economy, 40–45, 47, 56–58, 125, 132, 267–268
American foreign policy, 3–5, 9, 48, 64, 133–135, 140–142, 144, 148, 149–156, 222–223, 240–250, 254, 264
American power, 3, 218–219, 258–259, 266–267, 281
Armstrong, Hamilton Fish, 285
autarky, 149–150, 151, 152, 247, 262, 264

Bauer, P. T., 283
Beard, Charles, 134
Behrman, Jack, 276
Bentham, Jeremy, 135
Bismarck, Otto von, 132
Bowles, Chester, 282, 286
budget, 25, 28–29, 79, 105, 106–108, 113, 123–128, 280
budget cutting, 116–119, 123, 275

budgetary fears, 114–116, 258, 267–268
budgetary limits, 12–13, 23, 52, 80, 82–84, 103, 114–116, 127, 258, 267–268, 275
budgetary procedures, 109, 110–113, 125–127
budgeting concepts, 119–120, 123–125, 273, 275
Bureau of the Budget, 107, 112, 113, 116–120, 123
Burke, Edmund, 273–274
Burkhead, Jesse, 273
Byrd, Harry F., 274–275

Canada, 68, 145, 148, 155
Carney, Robert B., 17–18
Chamberlain, Neville, 59
Chavez, Dennis, 274
China, 42, 43, 46, 60, 68, 152, 188, 201–214, 216–221, 254, 285
Clausewitz, Karl von, 7, 70
colonialism, 10, 195, 229–230, 286–287
commercial policy, 133–134, 140–149, 241–242
Communist expansion, 5, 10–11, 46–47, 252–254
Communist goals, 5–7, 46–47, 98, 103, 152, 159, 168–169, 180–181, 185–186, 224–225, 252–254, 277–278, 279
complacency, 265–267